JOURNAL FOR THE STUDY OF THE OLD TESTAMENT SUPPLEMENT SERIES
302

Sheffield Academic Press

Mourning in the Ancient Near East and the Hebrew Bible

Xuan Huong Thi Pham

Journal for the Study of the Old Testament
Supplement Series 302

Copyright © 1999 Sheffield Academic Press

Published by
Sheffield Academic Press Ltd
Mansion House
19 Kingfield Road
Sheffield S11 9AS
England

Typeset by Sheffield Academic Press
and
Printed on acid-free paper in Great Britain
by Biddles
Guildford, Surrey

British Library Cataloguing in Publication Data

A catalogue record for this book is available
from the British Library

ISBN 1-84127-029-6

CONTENTS

PREFACE

Behind this book lies a history. In 1975, when the Vietnam War ended, I was reading Ezekiel in my devotions. I imagined Ezekiel carrying his exile bundle when my own husband, toting his bundle, said goodbye to me and our one-year-old son before he went on a forced ten-day re-education retreat. The ten-day retreat lasted for months, and then the months became years. Meanwhile, the wives and the children at home tried to survive as best they could.

I am grateful that my husband was released after almost three years in a re-education camp, and that my whole family was allowed to resettle in the USA. Both of us entered the Eastern Mennonite Seminary. Later, during my second year of course work at The Catholic University of America, my earlier life came vividly to mind as I read Lamentations 1–2. The scene is one of utter despair: Lady Jerusalem without hope. But that scene is reversed in the great poem of Isa. 51.9–52.2, where again the basic image is Lady Jerusalem engaged in mourning rites. Here the LORD becomes Jerusalem's comforter, the exiles will return and the city will be rebuilt. The period of mourning is over.

The focus of this study is the Israelite mourning ceremony and its ancient Near Eastern analogues as reflected in the three texts mentioned above. The mourning ceremony is a firmly rooted institution attached to the ultimate life-cycle event—death—and thus familiar to the whole of Israelite society. The recognition that Lamentations 1–2 and Isa. 51.9–52.2 are influenced by Israelite mourning rites for the dead is not new. My contribution to the study of these texts, however, is that I have been able to identify the role of the מנחם, 'comforter', in the Israelite mourning ceremony. This insight has made it possible to identify the speaking voices and clearly delineate the beginning and end of the speeches in each of the poems. I would say that the mourning ceremony setting is the key to the basic organization of each of these three texts.

The study is published here essentially as it was presented as a doctoral dissertation at The Catholic University of America in 1996. I have greatly benefited from Br Aloysius Fitzgerald's insights on Hebrew poetry, his wealth of knowledge, his patience and devotion. I am deeply indebted to Revd Alexander A. Di Lella who generously gave of his time to help me complete this dissertation. His vast erudition and unswerving dedication have been an inspiration. I am also grateful to Revd Joseph Jensen and Revd Christopher Begg who carefully worked through the drafts of this dissertation and offered many helpful suggestions. Revd Francis T. Gignac's interest and encouragement constituted the driving force behind this project.

Special thanks are due to Revd Patrick J. Madden for his help with computer matters. My mother, Nguyen Thi Khanh, also deserves grateful mention. She became a widow at 38, and raised all of us, eight children, through unceasing prayers. She has been a faithful מנחם to all of us, and especially to myself during the dark days of my mourning. My husband, Le Ngoc Can, and my son, Bao Quoc, as well as my sisters and brothers, have all lovingly borne their share of sacrifice and faithfully walked with me through the journey.

Finally, grateful acknowledgment is also due to the members of the JSOTSup editorial board and staff who have made this publication possible.

Xuan Huong Thi Pham
Fairfax, Virginia
April 1999

ABBREVIATIONS

AB	Anchor Bible
ABD	David Noel Freedman (ed.), *The Anchor Bible Dictionary* (New York: Doubleday, 1992)
ANET	James B. Pritchard (ed.), *Ancient Near Eastern Texts Relating to the Old Testament* (Princeton, NJ: Princeton University Press, 1950)
ASORSVS	American Schools of Oriental Research Special Volumes Series
ATD	Das Alte Testament Deutsch
BDB	Francis Brown, S.R. Driver and Charles A. Briggs, *A Hebrew and English Lexicon of the Old Testament* (Oxford: Clarendon Press, 1907)
BEATAJ	Beiträge zur Erforschung des Alten Testaments und des Antiken Judentums
BHS	*Biblia hebraica stuttgartensia*
Bib	*Biblica*
BibOr	Biblica et orientalia
BKAT	Biblischer Kommentar: Altes Testament
BZAW	Beihefte zur *ZAW*
CAD	Ignace I. Gelb *et al.* (eds.), *The Assyrian Dictionary of the Oriental Institute of the University of Chicago* (Chicago: Oriental Institute, 1964–)
CBQ	*Catholic Biblical Quarterly*
CEV	Contemporary English Version
CGTC	Cambridge Greek Testament Commentary
CTA	A. Herdner, *Corpus des tablettes en cunéiformes alphabétiques* (Mission de Ras-Shamra; Paris: Geuthner, 1963)
CurTM	*Currents in Theology and Mission*
GesB	W. Gesenius, *Hebräisches und aramäisches Handwörterbuch* (ed. F. Buhl; Leipzig: Vogel, 17th edn, 1921)
GHB	P. Joüon, *Grammaire de l'hébreu biblique* (Rome: Pontifical Biblical Institute, 1923)
GKB	Wilhelm Gesenius, E. Kautzsch and Gotthelf Bergsträsser, *Hebräische Grammatik* (Leipzig: J.C. Hinrichs, 1979)

GKC	*Gesenius' Hebrew Grammar* (ed. E. Kautzsch, revised and trans. A.E. Cowley; Oxford: Clarendon Press, 1910)
HALOT	*The Hebrew and Aramaic Lexicon of the Old Testament* (trans. and ed. M.E.J. Richardson *et al.*; 2 vols.; Leiden: E.J. Brill, 1994–95)
HAT	Handbuch zum Alten Testament
HSM	Harvard Semitic Monographs
HTR	*Harvard Theological Review*
IB	*Interpreter's Bible*
IDB	George Arthur Buttrick (ed.), *The Interpreter's Dictionary of the Bible* (4 vols.; Nashville: Abingdon Press, 1962)
IDBSup	*IDB*, Supplementary Volume
ISJ	Institución San Jerónimo
ITC	International Theological Commentary
JA	*Journal asiatique*
JANESCU	*Journal of the Ancient Near Eastern Society of Columbia University*
JBL	*Journal of Biblical Literature*
JR	*Journal of Religion*
JSOT	*Journal for the Study of the Old Testament*
JSOTSup	*Journal for the Study of the Old Testament*, Supplement Series
KAT	Kommentar zum Alten Testament
LD	Lectio divina
LHAVT	F. Zorell, *Lexicon hebraicum et aramaicum Veteris Testamenti* (Rome: Pontifical Biblical Institute, 1963).
NAB	*New American Bible*
NCBC	New Century Bible Commentary
NIV	New International Version
NJBC	R.E. Brown, J.A. Fitzmyer and R.E. Murphy (eds.), *The New Jerome Biblical Commentary* (Englewood Cliffs, NJ: Prentice–Hall, 1990).
NRSV	New Revised Standard Version
OBO	Orbis biblicus et orientalis
OTL	Old Testament Library
RB	*Revue biblique*
REB	Revised English Bible
SBLDS	SBL Dissertation Series
SBT	Studies in Biblical Theology
STDJ	Studies on the Texts of the Desert of Judah
STL	Studia theologica lundensia
TDNT	Gerhard Kittel and Gerhard Friedrich (eds.), *Theological Dictionary of the New Testament* (trans. Geoffrey W. Bromiley; 10 vols.; Grand Rapids: Eerdmans, 1964–)
TDOT	G.J. Botterweck and H. Ringgren (eds.), *Theological Dictionary of the Old Testament*

VT	*Vetus Testamentum*
WBC	Word Biblical Commentary
ZAW	*Zeitschrift für die alttestamentliche Wissenschaft*
ZDMG	*Zeitschrift der deutschen morgenländischen Gesellschaft*

Chapter 1

INTRODUCTION

The three texts of Lamentations 1 and 2 and Isa. 51.9–52.2 are closely related. All are dated by scholarly consensus between 587 and 538 BCE, the first two early and the last late in that period.[1] All share the same literary setting: personified Jerusalem is portrayed as sitting on the ground, mourning the events of 587 BCE and the exile. The setting is the mourning ceremony of biblical Israel, and, more generally, of the ancient Near East.

In this chapter, I will first state the purpose and contribution of this study; then I will give a description of the mourning rites practiced in the ancient Near East. Next, I will compare and contrast these mourning rites with those of biblical Israel by summary reference to the opening chapters of Job, which present in relatively ample detail a typical Old Testament mourning ceremony, and in addition throw light on the role of a מנחם, 'comforter', in such a ceremony. The need for a מנחם keeps coming back like a plaintive refrain in Lamentations 1. This figure likewise plays a significant role in Lamentations 2 and Isa. 51.9–52.2. A clear understanding of the term is thus essential to the interpretation of all three poems. The opening chapters in Job also mention what seems to be a frequent component of the mourning ceremony: the moment of silence, when Job's friends sit on the ground with him during seven days and nights, without speaking a word to him. Accordingly, I will devote a section to the role of the מנחם with particular attention to this moment of silence. Finally, I will list the editions of the primary texts used in my study.

The mourning ceremony in Job will set up the background for the

---

1. C. Westermann, *Lamentations: Issues and Interpretation* (Minneapolis: Fortress Press, 1994), pp. 54, 104; R.J. Clifford, *Fair Spoken and Persuading: An Interpretation of Second Isaiah* (New York: Paulist Press, 1984), p. 3.

exegesis in Chapters 2–4 of the texts of Lamentations 1 and 2, and Isa. 51.9–52.2. The resulting contributions to the field of biblical studies will be summarized in the concluding chapter.

Purpose and Contribution

The purpose of this study is to carry out a close reading of all three texts in the light of their common literary setting. The details of the rites of the mourning ceremony are well represented in the Old Testament and in the literature and art of the Near East more generally pertaining to the period 2500–500 BCE. Every line of the texts will be evaluated against this background.

Although the mourning ceremony setting of these texts has often been noticed,[2] my review of the literature indicates that they have never been studied systematically from this point of view. Such a systematic study throws clear light on points of detail. For example, the word ערותה, 'her nakedness', in Lam. 1.8 has been explained as 'the exposure of one's body', as in the story of Noah's drunkenness (Gen. 9.20-27), which brings great shame. Metaphorically, 'to see the nakedness' of a country means to spy out its weaknesses (Gen. 42.9, 12).[3] F.W. Dobbs-Allsopp suggests that this public exposure may allude to plunder and to rape,[4] the atrocious companions of war. It has never been suggested that, in the context of a mourning ceremony, 'her nakedness' may refer to the skirt of sackcloth, the mourning garment, that Jerusalem wears from her hips down, leaving the upper body bare (cf. Isa. 32.11-12). Similarly, the word טמאתה, 'her filth', in Lam. 1.9 has been invariably understood to refer to 'menstrual blood' or 'menstrual uncleanness'.[5] It

2.   D.R. Hillers, *Lamentations* (AB, 7A; New York: Doubleday, 2nd edn, 1992), pp. 6-7; Westermann, *Lamentations*, pp. 62-63; M.D. Guinan, 'Lamentations', *NJBC* (1990), pp. 558-62 (588); S.P. Re'emi, 'The Theology of Hope: A Commentary on Lamentations', in R.M. Achard and S.P. Re'emi, *God's People in Crisis: A Commentary on the Book of Amos; A Commentary on the Book of Lamentations* (ITC; Grand Rapids: Eerdmans, 1984), pp. 73-134 (78).

3.   Hillers, *Lamentations*, p. 86.

4.   F.W. Dobbs-Allsopp, *Weep, O Daughter of Zion: A Study of the City-Lament Genre in the Hebrew Bible* (BibOr, 44; Rome: Pontifical Biblical Institute, 1993), pp. 147-48.

5.   Hillers, *Lamentations*, p. 86; I.W. Provan, *Lamentations* (NCBC; London: Marshall Pickering; Grand Rapids: Eerdmans, 1991), pp. 44-45; Westermann, *Lamentations*, p. 129.

may, however, actually be the dirt on which Jerusalem has been sitting, mourning over her dead and exiled children.

On the level of macro-structure, the majority of exegetes fail to discern any consistent flow of ideas in Lamentations 1 and 2. They evade the difficult issue of structure by substituting comments on a verse-by-verse basis.[6] Commentators also disagree about the limits of the poem and its sub-units in Isa. 51.9–52.2.[7] However, the overall organization of the three texts becomes crystal clear once it is recognized that מנחם in Lam. 1.2b, 9b, 16b, 17a, 21a, and Isa. 51.12 is the technical mourning ceremony vocabulary for a friend who was expected to give the mourner comfort and advice.[8] We hear at least two voices in each poem. One voice is that of Jerusalem, the other voice is that of the מנחם, or 'comforter'. Claus Westermann questions the validity of analyzing the texts of Lamentations 1 and 2 according to the change of speakers. He and several other interpreters note only the disruptive effect of the change,[9] because they do not take into account the mourning ceremony setting where the mourners interact with one another.[10]

This study will clarify many of the problems in the three texts studied. It is worth noting that Lamentations 1 and 2 are sometimes described as lacking a coherent argument, and that lack is attributed to the difficulties of their alphabetic acrostic form.[11] Neither that description of these poems, nor its explanation, has any value. It will be shown below that Lamentations 1 and 2 show a clear flow of thought if they are read against the setting of a mourning ceremony. This study will also contribute to the understanding of a few other biblical texts that share the same mourning ceremony setting (e.g. Isa. 47.1-5; Jer. 48.16-20; Ezek. 26.16-17).

---

6. Westermann, *Lamentations*, pp. 63-64.

7. For example, C.R. North, *The Second Isaiah* (Oxford: Oxford University Press, 1964), pp. 211-20, gives an analysis of four different sections: 51.9-11, 12-16, 17-23; 52.1-6; Clifford, *Fair Spoken*, pp. 165-72, delimits the poem at 51.9–52.12, and the sub-units at 51.9-11, 12-16, 17-20, 21; 52.1-2, 7-12; 52.3-6.

8. J.J. Ferrie, Jr, 'Meteorological Imagery in Isaiah 40–55' (PhD dissertation, Washington, The Catholic University of America, 1992), p. 168.

9. Westermann, *Lamentations*, pp. 65, 139.

10. E. Jacob, 'Mourning', *IDB*, III, pp. 452-54, esp. p. 454.

11. Westermann, *Lamentations*, pp. 100, 130-31, 136-37.

The Mourning Rites of the Ancient Near East

Ancient Near Eastern literature has preserved a rich repertoire of mourning rites which doubtless reflect the funeral practice of the time.[12] Although some of these texts can be as far apart as 1500 years, the mourning rituals they describe have many common features, which attest to the conservative nature of the ritual practice, especially with regard to funeral rites.[13]

This section will look at the following texts: *The Curse of Agade*; *The Epic of Gilgamesh*; *The Poems about Baal and Anath*; and *The Tale of Aqhat*. I will also examine some texts pertaining to the process of mourning in international relations: a state-letter of Hattušili III, King of the Hittites; a state-letter of Tušratta, King of Mitanni; and *The Mother of Nabonidus*. All of these provide additional evidence on the role of the מנחם, although the concept of giving comfort is not explicitly mentioned.

The Curse of Agade

Written between 2200 and 2000 BCE, this poem tells the story of the rise and fall of the first great Mesopotamian empire. After the city was destroyed, the survivors mourned the death of the whole city, that is, the loss of human lives as well as the loss of physical structures such as temples, palaces, houses and gardens.

> The chief lamentation singer who survived those years,
> For seven days and seven nights,
> Put in place seven *balag*-drums, as if they stood at heaven's base, and
> Played *ub*, *meze*, and *lilis*-drums for him (Enlil) among them (the *balags*).
> The old women did not restrain (the cry) 'Alas my city!'
> The old men did not restrain (the cry) 'Alas its people!'
> The lamentation singer did not restrain (the cry) 'Alas the Ekur!'
> The young women did not restrain from tearing their hair,
> The young men did not restrain their sharp knives.[14]

---

12. E. Lipiński, *La liturgie pénitentielle dans la Bible* (LD, 52; Paris: Cerf, 1969), p. 30.

13. G.A. Anderson, *A Time to Mourn, a Time to Dance: The Expression of Grief and Joy in Israelite Religion* (University Park, PA: Pennsylvania State University Press, 1991), p. 60; Jacob, 'Mourning', p. 453.

14. *Agade* ll. 198-206. J.S. Cooper, *The Curse of Agade* (Baltimore: The Johns Hopkins University Press, 1983), pp. 59, 61.

'Seven days and seven nights' mark the ritual period of mourning during which people lament loudly, tearing their hair and cutting themselves with sharp knives. Several groups of people take turns in lamenting: the chief lamentation singer, the old women, the old men. Musical instruments accompany the loud wailing.

The Epic of Gilgamesh

This Akkadian epic, composed around the beginning of the second millennium BCE, relates the adventures of Gilgamesh, the two-third god and one-third human king of the southern Mesopotamian city of Uruk around 2600 BCE.

When his younger friend Enkidu dies, Gilgamesh covers the face of his friend and weeps aloud, calling the elders, the wailing women and the people of Uruk to lament. He walks back and forth in front of the dead body, pulling out his hair and tearing off his clothes. He weeps over Enkidu for seven days and seven nights, and will not give his friend's body up for burial until the corpse starts to decompose. Then he lets his hair grow uncut, puts on a lion skin, loosens his girdle, and roams the steppe, out of fear of death and in search of immortality. In his grief, Gilgamesh has identified himself with Enkidu's wild state at his initial creation:

> Shaggy with hair is his whole body,
> he is endowed with hair like a woman.
> The locks of his hair sprout like Nisaba.
> He does not know either people or land, garbed is he like Sumuqan.
> With the gazelles he feeds on grass,
> With the wild beasts he jostles at the watering place,
> With the teeming creatures his heart rejoices in water.[15]

Gilgamesh fears death. This becomes explicit in the following passage:

> For Enkidu, his friend, Gilgamesh
> Weeps bitterly, as he ranges over the steppe:
> 'When I die, shall I not be like Enkidu?
> Woe has entered my belly.
> Fearing death, I roam over the steppe.'[16]

---

15. *Gilg.* 1.2.35-41; Anderson, *A Time to Mourn*, pp. 76-77. When Anderson cites a text from Gilgamesh, he uses the edition of R.C. Thompson, *The Epic of Gilgamesh: Text, Transliteration, and Notes* (Oxford: Clarendon Press, 1930).

16. *Gilg.* 9.1.1-5; *ANET*, p. 88.

Gilgamesh wanders in search for life, yet his journey leads him into the steppe or wilderness/desert which is identified by the Mesopotamians as 'the area which leads to the nether world'.[17] By wandering in the steppe, clad in lion skins, with his hair uncut, Gilgamesh the mourner has cut himself off from the realm of ordinary human life; the lion skin covering may help him to roam unnoticed among the wild beasts of the steppe. When he arrives at the home of the innkeeper Siduri, he recounts his plight to her. She then advises him as follows:

> Gilgamesh, where are you wandering?
> The life you pursue, you shall not find.
> When the gods created humankind,
> Death for humankind they established,
> Life in their own hands they retained.
> So, Gilgamesh, let your belly be full,
> Rejoice continually day and night.
> Each day make a feast of rejoicing,
> Day and night dance and play!
> Let your garments be clean,
> May your head be washed; bathe yourself in water.
> Pay heed to the little one that grasps your hand,
> Let your spouse rejoice in your lap,
> For this is the task of [womankind].[18]

From the innkeeper's advice, it may be inferred that Gilgamesh has not been washing himself, and that his animal skins are far from clean. He is in a way identifying himself with the dead, as he himself advises Enkidu to do so before the latter descends to the underworld:

> Gilgamesh [says to him, to] Enkidu, [his servant]:
>   'If [you will go down] to the netherworld,
> [I will speak a word to thee, take my word];
>   my admonition[s] [may you heed well]:
> Clean raiment [you shall not put on],
>   as a sojourner they would ma[rk you].
> With sweet oil from the cruse do not anoint yourself,
>   at its fragrance they would gather about you.

---

17. S. Talmon, 'Wilderness', *IDBSup*, pp. 946-49 (946).

18. Frag. 3.1-14, translated by B. Meissner, *Ein altbabylonisches Fragment des Gilgamesepos* (M VAG 7.1; Berlin: Peiser, 1902); Anderson, *A Time to Mourn*, pp. 78-79; the Meissner Fragments have been translated by Anderson himself from the Old Babylonian version. See *A Time to Mourn*, p. 75 n. 53.

A throw stick into the netherworld do not toss,
  those struck with the throw stick would surround you.
A staff into your hands do not take,
  the spirits would tremble on your account.
Do not put sandals on your feet,
  nor make a sound against the netherworld.
Your wife whom you love, do not kiss.
  Your wife whom you hate, do not strike.
Your son whom you love, do not kiss.
  Your son whom you hate, do not strike.
For the wailing of the netherworld would seize you.'[19]

When Enkidu goes down to the realm of the dead, he must abstain from wearing clean clothes, anointing himself with oil and showing signs of affection to his wife or child, so as not to provoke 'the jealousy of the dead, who can no longer enjoy these pleasures'.[20]

Gilgamesh the mourner has in fact followed these proscriptions. He has identified himself with the dead in his state of mourning which lasts more than the usual period of seven days.

The Poems about Baal and Anath
This Ugaritic text from around the middle of the second millennium BCE relates the exploits and adventures of Baal, the storm god, on whom depends the fertility of the land, according to Canaanite beliefs.

El, the supreme god of the pantheon, goes into great mourning when the messengers announce the death of Baal:

Then El the kind, the compassionate,
  descends from the throne and sits on the footstool,
  from the footstool he [descends and] sits upon the ground.
He strews stalks of mourning on his head,
  the dust in which he wallows on his pate.
His clothing he tears, down to the loincloth,
  his skin he bruises with a rock by pounding,
  with a razor he cuts his beard and whiskers.
He rakes his upper arms,
  he plows his breast like a garden,
  like a valley he rakes his chest.

19. *Gilg.* 12.10-28; Anderson, *A Time to Mourn*, p. 75.
20. *CTA* 5.6.11-25. Anderson, *A Time to Mourn*, p. 76.

He raises his voice and shouts:
'Baal is dead: what will happen to the people?
    Dagon's son: what will happen to the masses?
I am descending to the underworld, after Baal.'[21]

The ritual mourning seat is the ground. El descends from the throne to the footstool, then from the footstool to the ground. There, El displays the ritual mourning behaviors: he puts dirt and dry stalks on his head, tears his clothes, shaves his face, gashes his body, and laments aloud.

Anath, Baal's consort, also puts on a loincloth and cuts herself. Weeping loudly, she wanders in search of Baal's body, locates it and takes it to the heights of Zaphon for burial. She slaughters cattle and sheep for Baal's funeral offering. Then she goes and prostrates herself at El's feet.

Toward the close of this narrative sequence, El sees in a vision that Baal has come back to life, and with him, nature and vegetation:

In a dream of El the kind, the compassionate,
    in a vision of the Creator of all,
the heavens rained down oil,
    the wadis ran with honey.
El the kind, the compassionate, was glad:
    he put his feet on a stool,
he opened his mouth and laughed;
    he raised his voice and shouted:
'I now take my seat and rest,
    my soul rests within me,
because Baal the conqueror lives,
    the Prince, the lord of the earth is alive!'[22]

The mourning process is over. El rejoices, gets back on the throne, and rests.

The Tale of Aqhat
The story begins with Danil at the temple, making sacrifices to the gods for seven days, groaning and spending the nights on sackcloth, pleading

---

21. Anderson, *A Time to Mourn*, pp. 60-63. Anderson's translation varies slightly from *ANET*'s (p. 139). Anderson supports his different renderings with convincing arguments: e.g. he reads 'stalks of mourning' because the Ugaritic root *'mr* is related to Hebrew, עָמִיר, 'sheaf', and עָמִיר, 'fallen grain'.

22. *CTA* 6.3.10-21; Anderson, *A Time to Mourn*, p. 67.

for the gift of a son. On the seventh day, Baal intercedes with El for Danil, and describes the latter's grief:

> Lo, on the seventh day,
> Baal drew near with his supplication:
> 'Danil the *rp i*—man is […],
> He is groaning, the Hero, the man of *Hrnm*.'[23]

The suppliant behaves like a mourner. He groans and wears sackcloth for a period of seven days. According to Anderson, the meaning of the first verb (*'abynt*) which describes Danil's state is uncertain. However, the second verb (*'anḫ*) is often translated 'to sigh, groan', like the Hebrew root אנח, and can similarly denote visible behavior,[24] as the following text in Ezek. 21.11-12 (NAB) shows:

> As for you, son of man, groan! with shattered strength groan bitterly while they look on. And when they ask you, 'Why are you groaning?', you shall say: Because of a report; when it comes every heart shall fail, every hand shall fall helpless…

Danil rejoices when his plea is granted:

> The face of Danil beamed,
>   the top of his forehead shone.
> He opened his mouth and laughed;
>   he put his feet on a stool,
> he raised his voice and shouted:
> 'I now take my seat and rest,
>   my soul rests within me,
> because a son will be born to me like my brothers,
>   and a root like my kinsmen.'[25]

When Danil hears the news that he will have a son, he laughs, gets back on the throne and shouts for joy. He behaves exactly like El after the vision of Baal coming back to life. In both cases, the idea of 'rest' is doubly emphasized:

23. *CTA* 17.1.16-19; Anderson, *A Time to Mourn*, p. 70. The translation in *ANET* (p. 150) is:

> But lo, on the seventh day,
>   Baal approaches with his plea:
> 'Unhappy is Daniel the Rapha-man,
>   A-sighing is Ghazir the Harnamiyy-man.'

24. Anderson, *A Time to Mourn*, p. 70, esp. n. 35.
25. *CTA* 17.2.8-15; Anderson, *A Time to Mourn*, p. 70.

> 'I now take my seat and rest,
>   my soul rests within me.'

The state of rest can be reached only after the mourning and/or lamenting period is over.

Later, Danil's joy is turned into mourning at the news of his son's, Aqhat's, death. Danil searches for the remains of Aqhat's body in the bellies of vultures, and, weeping, he buries them. Then he engages professional women who come to his palace and weep continually for Aqhat for seven years. At the end of the mourning period, the weeping women depart, and Danil makes offerings to the gods.

Mourning in International Relations

On the international level, allied countries were obliged to take part in the mourning for one another's kings or members of the royal household.

For example, the mourning of Hattušili III, King of the Hittites, over the demise of his brother-ally, Kadašman-Turgu (1297–1280), King of Kardunijaš (Kassite Babylonia), is described in a state-letter by the Hittite king addressed to Kadašman-Enlil II (1279–1265), the son and heir of the deceased.

In the letter, Hattušili III reminded the new king of the Hittite–Babylonian treaty between the latter's father and himself. Through that treaty, they had become 'good-willing brothers', and agreed that when one of them died, the survivor would protect the deceased's sons. Hattušili III assured the new king of his sympathy and his best intentions to implement the treaty regulations, especially his duty to ensure the peaceful and legal transfer of dynastic inheritance to the heir of the throne.[26]

Another example is that of the mourning of Tušratta, King of Mitanni, over the death of his brother-in-law and ally, Amenhotep III, King of Egypt. It is described in a state-letter by Tušratta to Amenhotep IV-Ehnaton, the eldest son and legitimate successor of the deceased.

Tušratta began the letter by reminding the new king that he and the latter's father had always fulfilled their obligations to each other promptly and fully. Tušratta was eager to continue this relationship

---

26. P. Artzi, 'Mourning in International Relations', in B. Alster (ed.), *Death in Mesopotamia* (Copenhagen Studies in Assyriology, 8; Copenhagen: Akademisk, 1980), pp. 161-70 (162-64).

with the new king. Then Tušratta recounted his mourning from the time he received the sad news of the death of Amenhotep III: he wept the whole day, did not eat or drink, stayed up all night, and so became ill. He next recited a lament to express his enduring love, which he now transferred in heightened measure to Amenhotep IV, who stood in his father's place and would consequently be bound by his father's words. Finally, he urged the new king to fulfil a promise made by his father, namely, the transfer of gold statue(s) and other gifts in their real value.[27]

The final example concerns the Mother of Nabonidus. When his mother died in the ninth year of his reign (i.e. 547 BCE), Nabonidus, King of Babylon,

> slaughtered fat rams and assembled into his presence [the inhabitants] of Babylon and Borsippa together with [people] from far off provinces, he [summoned even kings, princes] and governors from the [borders] of Egypt on the Upper Sea, to the Lower Sea, for the mourning and [...] they made a great lament, scattered [dust] on their heads. For seven days and seven nights they walked about, heads hung low, [dust strewn], stripped of their attire. On the seventh day [...] all the people of the country shaved and cleaned themselves, [threw away] their (mourning) attire [...] [I had] chests with (new) attire [brought] for them to their living quarters, [treated them] with food [and drink], provided them richly with fine oil, poured scented oil over their heads, made them glad (again) and looking presentable. I provided them well for their [long] journey and they returned to their homes.[28]

These three cases all show that international mourning was based on the concept of family kinship between countries bound by treaties to one another.

In summary, the mourning rites of the ancient Near East are closely related to the rites of supplication or lamentation (cf. Danil pleading for the gift of a son at the temple). They include loud weeping (usually aided by professional wailing women), the tearing of clothes and donning of sackcloth, sitting or lying on the dirt, gashing the body, strewing dirt on the head, fasting, abstaining from anointing with oil. There are also some variant actions with regard to the hair and beard. Gilgamesh let his hair grow, and the people who came to the funeral of

27. Artzi, 'Mourning', pp. 164-65.
28. *ANET*, pp. 561-62.

Nabonidus's mother also let their beards grow, but El cut his beard and whiskers while mourning for Baal.

The ritual mourning period lasts seven days and seven nights, after which the mourners return to normal life. Gilgamesh and Danil represent exceptions to this rule.

After mourning for seven days and nights, Gilgamesh was still unable to reincorporate himself into the human community. He kept roaming over the steppe for years, searching for immortality. He finally met Utnapishtim who told him of a thorny plant which was supposed to give new life. Gilgamesh was able to get the precious plant from the depths of the sea, but on his way home, while he was bathing in a well, a serpent carried the plant away.

As for Danil, he wept for his son Aqhat for seven years, after which he ended his mourning with offerings to the gods. Then Paghat, his daughter, asked for his blessings before she went and killed Aqhat's murderer.

The Mourning Rites of Biblical Israel

The mourning and lamentation rites in the Bible will be studied on the basis of the opening chapters of Job, with passing reference to a few other relevant texts when needed.

In Job 1, after Yahweh points out Job's faithfulness to 'the Satan, or heavenly adversary', the Satan suggests that Job's loyalty is only to be explained by the fact that Yahweh has blessed him so abundantly. But if Job were to lose all that he has, he would in fact curse Yahweh (1.9-11). Yahweh accepts the challenge and grants the Satan permission to deprive Job of his possessions, but commands him not to touch Job's person (1.12). The Satan departs and then messengers arrive in rapid succession to report to Job the loss of his livestock, his herdsmen and farmers, and finally the death of his sons and daughters (1.13-19). Job's reaction is immediate. He rises and tears (קרע) his cloak (מעיל, 1.20), using mourning ceremony vocabulary.

Similarly, when Jacob learns of the death of Joseph, he tears (קרע) his clothes, girds his loins with sackcloth (שׂק), and mourns (אבל) his son for many days (Gen. 37.34). 'All his sons and all his daughters' come to comfort (נחם) him, but he refuses to be comforted. He answers them by saying he will go down as a mourner to Sheol to his son. The scene closes with Jacob weeping (בכה) for his dead son (Gen. 37.35).

Other examples of tearing clothes at times of calamity can be cited. Joshua tears his clothes when he hears of the Israelites' defeat at Ai (Josh. 7.6). David and his men tear their garments when they learn of the death of Saul and his son Jonathan, and of the Israelite defeat (2 Sam. 1.11). Ezra tears his garment and his cloak when he learns of the mixed marriages of the returned exiles (Ezra 9.3). Mordecai tears his clothes when he learns of the king's decree, issued at Haman's advice, to destroy all the Jews in the empire (Est. 4.1).

After tearing his cloak, Job shaves (גזז) his head (1.20). This is also a mourning rite. In Jer. 7.29, Jerusalem is told to shave her sacred hair (גזרך) and to throw it away, and to raise a lament on the heights, because Yahweh has rejected Judah. In Mic. 1.16, Jerusalem is told to make herself bald (קרחה), to shave her hair (גזז), because her children will be taken into exile.

Next, Job falls (נפל) to the ground and prostrates himself in worship (חוה). The precise sense of the hishtaphel of חוה here is made clear by what Job says immediately afterwards. He acknowledges that Yahweh has given and Yahweh has taken away, and then concludes by blessing the name of Yahweh (1.21). The verb חוה, 'to bow down, to prostrate oneself in worship', is not such clearly mourning ceremony vocabulary as that cited above (קרע, 'to tear', אבל, 'to mourn', נחם, 'to comfort', בכה, 'to weep', גזז, 'to shave'). However, in Josh. 7.6-7, Joshua falls upon the ground and prays; in Ezra 9.5-6, Ezra bows down (כרע) upon his knees and prays; in 1 Macc. 4.36-40, when Judas and his brothers find the sanctuary desolate, they tear their clothes, make great lamentation, and then fall with their faces to the ground and pray. All these texts have clear mourning ceremony contexts.

Job has passed his first test, but the Satan again challenges Yahweh, saying that Job remains faithful only because Yahweh has not touched his person, and if Yahweh does so, Job will surely curse Yahweh (2.4-5). Yahweh accepts the challenge and puts Job in the Satan's hand, but instructs the Satan to spare his life (2.6). The Satan departs and strikes Job with terrible skin sores from the top of his head to the soles of his feet (2.7). Job picks up a potsherd to scrape himself as he sits on the ash heap (והוא ישב בתוך־האפר, 2.8). In the last clause, the *wayyiqtol* is purposely avoided because the act of sitting on the ash heap is contemporaneous with Job's taking up a potsherd to scratch himself. The word אפר could mean 'loose dirt' or 'dust', like עפר in 2.12, but a good case can be made for seeing אפר as the ash of the rubbish heap outside the gate of Job's town.[29] The supposition that Job is sitting on the rubbish heap explains how he can simply reach down and pick up a potsherd. Job has changed his physical position from prostrating himself on the ground before Yahweh to sitting on the ash heap.

This sitting on the ash heap or on the ground is a clear mourning ceremony rite. In Isa. 47.1, Lady Babylon is told to sit on the dirt (וּשְׁבִי עַל־עָפָר), to sit on the ground (שְׁבִי־לָאָרֶץ), for she is about to be conquered by her enemies. When the King of Nineveh hears that the city is about to be destroyed by God, he rises from his throne, removes his royal garments, puts on sackcloth and sits on ashes (וַיֵּשֶׁב עַל־הָאֵפֶר, Jon. 3.6).

It should be noted that some mourning rites may not be explicitly mentioned in a given description of a mourning ceremony, but are to be inferred from the context. Job 2, for example, does not mention Job putting on sackcloth, but Job 16.15 refers to Job wearing sackcloth around his hips, leaving his upper body bare. Job's bare upper body would explain the mention of Job scraping his exposed flesh with a potsherd in 2.8.

Job has now passed his second test, and so a new episode begins. News of his misfortune has reached his friends (2.11). These friends from different towns meet at an appointed place and come to Job to mourn with him (לָנוּד־לוֹ) and to comfort him (וּלְנַחֲמוֹ, 2.11). They catch sight of Job from a distance and can hardly recognize him. They weep out loud, tear their cloaks, sprinkle dirt on their heads (וַיִּזְרְקוּ עָפָר עַל־רָאשֵׁיהֶם), and sit with him on the ground for seven days and nights (2.12). For the most part these actions of Job's friends have been examined above and analyzed as rites of mourning. The one new feature is the sprinkling of dirt on the head, which is also a mourning rite. Joshua and the elders of Israel put dirt on their heads at the news of the defeat at Ai (Josh. 7.6). After the defeat of Israel by the Philistines and the loss of the ark, a messenger with his clothes torn and dirt (וַאֲדָמָה) upon his head, brings the news to Eli (1 Sam. 4.12). After the death of Saul and Jonathan, and the defeat of the Israelites, an Amalekite from Saul's camp, with his clothes torn and dirt on his head, brings the news to David (2 Sam. 1.2). After being maltreated by Amnon, Tamar puts ashes (אֵפֶר) on her head and tears her tunic (2 Sam. 13.19).

---

29. É. Dhorme, *A Commentary on the Book of Job* (New York: Thomas Nelson, 1967), pp. 18-19.

When the Israelites in Judea hear of what Holofernes, the commander in chief of Nebuchadnezzar, has done to the other nations, despoiling and destroying all their temples, they fear for Jerusalem and the temple of their God. All those who live in Jerusalem gird themselves with sackcloth, strew ashes on their heads, prostrate themselves in front of the temple and pray for God's protection (Jdt. 4.11-12).

Other mourning rites scattered throughout the Bible include fasting (e.g. Judg. 20.26; 1 Sam. 31.13; 2 Sam. 1.12; Jon. 3.7; Jdt. 4.13; 1 Macc. 3.47), shaving the beard (e.g. Isa. 15.2; Jer. 41.5), gashing the body (e.g. Hos. 7.14; Jer. 16.6; 41.5), beating the breast (e.g. Isa. 32.12; Nah. 2.8), striking the thigh (e.g. Jer. 31.19; Ezek. 21.17), walking about bowed down (e.g. Pss. 35.14; 38.7) and barefoot. The mourning rite of walking barefoot may be inferred from Ezek. 24.17, where the prophet Ezekiel is forbidden to mourn for his wife and is told to put his sandals on his feet. Similarly, in v. 23, the Judahites in exile are forbidden to mourn the destruction of the temple in Jerusalem and are told to keep their sandals on their feet. In 2 Sam. 15.30, David weeps ceaselessly and walks barefoot in his flight from Jerusalem, following the rebellion of his son Absalom. In Isa. 20.2-4, the prophet Isaiah is told to walk naked and barefoot as a sign of the future captivity and exile of Egypt and Ethiopia.

The biblical ritual mourning period lasted for seven days (Gen. 50.10; 1 Sam. 31.13 // 1 Chron. 10.12; Jdt. 16.24; Sir. 22.12).

On the whole, the mourning rites of biblical Israel are strikingly parallel to those of the ancient Near East.

The Role of the מנחם *in the Mourning Ceremony*

After describing the actions of Job's friends upon their arrival, namely, the mourning rites by which they express their participation in Job's own grief, the text continues with a nominal clause which indicates action contemporaneous with their sitting on the ground with Job. Not one of the friends spoke a word to Job because they saw his misery was too great (ואין־דבר אליו דבר כי ראו כי־גדל הכאב מאד, 2.13b). When Job finally breaks the silence and voices a lament in ch. 3, they take turns answering him in the ensuing chapters.

Job's friends have come with the express purpose to mourn with him and to comfort him (2.11). They are Job's 'comforters' (מנחמים). Based on what Job's friends did and said, and on some other relevant texts, this section will look at the role of the מנחם in terms of means and effect. I will first discuss the means or ways used by the מנחם to reach the desired goal of comforting the mourner, and then the resulting effects on the mourner, that is, whether the mourner's grief is alleviated or not.

Ways of Offering Comfort

The מנחם tries to comfort or to mitigate the mourner's grief in two main ways: first, by identifying with the mourner through participating in the mourning rites;[30] and, secondly, by speaking to the mourner, giving him or her advice on how to get over his or her pain.

Participation in the Mourning Rites

Visible Mourning Rites. Weeping, tearing clothes, gashing the body, shaving the head and beard—all these are mourning rites which are seen and heard by everyone. They are readily recognizable. When Job's friends see him, even from afar, they weep aloud, tear their cloaks and sprinkle dirt on their heads. Then they sit with Job on the ground for seven days and nights. By their actions, they show that they are mourning with Job; he is not alone in his sorrow. He has friends who love him and care for him. They are friends indeed according to the definition in Prov. 17.17 (NRSV):

> A friend loves at all times,
>   and kinsfolk are born to share adversity.

Participation in the mourning rites is especially commanded:

> Avoid not those who weep,
>   but mourn with those who mourn (Sir. 7.34; NAB).

> Weep with those who weep (Rom. 12.15; NAB).

By contrast, participation in the mourning rites is forbidden in Jer. 16.5-7 because Israel's failure to keep the covenant has nullified Yahweh's obligation of covenant loyalty:

> For thus says the LORD: Do not enter the house of mourning, or go to lament, or bemoan them [ואל־תנד להם]; for I have taken away my peace from this people, says the LORD, my steadfast love and mercy. Both great and small shall die in this land; they shall not be buried, and no one shall lament for them; there shall be no gashing, no shaving of the head

---

30. According to Anderson (*A Time to Mourn*, p. 84), this participation in the mourning rites reflects 'a processual usage' of the verb נחם.

for them. No one shall break bread for the mourner, to offer comfort
(לנחמו) for the dead; nor shall anyone give them the cup of consolation
to drink for their fathers or their mothers (NRSV).

In contrast, enemies do not share in the mourner's grief—they rejoice
instead. After Anat buries Baal and slaughters cattle and sheep for his
funeral offering, she goes to El's mountain, prostrates herself at his feet
and cries out:

> Now let Asherah and her sons rejoice,
> the goddess and her array of kinfolk.
> For Baal the Conqueror has died,
> the Prince, the Lord of the earth has perished.[31]

The psalmist is particularly distressed at the rejoicing of his enemies
over his sufferings:

> Yet when I stumbled they were glad
> and gathered together;
> they gathered together striking me unawares.
> They tore at me without ceasing;
> they put me to the test; they mocked me,
> gnashing their teeth at me (Ps. 35.15-16; NAB).

The psalmist prays in 35.19 and 24 (NAB):

> Let not my unprovoked enemies rejoice over me;
> let not my undeserved foes wink knowingly.
> Do me justice, because you are just, O LORD;
> my God, let them not rejoice over me.

The mourner's grief is greatly aggravated by the rejoicing of his
enemies.

Silence as a Mourning Rite. The nominal clause in Job 2.13b adds that
none of Job's friends spoke a word to Job. It may be safely inferred that
Job also keeps silent during all that time. This moment of silence has
been noted as a recognized part of the mourning ritual.[32] The initial
loud weeping and wailing, accompanied by visible ritual gestures such
as tearing clothes, strewing dirt on the head, gashing the body, and so
on, was usually followed by a period of stunned silence.[33]

31. *CTA* 6.1.39-43; Anderson, *A Time to Mourn*, p. 73.
32. N. Lohfink, 'Enthielten die im Alten Testament bezeugten Klageriten eine
Phase des Schweigens?', *VT* 12 (1962), pp. 260-77.
33. Lipiński, *La liturgie*, pp. 32-33.

These two phases are clearly reflected in the parallel commands to wail (הילילו) and to be still (דמו) over the fall of Tyre (Isa. 23.1-3a; NRSV):

> Wail, O ships of Tarshish,
>   for your fortress is destroyed.
> When they came in from Cyprus
>   they learned of it.
> Be still, O inhabitants of the coast,
>   O merchants of Sidon,
> your messengers crossed over the sea
>   and were on the mighty waters.

The mourning over the fall of Tyre is also recorded in Ezek. 26.15-17a (NRSV):

> Thus says the Lord GOD to Tyre: Shall not the coastlands shake at the sound of your fall, when the wounded groan, when slaughter goes on within you? Then all the princes of the sea shall step down from their thrones; they shall remove their robes and strip off their embroidered garments. They shall clothe themselves with trembling, and shall sit on the ground; they shall tremble every moment, and be appalled [ושממו] at you. And they shall raise a lamentation over you.

Like El at the news of the death of Baal, the 'princes of the sea', that is, the maritime partners of Tyre, descend from their thrones, remove their royal garments and sit on the ground. They are stunned into silence by the enormity of the destruction. The verbal root שמם, 'be appalled/horrified', connotes the idea of being speechless and motionless out of fear. This moment of silence helps to recollect the past, and to realize and accept the present. When the impact of the devastation has lessened, the princes intone a lament for Tyre.

Ezra the scribe also goes through the ritual mourning gestures and the moment of silence when he learns that the returned exiles, including the priests and the Levites, had intermarried with the indigenous population of Canaan:

> When I heard this, I tore my garment and my mantle, and pulled hair from my head and beard, and sat appalled [משומם]. Then all who trembled at the words of the God of Israel, because of the faithlessness of the returned exiles, gathered around me while I sat appalled [משומם] until the evening sacrifice (Ezra 9.3-4; NRSV).

By tearing his clothes, pulling hair from his head and beard, and sitting motionless in stunned silence Ezra is 'enacting mourning, as it were, for the death of the community', since the community deserves the judgment of death through its sin.[34]

Such ritual silence seems to be present whenever the mourning or supplication/lamentation is for a great and terrible event, as in the cases cited above.

Speaking and Giving Advice to the Mourner. In Job 3, Job breaks the mourning silence and begins to speak. He denies that suffering is the corollary of sin and that good fortune necessarily follows virtue. Job's friends think that he completely misunderstands God's governance of the world and seek to correct his view of providence in the ensuing chapters. In delivering their speeches, Job's friends act as מנחמים, 'comforters', for that is the title Job confers on them in Job 16.2 (NAB):

שמעתי כאלה רבות מנחמי עמל כלכם:

> I have heard this sort of thing many times.
> Wearisome comforters are you all!

The use of מנחמים in Job 16.2 may be compared with Isa. 40.1-2 (NAB) where נחמו, 'comfort', is used in interlinear parallelism with דברו על־לב, 'speak tenderly' (lit. 'speak to the heart of'):

נחמו נחמו עמי יאמר אלהיכם:
דברו על־לב ירושלם וקראו אליה
כי מלאה צבאה כי נרצה עונה
כי לקחה מיד יהוה כפלים בכל־חטאתיה:

> Comfort, give comfort to my people, says your God.
> Speak tenderly to Jerusalem, and proclaim to her
> That her service is at an end, her guilt is expiated;
> Indeed she has received from the hand of the LORD double for all her
>   sins.

The addressees here are presumably angels, messengers in Yahweh's heavenly court. They are to comfort Jerusalem in mourning, the symbol of the people of Israel in exile.

When Boaz gives Ruth permission to glean in his field, he advises her to keep close to the young women who work for him and not to glean in another field. He also commends her for her devotion to Naomi; then Ruth answers him (2.13; NRSV):

---

34. H.G.M, Williamson, *Ezra, Nehemiah* (WBC, 16; Waco, TX: Word Books, 1985), p. 133.

> May I continue to find favor in your sight, my lord, for you have com-
> forted me and spoken kindly to your servant [כי נחמתני וכי דברת על־לב
> שפחתך], even though I am not one of your servants.

The verb נחם is again paired with דבר על־לב in Gen. 50.21 when
Joseph reassures his brothers that he will continue to take care of them
and their children even after the death of Jacob:

> 'So have no fear; I myself will provide for you and your little ones.'
> In this way he reassured them and spoke kindly to them [וינחם אותם
> וידבר על־לבם].

To sum up, the act of comforting involves participation in the mourning rites and also speaking kindly and giving advice to the mourner.

Effects on the Mourner

The act of comforting can lead to two opposite reactions on the part of
the mourner. On the one hand, the mourner may be comforted, that is,
his[35] grief is alleviated. He accepts others' participation in the mourning
rites as a sign of sympathy and their words of comfort as good advice to
follow. On the other hand, the mourner may not be comforted. His pain
is still unbearable. He suspects that the true intention behind others'
participation in the mourning rites and their words of comfort are irrel-
evant to his grief. Whether the mourner is comforted or not, the verb
נחם in these cases has the nuance of 'bringing about the cessation of
mourning'.[36]

Positive Result: The Mourner Is Comforted. When the mourner is
comforted, his behavior changes—he stops mourning. The Old Testament relates a detailed change of behavior in the case of David. While
the child born by Bathsheba to David was ill, David prayed and fasted
and lay all night on the ground. But when the child died, David washed,
anointed himself, changed his clothes, went to worship in the house of
Yahweh, came back, and ate.

> Then David comforted [וינחם דוד] his wife Bathsheba. He went and slept
> with her; and she conceived and bore him a son, who was named
> Solomon (2 Sam. 12.24; NAB).

35. I am aware that the mourner may be a male or female figure. For the sake of
simplicity, I assume a male figure in general propositions so as to avoid possible
confusion with Jerusalem, the female mourner.

36. Anderson (*A Time to Mourn*, p. 84) calls this 'the resultative usage' of the
verb נחם.

The resumption of sexual relations also indicates the cessation of the mourning period for Ephraim. Ephraim mourned many days for his sons who were killed by the people of Gath. After Ephraim's brothers came to comfort him [לנחמו],

> Ephraim went in to his wife, and she conceived and bore a son; and he named him Beriah, because disaster had befallen his house (1 Chron. 7.23; NRSV).

Negative Result: The Mourner Is Not Comforted. When the mourner is not comforted, he keeps on mourning. He does not want to stop the mourning sequence and return to normal life. This is what the text probably means when it says that Jacob 'refused to be comforted' (וימאן להתנחם). Jacob's answer to his children, 'No, I shall go down to Sheol to my son, mourning' (Gen. 37.35; NRSV), shows that he intends to go on mourning until he dies. It may be inferred that in comforting Jacob, his children tried to persuade him to stop mourning for Joseph, but Jacob could not get over his grief. His answer recalls El's mourning cry over Baal: 'I am descending to the underworld, after Baal.'[37]

Yahweh says in Jer. 31.15: 'Rachel is weeping for her children; she refuses to be comforted for her children [מאנה להנחם], because they are no more.'

In the next two verses, Yahweh commands Rachel to stop weeping and promises that her children will return from exile. Thus the refusal to be comforted here means that Rachel does not want to or cannot stop mourning, that she is not comforted.

In Sir. 38.17-18,[38] Ben Sira advises against such excessive grief which may cause harm, even death:

> Weeping bitterly, mourning fully,
>> pay your tribute of sorrow, as he [the deceased] deserves,
> A day, two days, to prevent gossip;
>> then be comforted [παρακλήθητι] for your sorrow.
> For grief can bring on an extremity
>> and heartache destroy one's health.

The advice 'be comforted' here has the resultative meaning of 'stop grieving, stop the mourning process'.

37. CTA 5.6.25. Anderson, *A Time to Mourn*, p. 63.
38. I follow the translation in P.W. Skehan and A.A. Di Lella, *The Wisdom of Ben Sira* (AB, 39; New York: Doubleday, 1987), p. 439, except for the last colon of v. 17, where I give a literal translation of the Greek.

Job's friends do not succeed in comforting him. Instead, they are rebuked by Job who calls them 'wearisome comforters' (מנחמי עמל, Job 16.2). Later on, at the close of the story, they are rebuked by Yahweh for not speaking what is right concerning Yahweh (42.7-9).

The Old Testament records a case of international mourning where the comforters from abroad fail in their task of comforting, due to the misinterpretation of their mission by the host country:

> Some time afterward, the king of the Ammonites died, and his son Hanun succeeded him. David said, 'I will deal loyally with Hanun son of Nahash, just as his father dealt loyally with me.' So David sent envoys to console him concerning his father (2 Sam. 10.1-2a; NRSV).

In the ancient Near East, when a treaty partner died and his successor was enthroned, the other partner was expected to send emissaries.[39] An example of this protocol may be found here,[40] although the text does not mention explicitly any treaty between David and Nahash. David sends מנחמים, 'comforters', with the mission to comfort (לנחמו) Hanun the new king. Their presence at Hanun's court should show that David honors the deceased (2 Sam. 10.3), that he wishes to support Hanun's claim to the throne, and probably also that he wants to confirm the covenant bond with the new king.[41] David's genuine intention may be inferred from a related passage in 1 Kgs 5.15. King Hiram of Tyre hears of Solomon's enthronement and sends emissaries to Solomon, because Hiram had always been a friend (אהב) to David. The word 'friend' must refer to a former treaty relationship between Hiram and David.[42] The account goes on to relate that Hiram and Solomon made a treaty (1 Kgs 5.26). In the case of David and Hanun, the latter's advisers suspect David's intentions. The Ammonites consequently shame David's representatives by distorting a common rite of mourning. The mourner usually shaved off the edges of the beard (Lev. 19.27; 21.5) or the whole beard (Isa. 15.2; Jer. 41.5; 48.37). Here, half the beard of each envoy is shaved. Just as captives were led into exile naked (Isa. 20.1-6), so David's envoys were sent home with the lower halves of

39. W.L. Moran, 'The Ancient Near Eastern Background of the Love of God in Deuteronomy', *CBQ* 25 (1963), pp. 77-87 (80).

40. K.D. Sakenfeld, *The Meaning of Hesed in the Hebrew Bible: A New Inquiry* (HSM, 17; Missoula, MT: Scholars Press, 1978), p. 76.

41. S.M. Olyan, 'Honor, Shame, and Covenant Relations in Ancient Israel and its Environment', *JBL* 115 (1996), pp. 201-18 (212).

42. Moran, 'Love of God', p. 81.

their garments cut off, exposing their buttocks (2 Sam. 10.4).

To sum up, the מנחם carries out his function by participation in the mourning rites and by words of kindness and advice. His success or failure depends on the severity of the loss (especially from the mourner's viewpoint), on other external circumstances (such as the suspicion of Hanun's advisers) and on his own wisdom and power (e.g. Job's friends fail to comfort him because they are limited in their perception of God).

The mourning rites and the role of the מנחם analyzed above, particularly in the book of Job, provide a biblical basis for studying the three texts of Lamentations 1 and 2 and Isa. 51.9–52.2 against the literary setting of the Israelite mourning ceremony.

Text Editions Used in This Study

The primary text editions used in this study are as follows:

The Masoretic Text (MT):

Elliger, K., and W. Rudolph (eds.), *Biblia hebraica stuttgartensia* (Stuttgart: Deutsche Bibelgesellschaft, 1984 [1967–77]).

The Septuagint (LXX):

Rahlfs, A., *Septuaginta* (Stuttgart: Deutsche Bibelgesellschaft, 1979 [1935]).
Ziegler, J., *Isaias* (Septuaginta, 14; Göttingen: Vandenhoeck & Ruprecht, 1983).
—*Threni* (Septuaginta, 15; Göttingen: Vandenhoeck & Ruprecht, 1976).

The Vulgate (Vg):

Biblia Sacra iuxta latinam vulgatam versionem. XIII. Isaiae (Rome: Typis Polyglottis Vaticanis, 1969).
Biblia Sacra iuxta latinam vulgatam versionem. XIV. *Lamentationes* (Rome: Typis Polyglottis Vaticanis, 1972).

The Syriac Peshitta (Syr):

Brock, S.P. (ed.), *The Old Testament in Syriac.* III/1. *Isaiah* (Leiden: E.J. Brill, 1987).
Albrektson, B., *Studies in the Text and Theology of the Book of Lamentations* (STL, 21; Lund: C.W.K. Gleerup, 1963).

Albrektson provides a list of MSS containing the complete text of Lamentations.[43] Among these MSS, the oldest exhibiting a good type of text are as follows:

---

43. Albrektson, *Text and Theology*, pp. 8-17.

(1) MS D (British Museum, London): it is dated to the sixth century, and contains Jeremiah, Lamentations, the Epistle of Baruch and Baruch;

(2) MS A (Codex Ambrosianus B, Milan): also dated to the sixth century; it contains the Old Testament and Josephus's *Jewish War*, Book 6;

(3) MS P (Bibliothèque Nationale, Paris): it is dated to the seventh or eighth century and contains the complete Bible, although several leaves of the Old Testament and large parts of the New Testament are now missing;

(4) MS F (Biblioteca Medicea Laurenziana, Florence): it is dated in the ninth century and contains the greater part of the Old Testament;

(5) MS B (University of Cambridge): it is dated to the end of the twelfth century and contains a complete Bible, although the characters have become almost illegible in many places; fortunately, the text of Lamentations is in a fairly good state of preservation;

(6) MS O (Selly Oak Colleges Library, Birmingham): dated to the fifteenth or sixteenth century, it contains large portions of the Old Testament but with a great number of omissions of single words and phrases.

Since Codex Ambrosianus B (MS A) will be reproduced in the Leiden edition of the Old Testament Peshitta, Albrektson has chosen to present in his book (*Text and Theology*) an eclectic text based on the ancient MSS DAPF, followed sometimes by MSS BO, with a critical *apparatus*. However, his eclectic text differs from MS A only in the following passages, where [MS] A has either an obvious clerical error or a peculiar reading which there is no reason to regard as original against the evidence of other authorities: 1.10, 20; 2.7, 8, 17, 18, 19, 20; 3.21; 4.2, 4, 8, 18.[44]

Biblical texts are quoted from the NAB and NRSV when so indicated; otherwise, all other translations are my own.

<hr />

44. Albrektson, *Text and Theology*, p. 33.

Chapter 2

LAMENTATIONS 1

The book of Lamentations consists of five chapters, each of which is a self-contained poem. The first four chapters follow the alphabetic acrostic pattern: each is composed of 22 stanzas, and the first line of each stanza in chs. 1, 2 and 4 begins with a letter in the order of letters in the Hebrew alphabet; ch. 3 is peculiar in that all three lines of each stanza begin with the same letter of the alphabet which marks the given stanza. Chapter 5 has 22 lines, but the first letters in each line do not follow the sequence of letters in the Hebrew alphabet.

All five chapters are generally thought to be closely related to the destruction of Jerusalem in 587 BCE, and to have been composed shortly after this disastrous event recorded in 2 Kgs 25.1-4a, 8-12 (NAB):

> In the tenth month of the ninth year of Zedekiah's reign, on the tenth day of the month, Nebuchadnezzar, king of Babylon, and his whole army advanced against Jerusalem, encamped around it, and built siege walls on every side. The siege of the city continued until the eleventh year of Zedekiah. On the ninth day of the fourth month, when famine had gripped the city, and the people had no more bread, the city walls were breached.
>
> …On the seventh day of the fifth month (this was in the nineteenth year of Nebuchadnezzar, king of Babylon), Nebuzaradan, captain of the bodyguard, came to Jerusalem as the representative of the king of Babylon. He burned the house of the LORD, the palace of the king, and all the houses of Jerusalem; every large building was destroyed by fire. Then the Chaldean troops who were with the captain of the guard tore down the walls that surrounded Jerusalem.
>
> Then Nebuzaradan, captain of the guard, led into exile the last of the people remaining in the city, and those who had deserted to the king of Babylon, and the last of the artisans. But some of the country's poor, Nebuzaradan, captain of the guard, left behind as vinedressers and farmers.

W. Rudolph suggests by contrast that Lamentations 1 refers to the events of 597 BCE since this chapter does not mention the destruction of the city and its temple.[1] D.R. Hillers refutes this hypothesis on two counts: first, to say that ch. 1 does not mention the destruction of the city and its temple is 'essentially an argument from silence'; and secondly, the first siege in 597 BCE was too short[2] to fit the references to severe famine in vv. 11 and 19.[3] The majority of scholars agree that there are no objective criteria by which the specific date of composition can be determined for each of Lamentations' five poems; the general consensus is that all of them must have originated in the period between the fall of Jerusalem in 587 BCE and the Edict of Cyrus in 538 BCE. Claus Westermann suggests an even more specific *terminus ad quem*, around 550 BCE, the time when Deutero-Isaiah was active.[4]

The book of Lamentations provides a way for the catharsis of suffering. Indeed, it seems that the voices of eyewitnesses can still be heard through these laments.[5] They must have been sung by survivors at the mourning ceremonies which commemorated the catastrophe of 587 BCE, as can be inferred from the following texts:

> The second day after the murder of Gedaliah, before anyone knew of it, eighty men with beards shaved off, clothes in rags, and with gashes on their bodies came from Shechem, Shiloh, and Samaria, bringing food offerings and incense for the house of the LORD (Jer. 41.4-5; NAB).

> Thereupon this word of the LORD of hosts came to me: Say to all the people of the land and to the priests: When you fasted and mourned in the fifth and in the seventh month these seventy years, was it really for me that you fasted? (Zech. 7.4-5; NAB).

1.   W. Rudolph, *Das Buch Ruth, das Hohe Lied, die Klagelieder* (KAT, 17; Gütersloh: Gerd Mohn, 2nd edn, 1962), pp. 209-210. Rudolph still has a point. See my exegesis of vv. 10-11 (pp. 80-83).

2.   This siege lasted about two months, according to 'The Conquest of Jerusalem', in *ANET*, p. 564: 'Year 7, month Kislimu: The king of Akkad moved his army into Hatti land, laid siege to the city of Judah, and the king took the city on the second day of the month Addaru. He appointed in it a [new] king of his liking, took heavy booty from it, and brought it into Babylon.'

3.   Hillers, *Lamentations*, p. 10.

4.   Westermann, *Lamentations*, pp. 104-105; Westermann thinks that ch. 3 bears little relationship to the events of 587 BCE and therefore the limits of 587–550 BCE do not apply to ch. 3.

5.   Westermann, *Lamentations*, pp. 54-55, 61.

Thus says the LORD of hosts: The fast days of the fourth, the fifth, the seventh, and the tenth months shall become occasions of joy and gladness, cheerful festivals for the house of Judah; only love faithfulness and peace (Zech. 8.19; NAB).

In this chapter, I will first give a translation of Lamentations 1, followed by critical notes; then I will discuss the literary setting of the mourning ceremony and the problem of the chapter's address and structure. The exegesis forms the next section. The conclusion will summarize the fresh insights gained from reading Lamentations 1 against the setting of a mourning ceremony.

Translation and Critical Notes

Since the poem contains only cited speeches without narrative introductions, I indicate my understanding of who is speaking in parentheses before a given speech. One speaker is clearly Jerusalem personified as the chief mourner. The other speaker is then 'the second speaker', although he[6] speaks first in the poem. A full discussion will follow in the section on the address problem.

(The second speaker)

1   Alas, she sits alone,
         the city once full of people!
     She has become a widow,[a]
         she that once was great among the nations!
     Once a princess over the city-states,[b]
         she is now subjected to forced labor!

2   She weeps bitterly through the night,
         with tears on her cheeks.
     She has no one to comfort her
         among all [a]those who have loved her;[a]
     All her friends have dealt treacherously with her,
         they have become her enemies.

6.   For the sake of clarity, I have chosen to refer to the second speaker as 'he', so as to avoid any confusion with the use of 'she' for Jerusalem.

3   Judah has gone into exile
          after[a] having endured oppression and cruel enslavement.
    She sits [b]as a mourner[b] among the nations,
          she has found no rest.
    All those who hunted her down have overtaken her
          in [c]her difficult situation.[c]

4   The roads to Zion mourn
          for lack of pilgrims coming to the feast.
    All her gates are deserted,[a]
          her priests groan.
    Her virgins [b]have been led away,[b]
          and she herself is bitter.

5   Her foes have become masters,
          her enemies prosper,
    Because Yahweh has afflicted her
          for the multitude of her transgressions.
    Her children have departed,
          captives before the foe.

6   And departed from[a] daughter Zion
          is all her splendor.
    Her princes were like rams[b]
          that had not found pasture.
    They departed without strength
          before their captors.

7   Jerusalem remembers
          [a]the miserable days of the exile,[a]
    [b][All her treasures
          that were from days of old,][b]
    When her people fell into the hand of the foe,
          and she had no one to help her.
    The foes [c]gloated over[c] her,
          they laughed at her misfortune.[d]

8   Jerusalem sinned grievously,[a]
          therefore she has become [b]an object of head-wagging.[b]

All those who once honored her now despise her,
    for they have seen her nakedness.
She herself groaned,
    and turned away.

9   Her filth is on her skirt;^a
    she gave no thought to her future.
Thus ^bshe has fallen astoundingly,^b
    she has no one to comfort her.

(Jerusalem)
    O Yahweh, look at ^cmy affliction,^c
    for the enemy has gone too far!

(The second speaker)
10   The foes stretched out their hands
    for all her precious things.
Indeed she saw nations
    invade her sanctuary,
^aWhom you forbade
    to enter your assembly.^a

11   All her people groaned
    as they searched for bread.
They surrendered their treasures for food,
    to keep themselves alive.

(Jerusalem)
    Look, O Yahweh, and see
    how despised I am!

12   ^aCome, all you who pass by,^a
    look and see,
If there is any pain like my pain,
    which was inflicted upon me,
With which Yahweh afflicted me,
    on the day of his burning wrath.

13   From on high he sent fire,
    ^ahe brought it down^a into my bones.

He spread a net for my feet,
    [b]he turned me back in defeat.[b]
He left me appalled,
    in pain all day long.

14   [a]A watch was kept over my sins,[a]
    they were bundled together by his hand.
They went up my neck;
    he caused my strength to fail.
The Lord delivered me into their grip[b]
    [c]from which I cannot rise.[c]

15   The Lord heaped up[a] all my warriors
    in my midst.
He summoned against me an assembly
    to crush my young men.
The Lord trampled in a winepress
    virgin daughter Judah.

16   For these things I weep;
    my eyes[a] flow with tears.
But far from me is any comforter
    to save my life.
My children are appalled,
    for the enemy has prevailed.

(The second speaker)
17   Zion has stretched forth her hands;[a]
    still she has no one to comfort her.
Yahweh gave orders against Jacob
    that his neighbors be his foes.
Jerusalem has become
    [b]an object of head-wagging[b] among them.

(Jerusalem)

18   Yahweh is just,
    for I have rebelled against his word.
Listen, all you peoples,[a]
    and consider my pain!

My young women and my young men
  have gone into captivity.

19 I called to my lovers;[a]
      they deceived me.
    My priests and my elders
      perished in the city,
    Though they had sought food
      [b]to keep themselves alive.[b]

20 See, O Yahweh, how distressed I am:
      my inner parts are in ferment.
    My heart is convulsed[a] within me,
      [b]for I have rebelled stubbornly.[b]
    [c]Outside the sword has bereaved;
      death[d] is in the city.[c]

21 Hear[a] how I groan,
      I have no one to comfort me.
    All my enemies [b]rejoiced at the evil done to me.[b]
      that you yourself did it.
    [c]O, bring on[c] the day you have announced,
      so that they may be as I am!

22 Let all their wickedness come before you,
      and deal severely with them,
    As you have dealt severely with me,
      because of all my transgressions.
    For many are my groans,
      and my heart is in pain.

---

1 [a]The preposition כ in כאלמנה can mean 'exactly like' (e.g. Neh. 7.2, כי־הוא כאיש אמת, 'for he was a faithful man'; see *GHB*, §133g), and so does not need to be translated.

[b]The word מדינה occurs only in texts written about the time of Lamentations or later (e.g. 1 Kgs 20.14; Est. 1.1; Ezra 2.1; Neh. 1.3), and normally means 'province' in biblical Hebrew. It actually means 'city' in Aramaic. In the present context, it refers to 'city-states' in the golden era of Israel under David and Solomon, and other periods when Jerusalem was a dominant power.

2 [a-a]A distinction is to be made here between אהביה, 'those who have loved her' (v. 2b) and רעיה, 'her friends' (v. 2c). It is true that אהב can mean 'a friend' with the nuance of 'a treaty partner', as in the case of Hiram, King of Tyre, who is 'a friend' of David in 1 Kgs 5.15 (Moran, 'Love of God', p. 81). However, the distinction between אהביה and רעיה in this verse is that between family and blood relatives on the one hand, and friends on the other hand. See Deut. 13.7; Ps. 38.12; Job 42.11.

3 [a]*HALOT*, II, pp. 597-99, gives two interpretations for מן:

(1) local: 'out of', i.e. out of a state of sufferings, which Jerusalem had suffered at the hands of her oppressors;

(2) temporal: 'after', i.e. after having suffered x and y at the hands of the oppressors.

In the end, both local and temporal interpretations yield nearly the same meaning. The normal use of גלה מן seems to combine both local and temporal shades of meaning (e.g. 1 Sam. 4.21, 22; Ezek. 12.3; Hos. 10.5; Mic. 1.16). See Albrektson, *Text and Theology*, p. 57. The preposition מן in מעני and מרב is to be taken in the same composite sense.

[b-b]Implied meaning from the use of the same verb ישבה in v. 1a.

[c-c]Lit. 'between the straits'.

4 [a]The word שוממין is probably a dialectical 'nunation' for the sake of sound-patterning in v. 4b, which is accentuated by the presence of ו in the first colon: כל־שעריה שוממין כהניה נאנחים. Note the sounds *k, h, m, m, n* in the first colon, and *k, h, n, h, n, n, m* in the second.

[b-b]Read נהוגות with LXX (ἀγόμεναι). See exegesis below (pp. 65-66).

6 [a]The *kethib* מן־בת is the preferred reading here. Note the alliterative pattern in the first colon of v. 6a: yod, sade, nun in ויצא מן־, and sade, yod, nun in ציון.

[b]Both LXX κριοί, and Vg *arietes* vowel the consonants here as כְּאֵילִים, 'like rams', which seems better than MT כְּאַיָּלִים, 'like stags', since אַיִל is a title for leaders (e.g. Exod. 15.15; Ezek. 17.13; 2 Kgs 24.15). Jerusalem's leaders are depicted as being led off to exile like starved sheep. NAB also opts for LXX and Vg. See exegesis below (pp. 69-70).

7 [a-a]מרוד from רוד means 'wandering' like מחול, 'dancing' (e.g. Jer. 31.4; Lam. 5.15), and מבוא, 'entering' (e.g. 2 Sam. 3.25 *kethib*). The second colon lit. says: 'the days of her misery and her wandering.' The specific sense here of 'exile' is suggested by the first colon in v. 7c: בנפל עמה ביד־צר. But Lady Jerusalem has not gone anywhere. She is still in the same location. It is her citizens who are in exile. The phrase 'the miserable days of the exile' is an attempt to catch the sense of the colon in tolerable English.

[b-b]Verse 7b is a gloss. See the discussion below.

[c-c]Usually, the verbal phrase ראה ב means 'to gloat over' (e.g. Judg. 16.27; Mic. 7.10). Although the preposition ב is lacking here, the verb ראוה is parallel to שחקו

עַל and denotes the mocking glance of the enemy who rejoices over the misfortune of Jerusalem. See *HALOT*, III, p. 1158.

[d]The *hapax legomenon* מִשְׁבָּת is clearly derived from שָׁבַת, and means 'cessation, downfall, misfortune', or the like. 4QLam[a] reads מִשְׁבָּרִיה, 'her ruins', for מִשְׁבַּתָה, 'her misfortune'. F.M. Cross ('Studies in the Structure of Hebrew Verse: The Prosody of Lamentations 1.1-22', in C.L. Myers and M. O'Connor (eds.), *The Word of the Lord Shall Go Forth: Essays in Honor of David Noel Freedman in Celebration of his Sixtieth Birthday* [ASORSVS, 1; Winona Lake, IN: Eisenbrauns, 1983], pp. 129-55 [140-41]) favors מִשְׁבָּרִיה, and explains the reading in MT as a confusion of רִי for ת, which was common before the reduction of the size of י in the Jewish script. Both nouns make sense in the context, so I think it is unnecessary to emend MT.

8 [a]The infinitive absolute חָטֹא proposed by *BHS* is probably preferable, although the cognate accusative חֵטְא in MT is equally possible. See *GHB*, §125q.

[b-b]The *hapax legomenon* נִידָה is seen as deriving from נוּד which, in the qal, always conveys a sympathetic gesture and belongs in the mourning ceremony context (e.g. Jer. 15.5; 22.10; Job 2.11; 42.11). But in the hiphil, and combined with בְּרֹאשׁ, lit. 'at the head', the verbal clause means 'to shake, or wag the head', which is a gesture of scorn (e.g. Jer. 18.16). The same is true of the hithpolel in Jer. 48.27 where בְּרֹאשׁ is probably to be understood. Compare with מָנוֹד רֹאשׁ, 'object of head-wagging', in Ps. 44.15. See BDB, pp. 626-27; *HALOT*, II, pp. 678, 696; and the exegesis below (pp. 72-73).

9 [a]The plural noun שׁוּלִים in בְּשׁוּלֶיהָ, lit. 'on her skirts', is a plural of extension (see GKC, §124a-c); I therefore translate it as a singular, 'skirt'.

[b-b]LXX καὶ κατεβίβασεν ὑπέρογκα, 'and she has lowered her haughty tones', seems to have read a hiphil verb וַתֹּרֶד with the noun פְּלָאִים, 'wonders', as the direct object. The Masoretic pointing takes פְּלָאִים as an adverbial accusative, which is the only such use of this noun in the MT. On the use of the adverbial accusative, see *GHB*, §126c-d. Sym has καὶ κατήχθη ἐπὶ πλεῖον, 'and she was brought down still lower'. Basing itself on Sym and Vg *deposita est*, 'she is cast down', *BHS* suggests the reading וַתּוּרַד. Aq reads κατέβη θαυμαστά, 'she came down wondrously'. The Lucianic recension corrected LXX to πέπτωκεν θαυμαστῶς, 'she has fallen astoundingly'.

[c-c]LXX τὴν ταπείνωσίν μου, 'my affliction', Aq τὴν κακουχίαν μου, 'my misery', Vg *adflictionem meam*, 'my affliction', and Syr *šw'bdy*, 'my servitude', all read first-person possessive pronouns. *BHS*, in light of Bohairic and Ambrosius *humilitatem eius*, 'her abjection', suggests reading the third person (עָנְיָהּ, 'her affliction'), which makes the speaker the same as at the beginning of the verse. The readings of Bohairic and Ambrosius seem, however, to be cases of assimilation and facilitation (D. Barthélemy, *et al.*, *Critique textuelle de l'Ancien Testament*. II. *Esaïe, Jérémie, Lamentations* [OBO 50.2; Fribourg: Editions Universitaires, 1986], p. 868). NAB chooses the reading suggested by *BHS*. I retain MT with the majority of witnesses.

10 ᵃ⁻ᵃThe prohibition here refers to Deut. 23.4 where the assembly is called קְהַל יְהוָה, 'the assembly of Yahweh'. The speaker here is addressing Yahweh. The second-person pronoun in the first and the second cola of v. 10c refers to Yahweh. Thus, לֹא־יָבֹאוּ בְקָהָל לָךְ, lit. 'they shall not enter your assembly', cannot be a direct quotation.

12 ᵃ⁻ᵃMT לוֹא אֲלֵיכֶם, lit. 'not to/for you', yields no satisfactory sense. I follow the common emendation to לְכוּ, 'come', proposed by F. Praetorius ('Threni I, 12. 14. II, 6. 13', *ZAW* 15 [1895], pp. 143-46).

13 ᵃ⁻ᵃRead וַיֹּרִדֶנָּה, 'and he brought it down', instead of MT וַיִּרְדֶּנָּה, 'and he ruled it'. Both LXX κατήγαγεν αὐτό, 'he brought it down', and Syr *w'ḥtny*, 'and he brought me down', interpret MT as a hiphil from the root יָרַד, 'to come down', which makes more sense than the implied root רָדָה, 'to rule', of MT, or the implied Aramaic root רְדָא, 'to chastise', as interpreted by Vg (*et erudivit me*, 'and he chastised me'). In support of the root יָרַד used of fire from God, see 2 Kgs 1.10, 12, 14; 2 Chron. 7.1; and Hillers, *Lamentations*, p. 72.

ᵇ⁻ᵇFor the sense of defeat in the use of שׁוּב with אָחוֹר, see Pss. 9.4; 44.11; 56.10; Isa. 44.25.

14 ᵃ⁻ᵃMT נִשְׂקַד is a *hapax legomenon* from an unknown root שָׂקַד. Several MSS derive נִשְׂקַד from שָׁקַד, 'to keep watch, be wakeful'. LXX ἐγρηγορήθη ἐπί, 'a watch has been kept over', reflects the pointing נִשְׁקַד עַל which is followed in my translation. Vg *vigilavit*, 'has watched', also presupposes נִשְׁקַד instead of MT נִשְׂקַד. It seems that Syr *'tt'yrw 'ly ḥṭhÿ*, 'my sins were stirred up/aroused against me', is also based on the root שָׁקַד, although Syr makes פִּשְׁעַי the subject and consequently has a plural verb.

ᵇThe word יְדֵי does not refer to the hands of the foes who have not been mentioned since v. 10 (contra several commentators, e.g. Westermann, *Lamentations*, p. 133; W.D. Reyburn, *A Handbook on Lamentations* [United Bible Societies Handbook Series; New York: United Bible Societies, 1992], p. 32; J. Hunter, *Faces of a Lamenting City: The Development and Coherence of the Book of Lamentations* [BEATAJ, 39; New York: Peter Lang, 1996], p. 96). The 'hands' here are most easily understood rather as the 'grip' of the sins (mentioned in v. 14a) which become a weight on Jerusalem's neck (v. 14b). The word יַד is used in the construct state with פֶּשַׁע also in Job 8.4: אִם־בָּנֶיךָ חָטְאוּ־לוֹ וַיְשַׁלְּחֵם בְּיַד־פִּשְׁעָם, 'If your children have sinned against him [Shaddai], he would have sent them away into the grip of their guilt.'

ᶜ⁻ᶜFor an asyndetic relative clause as a virtual genitive after a construct noun, see Exod. 4.13 and *GHB*, §129q.

15 ᵃThis verb has been traditionally connected with סָלָה I (BDB, p. 699), which occurs only once more in the MT, i.e. in the qal in Ps. 119.118, probably with the meaning 'to make light of, to hold in contempt'. LXX ἐξῆρε, 'he removed', Vg *abstulit*, 'he has taken away', and Syr *kbš*, 'he trampled down', are attempts to interpret a rare verb. Hillers (*Lamentations*, pp. 74-75) looks for a consistency of imagery in the verse and suggests that סלה here is a biform of סלל, 'to heap up', used in Jer. 50.26. The imagery throughout the verse is that of harvest. Hunter (*Faces*, p. 116) also adopts Hillers' suggestion. See exegesis below (pp. 86-87).

16 ᵃDittography in MT. Read a single עיני with a few MSS, LXX, Syr and Vg.

17 ᵃThe ב in בידיה introduces the object as a means or instrument with which the action is performed. For this ב *instrumenti*, see *GHB*, §125m; GKC, §119q.

ᵇ⁻ᵇThe word נדה sometimes means 'menstruation, menstruating woman', but it is not restricted to that meaning. Marrying a brother's wife is נדה, 'a horrible deed' (Lev. 20.21). King Hezekiah told the Levites to carry out the נדה, 'things involved in idolatrous worship', from the holy place (2 Chron. 29.5). The house of David and the inhabitants of Jerusalem will get a fountain that removes לחטאת ולנדה, 'sin that defiles' (Zech. 13.1). The land of the Canaanites is a land נדה היא בנדת עמי הארצות בתועבתיהם אשר מלאוה מפה אל־פה, 'unclean with the filth of the peoples of the land, with the abominations with which they have filled it from one end to the other' (Ezra 9.11; NAB). In all the above texts, the word נדה involves real moral turpitude, not the ritual/legal 'impurity' connected with menstruation. Similarly, in this context, נדה means something different than the impurity associated with menstruation. Jerusalem sinned by breaking the covenant with Yahweh and was consequently punished by Yahweh. Now she sits on the ground, mourning the loss of her children. This humiliated Jerusalem has come to be regarded as a worthless person, 'an object of head-wagging', in the eyes of the passers-by.

18 ᵃRead the *qere* העמים with many MSS, LXX and Targums.

19 ᵃThe piel participle מאהבים, 'lovers', is to be distinguished from the qal participle אהבים (v. 2b), which represents, in the context, family and blood relatives. The piel stem carries an intensive nuance. The piel participle of אהב, 'to love', occurs 16 times in the MT (Jer. 22.20, 22; 30.14; Ezek. 16.33, 36, 37; 23.5, 9, 22; Hos. 2.7, 9, 12, 14, 15; Zech. 13.6; Lam. 1.19) with the pejorative sense of 'inconstant lovers' who constantly change the objects of their love. See E. Jenni, *Das hebräische Piel* (Zürich: EVZ Verlag, 1968), p. 158.

ᵇ⁻ᵇThe indirect volitive after a past tense to express purpose is extremely rare. *GHB*, §116e, so identifies the form here, as does S.R. Driver, *A Treatise on the Use of the Tenses in Hebrew and Some Other Syntactical Questions* (Oxford: Clarendon Press, 2nd rev. edn, 1881), §63. At the end of v. 19c, LXX reads καὶ οὐχ εὗρον, 'but they found none'. This added clause is not found in the Hebrew *Vorlage* which Origen used. Nor is it present in either Vg or Targums. But Syr has it as *wl' 'škhw*, 'but they found none'. This addition may have been an early gloss in the *Vorlagen* of LXX and Syr, which was subsequently removed by the Masoretes in their critical recension of the text. See Albrektson, *Text and Theology*, p. 80.

20   ᵃLit. 'is turned upside down'.

ᵇ⁻ᵇVg *amaritudine plena sum*, 'I am full of bitterness', seems to have read the root מרר, 'to be bitter', instead of the MT root מרה, 'to be rebellious'. C.L. Seow ('A Textual Note on Lam 1.20,' *CBQ* 47 [1985], pp. 416-19) argues for מרר by suggesting that Syr *mmrmrw mrmrt*, from the root *mr*, 'to be bitter', and perhaps also LXX παραπικραίνουσα παρεπίκρανα, from παραπικραίνω, 'to embitter', may have read the same root מרר. Actually, Syr uses the intensive conjugation palpal, and LXX the active voice; thus the verbs in both Syr and LXX mean 'to make bitter, to rebel against'. Both readings (מרה or מרר) make sense, and the evidence from the versions is not strong enough to support an emendation of MT.

ᶜ⁻ᶜThe opposition בבית/מחוץ distinguishes the countryside from Jerusalem. See Ezek. 7.15 where בחוץ is defined by בשדה, 'in the field', and מבית by בעיר, 'in the city'. See also Jer. 14.18 which makes a similar contrast between השדה and העיר.

ᵈFor the prepositionally introduced subject כמות, lit. 'like the death', of this nominal sentence, see *GHB*, §154b. The preposition כ here means 'exactly like' and, as in v. 1, is best omitted in English (*GHB*, §133g).

21   ᵃRead שמע, imperative singular, with Syr *šmʿ*, 'hear'.

ᵇ⁻ᵇThe first colon of v. 21b, as has been noted by many commentators, seems excessively long. Hillers (*Lamentations*, pp. 77-78) views it as a conflate text: 'All my enemies heard of my trouble/All my enemies rejoiced.' Another way of handling the problem is to regard שמעו as a dittography from the preceding line and to read כל־איבי ברעתי ששו, 'all my enemies rejoiced at the evil done to me'. The ב before רעתי may have dropped out due to haplography.

ᶜ⁻ᶜRead את הבא, imperative singular, with Syr *ʾyt*, 'bring on'. The second א may have dropped out through haplography. The imperative is the form suggested by the following ויהיו, 'that they may be'. See *GHB*, §116d.

The Mourning Ceremony Setting

Lamentations 1 presents a long series of woes that have befallen Jerusalem comparable to the woes that befall Job. In the face of these woes, what else could Lady Jerusalem do in the society of ancient Israel but begin a mourning ceremony? That is clear from the opening colon of the opening line: איכה ישבה בדד, 'Alas, she sits alone!'

Not only humans are described as sitting on the ground mourning. Capital cities as literary figures can also be described in that way; for example, personified Jerusalem in Isa. 3.26 (NRSV):

ואנו ואבלו פתחיה ונקתה לארץ תשב:

And her gates shall lament and mourn;
    ravaged, she shall sit upon the ground.

In Jer. 48.18a, in view of the disasters that await her, Dibon, the capital city of Moab, is told to come down from its glory and sit on the ground:[7]

רדי מכבוד ישבי בצמא ישבת בת־דיבון

> Come down from glory,
>> and sit on the parched ground,
>> enthroned daughter Dibon! (NRSV)

The mourning rite of sitting on the ground (as Job did) is, in turn, linked to weeping in Lam. 1.2a, 16a:

> She weeps bitterly through the night,
>> with tears on her cheeks.

> For these things I weep;
>> my eyes flow with tears.

Verse 2a presumes that the mourning ceremony goes on day and night, which recalls Job's friends sitting with him seven days and nights before he intones his lament. Job is not described as weeping, but his friends weep (Job 2.12). Jacob also weeps for Joseph (Gen. 37.35).

Lady Jerusalem weeps, seated on the ground, presumably girded with a skirt of sackcloth around the hips (v. 9a), leaving the upper body bare, for her 'nakedness' is seen (v. 8b). Her skirt is filthy (v. 9a) from the dirt which she is sitting on and which possibly she has sprinkled on her head.

When Job's friends hear of his tragic loss, they come to comfort him. Jacob's sons and daughters also come to comfort him at the news of Joseph's death. But Lady Jerusalem has no comforter (vv. 2b, 9b, 16b, 17a, 21a). Her children have been led into exile (v. 5c), and her friends have become her enemies (vv. 2c, 17b). Jerusalem is alone, forlorn (v. 1a).

Some priests may be present (v. 4b), but they are themselves groaning from sorrow and therefore cannot comfort Lady Jerusalem. She is appalled, transfixed in her grief (v. 13c). One of the few mourners on the scene, the 'second speaker', intones a lament. He may act like the chief lamentation singer in *The Curse of Agade*, or like one of those male singers who recite lamentations at mourning ceremonies (cf. 2 Chron. 35.25). He does not address Jerusalem, but describes her

---

7.   Read with many MSS, the Versions, and *qere*: וישבי; *kethib* ישבי is a copyist's error. W.L. Holladay, *Jeremiah 2* (Hermeneia; Minneapolis: Fortress Press, 1989), p. 342.

plight with sympathy and understanding. His lament helps Lady Jerusalem to release her pent-up feelings of bitterness and worthlessness. She finally appeals to Yahweh (vv. 9c, 11c, 20-22) and pours out her heart to outsiders (vv. 12-16, 18b-19).

Poetic Structure and Address

Lamentations 1 is an alphabetic acrostic poem with 22 verses. Each verse is a stanza of three lines or bicola, except v. 7, which has four bicola, one of which is considered a gloss (see exegesis below, pp. 69-70). The *qinah* (lamentation) meter (3+2 accents) accounts for roughly one-third of the poem (28 out of a total of 67 bicola).[8] Some lines may be described as 2+2, others as 3+3. Cases of assonance, alliteration, rhyme, chiasm and *inclusio* will be pointed out below and in the course of the exegesis.

Poetic Structure

Lamentations 1 can be neatly divided into two sections of 11 verses each:

Verses 1-11. The 'second speaker' (Jerusalem is the first speaker since she is the chief mourner and readily identified) speaks with two brief interruptions by Jerusalem in vv. 9c and 11c:

1. *Verses 1-9b: lament of the second speaker.*

> vv. 1-2: Jerusalem's mourning
> vv. 3-6: cause of her mourning
> > vv. 3-4: events outside the city
> > vv. 5-6: events in the city
> vv. 7-9b: Jerusalem's mourning

This lament by the second speaker is marked by the refrain: אֵין־לָהּ מְנַחֵם, lit. 'there is not to her a comforter' (v. 2b), forming an *inclusio* with אֵין מְנַחֵם לָהּ, lit. 'there is not a comforter to her' (v. 9b).

The opening stanza (v. 1) is remarkably structured. The three bicola are parallel to each other. The first two are linked by the word רַבָּתִי, while the second and the third bicola form an a:b::b´:a´ chiastic pattern:

היתה כאלמנה::רבתי בגוים::שׂרתי במדינות::היתה למס

She has become a widow: she that once was great among the nations::
once a princess over the city-states: she is now subjected to forced labor.

The whole stanza is skillfully based on assonance involving *a* (24 times) and *i* (6 times). The sound *i* occurs three times in the *hireq compaginis* used in a poetic form of the construct state in רבתי עם, 'full of people', רבתי בגוים, 'great among the nations', and שׂרתי במדינות, 'princess over the city-states'.

Another a:b::b′:a′ chiastic pattern is found in the last two bicola of the second stanza:

אין־לה מנחם::מכל־אהביה::כל־רעיה בגדו בה::היו לה לאיבים

She has no one to comfort her: among all those who have loved her::all her friends have dealt treacherously with her: they have become her enemies.

The segment on the cause of Jerusalem's mourning (vv. 3-6) shows the following poetic features:

Verse 3 has an *o* assonance and an internal rhyme in ישׁבה and מצאה in v. 3b. Moreover, בגוים in v. 3b rhymes with המצרים in v. 3c. Verse 4 also shows an *o* assonance with a rhyme in אבלות (v. 4a) and נוגות (v. 4c). Verse 5 displays an internal rhyme in צריה and איביה (v. 5a) and an end rhyme in הוגה and פשׁעיה (v. 5b). The three bicola of v. 6 all begin with a predicate verb.

The closing section of the speaker's lament reverts to a description of Jerusalem in mourning, silently reflecting on past events.

Verse 8 has an *a* assonance (21 times) and an end rhyme in הזילוה and ערותה (v. 8b). The first two bicola in v. 9 display a syntactic a:b::b:a chiastic structure, namely, nominal clause:verbal clause::verbal clause:nominal clause, טמאתה בשׁוליה::לא זכרה אחריתה::ותרד פלאים::אין מנחם לה, 'her filth on her skirt:she did not remember her future::she has fallen astoundingly:no comforter to her'.

2. *Verses 9c-11: plea addressed to Yahweh.*

> v. 9c: started by Jerusalem
> vv. 10-11b: continued by the second speaker
> v. 11c: closed by Jerusalem

Jerusalem opens and closes her prayer with a painful cry to Yahweh to look at her. The *inclusio* is formed by ראה יהוה, 'look, O Yahweh', in v. 9c and v. 11c. Verse 10 has an *a* assonance (22 times) and an enjambment between v. 10b and v. 10c. Verse 11c shows an end rhyme in והביטה and זוללה.

Behind the lament (vv. 1-9b) and the plea to Yahweh (vv. 9c-11) can be discerned a description of Jerusalem that follows a chiastic pattern.[9]

A   (vv. 1-2): political desolation
  B   (vv. 3-4): defeat and exile
    C   (v. 5): Yahweh the aggressor
      D   (v. 6): daughter Zion, heroine and victim
    C′   (v. 7): gloating of the enemy
  B′   (vv. 8-9): break with Yahweh
A′   (vv. 10-11): cultic desolation

The above motifs stand out like heavy brush-strokes in a painting.

Verses 12-22. Jerusalem speaks with a sympathizing remark by the second speaker in v. 17.

1. Verses 12-16: Jerusalem's address to the passers-by
      vv. 12-14: her mourning
        v. 15: cause of her mourning, events in Judah
        v. 16: her mourning

2.   Verse 17: remark by the second speaker

3.   Verse 18a: Jerusalem's reaction to the charge in v. 17b

4. Verses 18b-19: Jerusalem's address to all peoples
      v. 18bc: her mourning
        v. 19: cause of her mourning, events in the city

5. Verses 20-22: Jerusalem's plea to Yahweh

In this second section, Jerusalem pours out her grief almost vehemently. Her sufferings are so great that she keeps throwing out 'accusations' against Yahweh.[10] Yet she acknowledges her sins and the justice of Yahweh. Finally, she pleads with Yahweh to intervene on her behalf and to deal justly also with her enemies.

---

9.   Jean-Marc Droin, *Le livre des Lamentations: 'Comment?' Une traduction et un commentaire* (Geneva: Labor et Fides, 1995), pp. 32-33.

10.   The 'accusation against God' is a characteristic element of the lament in which an incomprehensible pain is expressed through a direct address to God or through a discourse with God as subject. See Westermann, *Lamentations*, p. 92.

Jerusalem's address to the passers-by (vv. 12-16) is marked by the following poetic features:

Verse 13 has alliteration in *m* and *r* and an end rhyme in שממה and דוה (v. 13c). Verse 15 has alliteration in *b* and *r*. The words אבירי (v. 15a), אדני (v. 15ac), עלי and בחורי (v. 15b) have assonance in *ay*. Verse 16 shows alliteration in *m* and *n* and assonance in *i* and an internal rhyme in אני and עיני (v. 16a). The last words in the second colon of v. 16a (מים), in the first colon of v. 16b (מנחם), and the first colon of v. 16c (שוממים) all end with mem.

The comment by the second speaker has an *a* assonance, an end rhyme in בידיה and לה (v. 17a), and a rhyme at the beginning of the cola of v. 17c with היתה and לנדה.

Jerusalem's address to the nations has assonance in *i* and *u* in v. 18. There is an internal rhyme in הוא and פיהו in v. 18a, and an opening rhyme in שמעו and וראו in v. 18b. Verse 19c shows an internal rhyme in בקשו and וישיבו.

Jerusalem's plea to Yahweh has alliteration in *m* and *r*, and *i* assonance throughout v. 20, an end rhyme in בקרבי and מריתי (v. 20b), and a near end rhyme in חרב and כמות (v. 20c). Verse 21a also shows an end rhyme in אני and לי. Verse 22 presents two a:b::b':a' chiastic patterns, one in the first two bicola, and one in the last bicolon: (1) כל־רעתם:ועולל למו::עוללת לי:כל־פשעי, 'all their wickedness: deal severely with them::dealt severely with me: all my transgressions'; (2) רבות:אנחתי::ולבי:דוי, 'many: my groans::my heart: in pain'.

The first two bicola in v. 22 are marked by alliteration in *l*. Verse 22c has an end rhyme in אנחתי and דוי.

The plea to Yahweh is enclosed within the *inclusio* formed by לבי in v. 20b and v. 22c.

Lamentations 1 follows the order of the Hebrew alphabet, that is, ע preceding פ, in vv. 16 and 17. The reverse order, פ before ע, is found in 4QLam[a].[11] Jean-Marc Droin believes this reverse order represents the original reading: v. 17, spoken by the second speaker and coming before v. 16, would then divide the section vv. 12-20 into two equal parts of four stanzas each, spoken by Jerusalem. Verse 17 would also become the center of a chiastic structure.[12]

11. Hillers, *Lamentations*, pp. 30, 48.
12. Droin, *Lamentations*, pp. 25, 37.

> A (v. 12): call on the passers-by to look
> B (v. 13): Yahweh afflicts me
>   C (v. 14): my sins
>   D (v. 15): destructive assembly
>   E (v. 17): no comforter
>   D′ (v. 16): my tears
>   C′ (v. 18): my rebellion
> B′ (v. 19): my lovers deceive me
> A′ (v. 20): call on Yahweh to look

This chiastic structure reveals some interesting links between verses (e.g. between vv. 13 and 19, 14 and 18), yet it fails to maintain the unity and continuity of Jerusalem's prayer to Yahweh (vv. 20-22) by cutting this off after v. 20 and making vv. 21-22 a distinct section.

Address
This section analyzes briefly the reasons for my identifying the speakers of each unit of speech as I do.

Verses 1-9b: Lament of the Second Speaker. The second speaker laments the plight of Jerusalem. Yahweh and Jerusalem are in the third person throughout, so they are not explicitly addressed. However, the second speaker knows that Yahweh hears his lament, since all laments are ultimately directed toward God, as in the case of Hagar and her son in Gen. 21.15-17.[13] Hagar and her son have been cast out of Abraham's tent. They have been wandering in the desert, and the water in the skin jar is gone. They are dying of thirst. Hagar weeps. The boy must have cried, for the text says, 'God has heard the voice of the boy where he is' (Gen. 21.17c).

It is clear that this second speaker is part of the mourning ceremony which he describes. When Jerusalem prays to Yahweh in v. 9c, and cannot continue her prayer, he finishes that prayer for her in vv. 10-11b. Jerusalem then adds the final line, v. 11c, to the prayer. He speaks again in v. 17, apparently blamimg Yahweh for Jerusalem's problems. Jerusalem reacts to that accusation in v. 18a; she wants to set that remark in the right perspective and says, 'Yahweh is just, for I have rebelled against his word'.

Who is the second speaker? First, he is present at the mourning ceremony and describes Jerusalem mourning. Secondly, he is obviously

---

13. Westermann, *Lamentations*, p. 91.

sympathetic toward Jerusalem: that is clear right at the start, from v. 1. Thirdly, he is a person of some stature, presented as speaking at a public assembly, though no one is addressed in particular. Those left behind in Jerusalem can easily be presumed to be present at the ceremony (v. 4; 2.10).

Finally, a person of stature, a friend of the mourner present at the mourning ceremony, would be expected to be a מנחם at the rite, that is, he would be expected to advise and comfort Jerusalem, to help her. But like Job's מנחמים (Job 2.13; 16.2), this speaker has nothing useful to say to Jerusalem, and so does not address her. His speeches are peppered with the refrain אין־לה מנחם (vv. 2b, 9b, 17a), a point of view shared by Jerusalem herself (v. 16b, a variation, and v. 21a). This refrain is really the leitmotif of the whole poem. Note that Job's friends only open their mouths after Job breaks the ice, and the conversation between Job and his friends is a conversation between the mourner and his מנחמים. The second speaker here eliminates himself as a possible מנחם, because he has nothing to say by way of advice or comfort.

Verse 9c: Appeal to Yahweh. The speaker here cannot be the second speaker, for the appeal to Yahweh is to look at עניי, 'my affliction'. The poem is wholly concerned with the affliction of Jerusalem; the pain of the second speaker is never mentioned. Thus the appeal to Yahweh must come from personified Jerusalem.

The second speaker has said in vv. 1-9b that Jerusalem has no מנחם. Jerusalem hears his comment and thinks: 'Perhaps Yahweh could be my מנחם!' But Jerusalem gets out only one line:

> 'O Yahweh, look at my affliction,
>   for the enemy has gone too far!'

Jerusalem, exhausted in her grief, cannot finish the prayer. She has a lot more to say, I suppose. There is a hint here that she does not believe her prayer will be heard. Yahweh did it. She deserved it (v. 18a). And that is that.

Verses 10-11b: Appeal to Yahweh Continued by the Second Speaker. Jerusalem leaves her prayer unfinished. The second speaker jumps in to help her. He divines what Jerusalem must have meant by 'the enemy has gone too far', and describes for Yahweh's benefit the loss of the temple vessels. The thought behind vv. 10-11b runs like this: 'Please, Yahweh, save Jerusalem, not because she deserves it, but for your own sake! The enemy dishonored you by bringing to an end worship in your house!' The logic in this prayer is similar to that in Ps. 79.9 (NRSV):

> Help us, O God of our salvation,
>   for the glory of your name;
> Deliver us, and forgive our sins,
>   for your name's sake.

Verse 11c: Appeal Ended. Jerusalem closes the prayer she began in v. 9c. The 'I' who is זוללה, 'despised, worthless', cannot be the second speaker, whose social standing is never a concern in Lamentations 1. Moreover, the qal participle זוללה is feminine. The focus falls on Jerusalem's social standing.

When Jerusalem complains about being despised at this point in the prayer, which deals with the plunder of the temple vessels and the desecration of the temple itself (v. 10bc), she cites her 'being despised' as a sign that the worship of Yahweh in Jerusalem is at an end. Her concern is Yahweh's honor, her honor is Yahweh's honor, and therein lies the seed of hope.

Verses 12-16: Address to the Passers-by. The speaker here is feminine, for the qualifying adjectives are feminine: שממה, 'appalled/desolate', and דוה, 'faint/in pain' (v. 13c), בוכיה, 'weeping' (v. 16a). The speaker can only be Jerusalem. The picture is of Jerusalem as a mother who grieves over her dead children (vv. 15, 16).

In v. 11c, Jerusalem completed the prayer to Yahweh that she had begun in v. 9c. However, she still has no great hope that her prayer to Yahweh will help: uppermost in her mind is still the viewpoint of v. 18a, that is, she has sinned, and she deserves what she got. Discouraged, she breaks off the prayer and addresses the passers-by in v. 12a. From what she says in v. 16b ('far from me is any comforter', i.e. 'I don't have any comforter'), it is clear what she is looking for among the passers-by: Jerusalem is looking for a comforter.

Verse 17: Sympathetic Remark. Jerusalem and Yahweh are in the third person, so the speaking voice is the second speaker, the potential מנחם who has decided he cannot advise Jerusalem, and, in fact, never does. He simply remarks that the appeal to the passers-by in vv. 12-16 got no response. The סביביו, 'his neighbors', of v. 17b are the people from among whom the עברי דרך, 'passers-by', of v. 12a would have come.

The neighbors of Jacob have now become his foes, by Yahweh's command. Jerusalem cannot find any comforter among them. Lady Jerusalem, the chief mourner, is still without a מנחם.

Verse 18a: Reaction to the Charge in Verse 17b. Jerusalem reacts to what the second speaker said in v. 17b: 'Yahweh did it!' Jerusalem believes this too, but she wants that statement nuanced: 'It is true that Yahweh did it, but I revolted against Yahweh, and I deserve to be punished.'

Verses 18b-19: Address to All Peoples. At this point, Jerusalem still does not believe that recourse to Yahweh will help. She has found no מנחם among her own family (v. 2b), among the states that once respected her (vv. 8b and 9b), among the passers-by/neighbors (vv. 12a, 17ab). In one last desperate attempt to find a מנחם, she cries out to כל־העמים, 'all the peoples' (v. 18b), of the world and describes for them her misery.

This address to the nations (5 bicola) is considerably shorter than that to the passers-by (15 bicola), and there is no comment by the second speaker on this speech as there was (v. 17) on her previous speech.

In mid-speech to the nations, Jerusalem realizes that she has no hope anywhere, in any human person. Her one and only hope is in Yahweh, who inflicted all these calamities upon her because of her rebellion, and come what may, she must appeal to him.

Verses 20-22: Plea to Yahweh. Jerusalem shifts from addressing the nations and makes a proper prayer to Yahweh. It also begins with ראה יהוה, 'O Yahweh, look', like the tentative one-line prayers that Jerusalem was able to whisper in vv. 9c and 11c. Once again, it is clear what she is looking for. She is asking Yahweh to be her מנחם when she acknowledges her need, אין מנחם לי, in v. 21a. No one else could solve her problems. Yahweh is her only hope. She calls on Yahweh to look at her devastated state—death is everywhere (v. 20c)—and to deal justly with her enemies. Only Yahweh can comfort when justice is at issue.

Exegesis

Lament of the Second Speaker (Verses 1-9b)
The second speaker begins to lament the ruins of Jerusalem which he personifies as a widow in mourning posture. He goes on to give the

cause of Jerusalem's mourning, then returns in closing to the description of Jerusalem, a solitary and despondent mourner.

The Mourning of Jerusalem (Verses 1-2). The second speaker, who is present at this mourning ceremony, describes Jerusalem in ruins as a widow in mourning: איכה ישבה בדד, 'alas, she sits alone!' The characteristic word איכה (or its shortened form איך), 'how, alas', usually occurs at the beginning of a funeral dirge,[14] although some funeral laments do not begin with, or even contain, the word (e.g. David's lament over Abner in 2 Sam. 3.33-34). The vast majority of the 78 instances of איכה or איך in the MT occur in regular narratives or discourses, and serve merely as adverbial interrogatives.[15] The word איכה here, as in Lam. 2.1 and 4.1, is an exclamation of grief at the striking change from the glorious past to the present state of humiliation.[16] It may also have an interrogative nuance, that is, it can express human incomprehension in the face of the impossible: 'How could it happen?' 'Why did it happen?' Lamentations 1 is not a funeral lament per se (i.e. a lament over a dead person, as is 2 Sam. 1.19-27), but a related genre,[17] where the prime concern is for the mourner who is mourning dead and exiled children.

The verb ישבה here is short for ישבה לארץ, 'sits on the ground', a posture of mourning (e.g. Isa. 3.26; Lam. 2.10; Job 2.8, 13; Jon. 3.6). A widespread custom among the Semitic peoples was to sit on the ground in times of mourning.[18]

The word בדד is technically a noun (solitude) used as an adverb (in a solitary manner).[19] It occurs with the root ישב in three other passages. Leviticus 13.46 states that the person with the 'leprous' disease shall

14. H. Jahnow, *Das hebräische Leichenlied im Rahmen der Völkerdichtung* (BZAW, 36; Giessen: Alfred Töpelmann, 1923), p. 136.

15. P.W. Ferris, Jr, *The Genre of Communal Lament in the Bible and the Ancient Near East* (SBLDS, 127; Atlanta: Scholars Press, 1992), p. 139.

16. Jahnow (*Das hebräische Leichenlied*, p. 99) calls this 'das Schema "Einst und Jetzt"'.

17. Westermann (*Lamentations*, pp. 11, 98) calls the poems in the book of Lamentations 'a distinctive group of communal laments' enriched with motifs from the dirge.

18. M. Dahood, 'Textual Problems in Isaiah', *CBQ* 22 (1960), pp. 400-409, esp. p. 401.

19. *HALOT*, I, p. 109.

live alone (בדד ישׁב), outside the camp. The prophet Jeremiah complains that Yahweh's word of judgment, which he was commanded to proclaim, caused him to live alone (בדד ישׁבתי, Jer. 15.17), isolated from human company, like a 'social leper'.[20] According to Lam. 3.28, the person on whom Yahweh's yoke is laid should ישׁב בדד, 'sit alone', in silence. All of the above instances of separation from human fellowship also imply isolation from God. Indeed the 'leper' is טמא, 'unclean, defiled', and must remain outside the camp, because God dwells among the people inside the camp (Num. 5.3). God and טמאה, 'uncleanness, defilement', are incompatible (Lev. 11.43-45).[21] While Jeremiah experienced ostracism from his people, he went through a period of doubt, felt that God had failed him, and was consequently isolated from God (Jer. 15.15, 18). Again, the person who bears Yahweh's yoke of chastisement has incurred divine wrath, and is isolated from God.[22]

The word בדד is ambiguous. It can convey the sense of chastisement by God as in the texts cited above, and in Isa. 27.10, כי עיר בצורה בדד, 'for the fortified city shall be desolate' (NAB). It can also carry the nuance of election, of being set apart by God for his special care, as in the blessing pronounced by Balaam, הן־עם לבדד ישׁכן, 'here is a people that lives apart' (Num. 23.9; NAB), and Moses, בדד עין יעקב, 'and the fountain of Jacob has been undisturbed' (Deut. 33.28; NAB). The following imagery of אלמנה, 'widow' (v. 1b), supports the understanding of בדד as loneliness, desolation in our passage. Nevertheless, the opening איכה, exclamatory and interrogative at the same time, does not rule out the nuance of election. Rather, it implies the burning question: How could it be that this city, which once was 'the city of our God', 'the joy of all the earth' (Ps. 48.2-3; Lam. 2.15), has now become desolate and deserted? The one word בדד, with its ambivalent meaning, conveys the contrast between the former state of election of the city and its present state of isolation.

The word רבתי carries two meanings: 'great' in the sense of 'populous' as in v. 1a, and 'great' in the sense of 'renowned and powerful' as in v. 1c. The preposition ב could mean 'among' or 'over'. Expressions

20. W.L. Holladay, *Jeremiah 1* (Hermeneia; Philadelphia: Fortress Press, 1986), p. 460.

21. E. Feldman, *Biblical and Post-Biblical Defilement and Mourning: Law as Theology* (New York: Ktav, 1977), pp. 31, 52.

22. H.-J. Zobel, 'בדד', *TDOT*, I, pp. 473-79 (478).

with 'among' used for individuals can imply 'eminence' and are equivalent to the superlative,[23] for example: כִּי־הִנֵּה קָטֹן נְתַתִּיךָ בַּגּוֹיִם, 'for I will make you least among the nations' (Jer. 49.15; NRSV); לַיִשׁ גִּבּוֹר בַּבְּהֵמָה, 'the lion, which is mightiest among wild animals' (Prov. 30.30; NRSV); הַיָּפָה בַּנָּשִׁים, 'fairest among women' (Cant. 1.8; NRSV). 'Over' implies 'ruling over', and the noun שַׂר, 'prince', is often used in construct before the thing ruled: שָׂרֵי הַמְּדִינוֹת, 'governors/officials of the provinces' (1 Kgs 20.14, 15, 17, 19; Est. 8.9; 9.3).[24] Because of the close parallelism between the three bicola, Hillers prefers to render בּ in the same way in רַבָּתִי בַגּוֹיִם, 'the greatest among nations', and in שָׂרָתִי בַּמְּדִינוֹת, 'the noblest of states'.[25] The element of hyperbole involved in this description of Jerusalem is characteristic of the funeral dirge which usually sings the exploits or virtues of the deceased in extravagant terms: for example, the elegy of David for Saul and Jonathan in 2 Sam. 1.23 (NAB):

> Saul and Jonathan, beloved and cherished,
>> separated neither in life nor in death,
>> swifter than eagles, stronger than lions!

This hyperbolic description presents Jerusalem not as she ever was in fact, but as she was in the eyes of those who loved her and believed her to be the chosen city of God.

Antithetic parallelism runs through every line of v. 1: between בָּדָד and רַבָּתִי עָם, 'full of people' (v. 1a; cf. 1 Sam. 2.5, רַבַּת בָּנִים, 'full of children'); between אַלְמָנָה, a woman without a male protector (husband, sons or even brothers), money or influence,[26] and רַבָּתִי בַגּוֹיִם, 'great among the nations' (v. 1b); finally, between שָׂרָתִי בַּמְּדִינוֹת, 'princess over the city-states', and מַס, 'forced labor' (v. 1c). The same word מַס describes the hardships of bondage in Egypt (Exod. 1.11).

Moreover, there is also semantic parallelism between בָּדָד and אַלְמָנָה (i.e. the widow is lonely and desolate), and between אַלְמָנָה and מַס (i.e. the helpless widow has no financial support and is forced into slavery). The elaborate structure of the first stanza focuses on Jerusalem as a mourning widow. She is a widow because she has lost her husband. And what a husband! She has lost Yahweh, not because he is dead, but

23. BDB, p. 88; Hillers, *Lamentations*, p. 65.
24. Hillers, *Lamentations*, p. 65.
25. Hillers, *Lamentations*, p. 61.
26. H.A. Hoffner, 'אַלְמָנָה', *TDOT*, I, pp. 287-91 (288).

because she has been cast off, abandoned, by Yahweh (cf. Isa. 54.5-7). She has lost all prestige and power. She is now confined to hard tasks under harsh treatment. Her present is bleak. Her future does not look better.

Lady Jerusalem sits alone and weeps. When Jacob mourns for Joseph, his other children come to comfort him (Gen. 37.35). Ephraim's brothers also come to comfort him at the death of his sons (1 Chron. 7.22). The mourner needs a comforter. But Jerusalem has no one to comfort her (אֵין־לָהּ מְנַחֵם, v. 2b). Her children and blood relatives (אֹהֲבֶיהָ) are gone. Her friends (רֵעֶיהָ) have turned against her instead of coming to her help in her time of adversity. The root בגד is used when a person does not honor an agreement.[27] Covenantal allies honor one another by sending comforters in times of mourning. David did just that at the death of Nahash, King of the Ammonites (2 Sam. 10.1-3). Jeremiah 27.3 mentions an anti-Babylonian alliance between Judah and Edom, Moab, Ammon, Tyre, and Sidon. Jerusalem's friends or allies have not honored her by sending comforters at this time of mourning. They have publicly violated their agreement with her. This covenant violation is behind the complaint of having no helper in v. 7c, of being despised in v. 8b, and of being deceived in v. 19a. She is cut off from God and from human company. What can she do but weep? And this she does, profusely (וְדִמְעָתָהּ עַל לֶחֱיָהּ, 'with tears on her cheeks', v. 2a), continually (בַלַּיְלָה, 'through the night', v. 2a), bitterly (בָכוֹ תִבְכֶּה, the emphasis on the act of weeping being brought out here by the infinitive absolute of the same verbal root בכה, 'to weep'). The comforter gives moral support and encouragement to go on in life; he makes life meaningful.[28] Verse 2b, which expresses Jerusalem's need of a comforter, shows only synthetic parallelism; it is enclosed, however, within vv. 2a and 2c, which present internal semantic parallelism:

בכו תבכה בלילה ודמעתה על לחיה
אין־לה מנחם מכל־אהביה
כל־רעיה בגדו בה היו לה לאיבים:

She weeps bitterly through the night with tears on her cheeks.
She has no one to comfort her among all those who have loved her;
All her friends have dealt treacherously with her, they have become her enemies.

---

27. S. Erlandsson, 'בגד', *TDOT*, I, pp. 470-73 (470).
28. Droin, *Lamentations*, p. 34.

The double repetition of כל, 'all', and the chiastic pattern[29] of vv. 2b and 2c give extra emphasis to the loneliness of Jerusalem and her need of a comforter.

The whole stanza is marked by assonance in *a* (17 times) and in *e* (8 times), and alliteration in *b* (7 times) and in *l* (9 times).

The Cause of Jerusalem's Mourning (Verses 3-6). The distinction between Judah (vv. 3-4) and Jerusalem (vv. 5-6) reflects the course of the Assyrian invasion, as recorded in Isa. 1.7-8 (NRSV):

> Your country lies desolate,
>   your cities are burned with fire;
> In your very presence
>   aliens devour your land;
> It is desolate, as overthrown by foreigners.
> And daughter Zion is left
>   like a booth in a vineyard,
> Like a shelter in a cucumber field,
>   like a besieged city.

The capital is often distinguished from the territory (e.g. Isa. 44.26; Jer. 7.34; 9.10-11; 14.18-19).

1. *Events outside the city (vv. 3-4).* Verse 3 recalls the political defeat. Judah is the kingdom, the territory around the capital city of Jerusalem. The root גלה means both 'to uncover' and 'to go into exile'. The first meaning is evidenced by verbs in synonymous parallelism with גלה such as חשׂף, 'to strip off' (e.g. Isa. 47.2, חשׂפי־שׁבל גלי־שׁוק, 'strip off your robe, uncover your legs'); ראה, 'to see' (e.g. Isa. 47.3, תגל ערותך גם תראה חרפתך, 'your nakedness shall be uncovered, and your shame shall be seen'). Verbs in antithetic parallelism to גלה bring out its meaning even more clearly, for example, כסה, 'to cover', in Isa. 26.21 (NRSV):

וגלתה הארץ את־דמיה ולא־תכסה עוד על־הרוגיה׃

> The earth will disclose the blood shed on it,
>   and will no longer cover its slain.

The second meaning is found in the phrase גלה מעל אדמתו, 'to go into exile away from one's land' (e.g. 2 Kgs 17.23; 25.21; Amos 7.11, 17).[30]

---

29. See my section 'Poetic Structure', p. 50 above.
30. H.-J. Zobel, 'גלה', *TDOT*, II, pp. 476-88 (478-79).

It should be noted that captives were led into exile, naked and barefoot (Isa. 20.4).

The people of Judah have gone into exile. Besides the meaning 'to be taken away into exile', the verb גלתה may carry the nuance of 'voluntary exile',[31] that is, some people might have left their homeland in order to escape from the harsh conditions, 'oppression and cruel enslavement' (v. 3a), that resulted from serving Assyria, Egypt and Babylon (see Jer. 2.16-18, 36-37; 2 Kgs 23.33-35; 24.7).[32]

The first colon of v. 3b, היא ישבה בגוים, 'she sits [as a mourner] among the nations', describes the spirit of the people in exile: they are also mourning, since the verb ישב carries the same connotation of mourning as in v. 1a. Life in exile is even harsher than the oppression and servitude at home, since it implies living among the גוים, 'nations'. Although the Old Testament asserts that Israel became a גוי at Sinai (Exod. 19.6) or at the exodus (Deut. 26.5), Israel is more often called עם־יהוה, 'the people of Yahweh' (e.g. 2 Sam. 1.12; Ezek. 36.20). The word גוים takes on a hostile implication when it designates the nations that had previously lived in the land of Canaan and with whom Israel was to make no religious or political treaties (e.g. Deut. 7.1-11). It also carries a strong negative nuance when applied to the nations responsible for the downfall of the northern kingdom through their abhorrent religious practices displeasing to Yahweh (see Deut. 18.9; 2 Kgs 17.8, 11, 15, 33; 21.2).[33]

The word מנוח, 'rest', has three of the same consonants as מנחם, 'comforter'. The Old Testament concept of 'rest' is bound up with 'land, inheritance, possession, safety from surrounding enemies' (cf. Deut. 12.9-10; 25.19). Yahweh gives 'rest' from 'pain, turmoil, and hard service' (Isa. 14.3). Judah in exile, away from its homeland, could not find rest. There is also no rest in mourning. El can rest only when he knows that Baal lives; it is then that he stops mourning for Baal.[34] A widow has no 'rest' until she gets married again. Naomi prayed that Yahweh might grant each of her daughters-in-law to find 'rest' in the home of

31. R.B. Salters, 'Lamentations 1.3: Light from the History of Exegesis', in J.D. Martin and P.R. Davies (eds.), *A Word in Season* (JSOTSup, 42; Sheffield: JSOT Press, 1986), pp. 73-89.

32. J.M. Miller and J.H. Hayes, *A History of Ancient Israel and Judah* (Philadelphia: Westminster Press, 1986), pp. 388-91.

33. R.E. Clements, 'גוי', *TDOT*, II, p. 426-33 (432).

34. Anderson, *A Time to Mourn*, p. 67.

another husband (Ruth 1.9); she sought 'rest' for Ruth by giving her advice on how to approach Boaz (Ruth 3.1-4). Yahweh's promise of restoration for Israel employs the imagery of marriage:

> You shall no more be termed Forsaken,
>   and your land shall no more be termed Desolate;
> But you shall be called My Delight Is in Her,
>   and your land Married;
> For the LORD delights in you,
>   and your land shall be married (Isa. 62.4; NRSV).

The roots רדף, 'to pursue', and נשׂג, 'to overtake', are often used together in a context of enmity. Laban pursued Jacob and overtook him in the hill country of Gilead (Gen. 31.23-25). The Egyptians pursued the Israelites and overtook them camped by the sea (Exod. 14.9). The covenant curses will pursue and overtake the people of Israel in cases of disobedience (Deut. 28.45). The word המצרים (from the root צרר, 'to be restricted, hemmed in') means 'straits/difficult situation', and may refer both to the siege and the fighting before the exile, as well as to the people's escape (the fugitives were captured by the Edomites on their flight during the fighting; see Obad. 14), and their present condition in exile.

This understanding discloses a double semantic parallelism within and among the bicola of v 3:

> v. 3a   Judah is in exile // she suffered enslavement
> v. 3b   She sits among the nations // she has no rest
> v. 3c   She was cornered by foes, // defeat in war
>   by conquerors // defeat in exile

The entire verse is built on assonance in *a* (16 times), and in *o* (7 times). The realities of hardship, war and exile affect the whole population. That is why Lady Jerusalem is mourning.

Verse 4 focuses on the effects of war and defeat on the religious life of the population.

'Zion' was originally the name of a fortress in Jerusalem before David captured the city from the Jebusites. David changed the name from 'the stronghold of Zion' to 'the city of David' (2 Sam. 5.7-9). Later, Solomon, David's son and successor, expanded Jerusalem to the northwest, and built the temple of Yahweh on a hill that came to be known as 'Mount Zion' (e.g. Ps. 78.68-69). Eventually, 'Zion' came to refer to Jerusalem, the entire temple city.[35]

---

35. J.D. Levenson, 'Zion Traditions', *ABD*, VI, pp. 1098-1102 (1098).

As a result of the exile, even the roads from the surrounding villages and cities of Judah leading to Zion, the city of God (cf. Pss. 48.2; 74.2), are mourning (אֲבֵלוֹת). Instead of the joyous throng walking in procession to the house of God (Ps. 42.4), the roads are now deserted. No one walks along these roads to appear before Yahweh at the three great yearly festivals (see Deut. 16.16; Ps. 122.1-4).

Consequently, the gates are שׁוֹמֵמִין, 'deserted/appalled'. The gates— or rather, their remains—stand motionless; they do not open or shut because they are broken, and because no one is entering or going out of the city. To be motionless is to be silent, a sign of mourning.[36] The city gate is the place where the elders and judges or kings sit to render judgment (e.g. Gen. 19.1, 9; Deut. 21.19; 2 Sam. 15.1-6; Prov. 31.23). The fact that the gates are deserted also means that there is no one to render justice.

The priests 'are groaning', נֶאֱנָחִים, instead of teaching the people the ways of God (cf. Jer. 18.18; Mal. 2.6-7). No worshiper comes to receive instruction.

What happens to the virgins is ambiguous. MT נוּגוֹת has been understood as the niphal participle of יגה; נוֹגוֹת becomes נוּגוֹת by dissimilation, yielding 'her virgins grieve'. The only other instance of niphal יגה is נוּגֵי מִמּוֹעֵד, 'those who grieve because the festival could not be celebrated' (Zeph. 3.18), which is probably a scribal error for כְּיוֹם מוֹעֵד, 'as on a day of festival' (see LXX; *BHS*; *HALOT*, II, p. 385). So analyzed, the semantic parallelism is with the preceding and following cola: her priests groan; her virgins grieve; and she herself is bitter. This solution to the problem is favored by the presence of the root יגה in vv. 5 and 12. In this case, the virgins are the young women who sing and dance at liturgies, as Rudolph suggests.[37]

The common alternative interpretation of MT is to derive the form from נהג, 'to drive, lead'. The text is corrected to נְהֻגוֹת (see *BHS*), or the form נוּגוֹת is explained as נְהֻגוֹת with the syncope of intervocalic ה as in לָבִיא (Jer. 39.7; see *HALOT*, I, p. 114). This interpretation is reflected in the LXX (ἀγόμεναι, 'led away'), and Sym (αἰχμαλώται, 'captive'), and is adopted here on the basis of the semantic parallelism that runs through the three bicola of v. 4:

---

36. Lipiński, *La liturgie*, p. 33.
37. Rudolph, *Klagelieder*, p. 212. See Judg. 21.19-21; Jer. 31.4, 13; Ps. 68.24-27.

v. 4a	(result)	(cause)
	Roads to Zion mourn	No pilgrims on the roads
v. 4b	(cause)	(result)
	Gates are empty	Priests groan
v. 4c	(cause)	(result)
	Young women exiled	Situation is bitter for Jerusalem

This reading of v. 4 uncovers a tragic contrast. At the time of the festival (מועד), when the Judahites should be marching along the roads toward Jerusalem and be present at her gates to be welcomed in by the priests, they have already been marched off far away from Jerusalem into exile.

I have presumed that בתולתיה נוגות, 'her virgins have been led away' (v. 4c), means the same thing as גלתה יהודה, 'Judah [i.e. the population of Judah] has gone into exile' (v. 3a), and בתולתי ובחורי הלכו בשבי, 'my young women and my young men have gone into captivity' (v. 18c). In the last two cases, it is clear that the reference is to both male and female deportees. Why, then, is there mention only of young women in v. 4c?

The problem could readily be resolved if the reference of בתולות is to the daughter cities of Jerusalem, the outlying towns of Jerusalem in Judah (e.g. עקרון ובנתיה, 'Ekron and her daughter cities', Josh. 15.45). But the vocabulary used for this meaning is invariably בנות, 'daughters'. It is true that בתולה can be used for a capital city like Jerusalem (e.g. בתולת בת־ציון, 'virgin daughter Zion', 2 Kgs 19.21; Isa. 37.22; Lam. 2.13). But בתולות is never used for daughter cities, and so this explanation of the reference to young females alone in Lam. 1.4c seems improbable.

The presence of young women in v. 4c is climactic. In v. 3 the deportees are simply referred to as Judah. In v. 4a, they are nameless pilgrims; in v. 4b, nameless priests mourn their absence. In v. 4c, attention is drawn to the young female deportees and their fate at the hands of their male captors in exile. What the poet attempts here is to rouse the sympathy of his audience for the fate of these women and for their grieving. The picture of males going into exile is not so well calculated to effect that arousal. Press reports about Serbs systematically raping Bosnian women roused horror throughout the world significantly more effectively than reports of Serb tanks shelling Bosnian army positions (War in Bosnia: 1992–95).

The poet does the same thing in presenting Jerusalem personified as a widow mourning the capture of Jerusalem and the exile of its inhabitants (including the population of Judah) in Lamentations 1 and 2. This would not be nearly as effective if the picture throughout Lamentations were of some priest mourning for his absent congregation!

Verse 4 shows significant syntactic balance. The first colon in v. 4a, the two cola in v. 4b, and the first colon in v. 4c follow the same pattern: subject + participial predicate. Assonance in *ê, e* (10×) and in *ô, o* (7×) runs through the whole stanza.

In summary, the cause of Jerusalem's mourning in vv. 3-4 is the exile of the population of Judah, which results in the emptiness of the roads leading to Jerusalem and the interruption of the temple worship.

2. *Events in the city (vv. 5-6)*. The pronominal suffix הָ, 'her', in v. 5 refers to Zion in v. 4a. In one of the covenant blessings, Yahweh promises to make his people לראש, 'into the head' (Deut. 28.13). Disobedience or breach of the covenant brings about the reverse: the foes have become masters. The parallel colon איביה שלו, 'her enemies prosper' (v. 5a), accentuates the thriving situation of the foes and adds to the bitterness of Jerusalem. It may also suggest hidden questions like those in Jer. 12.1 and Psalm 73, namely, 'why do the wicked prosper?'

The agent who brought about all this desolation and servitude on Jerusalem (and Judah) is clearly spelled out: it is none other than Yahweh himself. Yahweh's punishment is comprehensible in this case: Jerusalem has sinned, she has committed rebellion. The root פשע, 'to rebel, transgress', is used in political contexts of revolt against a suzerain (e.g. 2 Kgs 1.1, וישפע מואב בישראל, 'Moab rebelled against Israel'). Jerusalem did not keep the covenant stipulations; therefore, she must incur the covenant curses. The phrase רב־פשעיה, 'the multitude of her transgressions' (v. 5b), harks back to רב עבדה, lit. 'much toil' (v. 3a). There seems to be a correspondence of sin and judgment.[38]

Not only the population of Judah, but also the inhabitants of Jerusalem (עולליה, 'her children', v. 5c) have been led away into captivity. The covenant curse in Deut. 28.32, 41 has been fulfilled. A slight touch of irony can be detected here: the captives walk ahead of the masters who are 'the heads'. The word עולליה may also refer to the younger age group of the Jerusalem population.[39] This understanding emphasizes the

---

38. P.D. Miller, Jr, *Genesis 1–11: Studies in Structure and Theme* (JSOTSup, 8; Sheffield: JSOT Press, 1978), pp. 27-36.

39. E.g., Hunter, *Faces*, p. 113; Reyburn, *Lamentations*, p. 21; Westermann, *Lamentations*, p. 127.

harsh consequences of sin. Even the children must suffer exile. Verse 5a is in antithetic parallelism with v. 5c: Jerusalem's foes have become masters while her children have become captives. Enclosed between these two bicola is what Westermann calls 'an accusation against God',[40] since God is the subject of the discourse: כִּי־יְהוָה הוֹגָהּ עַל רֹב־ פְּשָׁעֶיהָ, 'because Yahweh has afflicted her for the multitude of her transgressions'. Droin calls the first colon of v. 5b 'a statement of faith', and the second colon 'a confession of sins'.[41] Faith acknowledges Yahweh as the true agent behind the human enemy, the human instrument in the hand of Yahweh.

The word צָר in the last colon forms an *inclusio* with צָרֶיהָ, 'her foes', in the first colon of v. 5a. The foes have closed their grip on Jerusalem: there is no escape.

Verse 6 continues the description of events in the city. The expression בַּת־צִיּוֹן, 'daughter Zion', used to personify the city of Jerusalem, originates from West Semitic thought patterns which regarded a capital city as a goddess married to its patron god. It has been noted that this use of the titles בַּת־, 'daughter', or בְּתוּלַת, 'virgin', plus the name of the city, is limited to situations in which the city is presented as having suffered or being about to suffer a disaster.[42] The word בַּת־ in this context simply means a 'girl, young woman, or woman' in a very general sense.[43] Similarly, the word בְּתוּלַת represents only an expansion or a modification of the personifying title.

The beginning phrase וַיֵּצֵא, 'and departed', recalls Ezek. 10.18 which describes the departure of the glory of Yahweh from the temple. Here, כָּל־הֲדָרָהּ, 'all her splendor/majesty', departs from daughter Zion. In Prov. 31.25, עֹז־וְהָדָר לְבוּשָׁהּ, 'strength and dignity are her clothing', the word הָדָר denotes the external appearance of the efficient housewife,[44] her distinctive mark, that by which she is seen and recognized. The Servant of Yahweh 'had no form or majesty that we should look at him' (לֹא־תֹאַר לוֹ וְלֹא הָדָר וְנִרְאֵהוּ, Isa. 53.2). Zion was 'the joy of all the earth' (Ps. 48.3), 'the perfection of beauty' (Ps. 50.2; Lam. 2.15). Zion was renowned among the nations on account of her perfect beauty, due

40. Westermann, *Lamentations*, p. 92.

41. Droin, *Lamentations*, pp. 34-35.

42. A. Fitzgerald, 'BTWLT and BT as Titles for Capital Cities', *CBQ* 37 (1975), pp. 167-83.

43. H. Haag, 'בת', *TDOT*, II, pp. 332-38 (334).

44. G. Warmuth, 'הדר', *TDOT*, III, pp. 335-41 (339).

to the splendor Yahweh had given her (בהדרי אשר־שמתי עליך נאם אדני
יהוה, 'because of my splendor that I had bestowed on you, says the Lord
GOD', Ezek. 16.14 [NRSV]). The הדר Yahweh gave to Zion, that made
her beautiful, consisted of embroidered garments, gold and silver orna-
ments, and choice food (Ezek. 16.10-13). So when the הדר departed
from Zion, her princes went hungry: לא־מצאו מרעה, 'they had not
found pasture' (v. 6b). The nobles also go hungry in Yahweh's judgment proclaimed in Isa. 5.13 (NAB):

לכן גלה עמי מבלי־דעת
וכבודו מתי רעב והמונו צחה צמא:

> Therefore my people will go into exile,
>> because they do not understand;
> Their nobles die of hunger,
>> and their masses are parched with thirst.

The word המונו (lit. 'its masses') is parallel to and paired with כבודו
(lit.; 'its glory'; nobles). In Isa. 5.14, המונה, 'her masses', is paired with
הדרה, 'her splendor', which in context refers to the nobles of v. 13.
Thus the princes or leaders of Jerusalem were also part of her הדר.
When Yahweh brings back the exiles to Zion, they will find pasture on
all the bare heights (Isa. 49.9), they will not hunger or thirst, and Zion
will 'put all of them on like an ornament' (Isa. 49.18). When the הדר
departed from Zion, she lost her wealth and riches, temple and palaces,
people and princes.

If אֵילִים, 'rams', is read instead of אַיָּלִים, 'stags', the word pun is preserved, since the ram is the leader of the flock. The people of Israel
often call themselves in relation to God 'the sheep of your pasture'
(צאן מרעיתך, Pss. 74.1; 79.13), 'the sheep of his pasture' (Ps. 100.3).
The princes were אילים, 'leaders', in Jerusalem; now they are starved
אילים, 'rams', being led away into captivity.

Rich pastures, good grazing lands, not only promise food in plenty,
but also evoke rest and contentment:

> In good pastures [במרעה־טוב] will I pasture them, and on the mountain
> heights of Israel shall be their grazing ground. There they shall lie down
> on good grazing ground, and in rich pastures [ומרעה שמן] shall they be
> pastured on the mountains of Israel. I myself will pasture my sheep; I
> myself will give them rest, says the Lord GOD (Ezek. 34.14-15; NAB).

The colon לא־מצאו מרעה, 'they had not found pasture', in v. 6b
recalls לא מצאה מנוח, 'she has found no rest', in v. 3b. Defeated and

exiled, the princes of Jerusalem as well as the people of Judah cannot satisfy their hunger and cannot rest from their hardships. Just as the children of Jerusalem march to their exile before the enemy (v. 5c), the princes march before their captors (רוֹדֵף לִפְנֵי, v. 6c), not as 'leaders', but as captives.

Verses 3-6 explain the cause of Jerusalem's mourning. While vv. 3-4 lament the exile of the whole population of Judah and the discontinuance of the temple worship, vv. 5-6 bemoan the exile of the inhabitants of Jerusalem and the loss of all that constituted her splendor and beauty. This section is marked by the *inclusio* formed with the roots מצא, 'to find', and רדף, 'to pursue', in v. 3bc and v. 6bc.

The Mourning of Jerusalem (Verses 7-9b). Verse 7 has four lines instead of the usual three. It seems odd that the poet would have deliberately gone beyond the metrical law that governs the structure of the rest of the whole poem and composed an extra line here. The fact that all four lines are present in LXX, Vg and Syr does not rule out the theory of a gloss, 'since there are several centuries between the time when the book was written and the time when it was translated'.[45] Most commentators[46] agree that one of the verses' bicola is a gloss; the question is which one should be omitted. Verse 7a must be kept in view of the alphabetic acrostic. Some scholars[47] leave out v. 7b which seems to interrupt the thought sequence. Others[48] keep v. 7b as the direct object of the verb זכרה, '[she] remembers', and delete v. 7c which does not

45. Albrektson, *Text and Theology*, p. 62.

46. D.N. Freedman ('Acrostics and Metrics in Hebrew Poetry', *HTR* 65 [1972], pp. 367-92, esp. p. 374) accepts all four lines on account of the overall length of the poem. Provan (*Lamentations*, p. 42) does not see any justification for omitting one line, considering our present limited knowledge of ancient Hebrew poetry. I agree with Hillers (*Lamentations*, p. 69) that the original composition was most probably characterized by a uniform stanza pattern, which has been disrupted in this case by a marginal note during the process of textual transmission.

47. Provan, *Lamentations*, p. 42, cites, e.g., H.-J. Kraus, *Klagelieder* (BKAT, 20; Neukirchen–Vluyn: Neukirchener Verlag, 3rd edn, 1968), p. 22; O. Plöger, 'Die Klagelieder', in E. Würthwein *et al.*, *Die fünf Megilloth* (HAT, 1.18; Tübingen: Mohr Siebeck, 2nd edn, 1969), pp. 127-64 (134); O. Kaiser, *Klagelieder* (ATD, 16; Göttingen: Vandenhoeck & Ruprecht, 3rd edn, 1981), p. 318 n. 59.

48. E.g. Rudolph, *Klagelieder*, p. 206; Albrektson, *Text and Theology*, pp. 62-63.

seem to add anything new,[49] and which probably was a marginal note on the rare word מרודיה (lit. 'her wandering') in v. 7a.[50] If v. 7b is omitted, the direct object of זכרה would be the second colon of v. 7a, namely, ימי עניה ומרודיה (lit. 'the days of her misery and her wandering'). That would mean these miserable days would belong to the past, which is not, however, the situation in Lamentations 1. Thus the second colon of v. 7a should be regarded as a temporal accusative: 'in the days of...'[51] However, these days are further explained by v. 7c, בנפל עמה ביד־צר, 'when her people fell into the hand of the foe', that is, they refer to the actual days of the fall of the city and the beginning of the exile, which have already happened, and are now in the past, as viewed by the mourners at the present mourning ceremony. Hillers[52] thinks the text makes sense with the omission of either v. 7b or v. 7c. He further agrees with T.J. Meek[53] that both lines represent variant readings which have become a conflate text in the course of the text's transmission. I think v. 7b is a gloss for the following reasons:

1. If v. 7b is connected to v. 7a as the second object of זכרה, one would have a case of enjambment where the sentence or clause extends beyond the boundaries of a line. Instances of enjambment are rare in Hebrew poetry, especially in Lamentations 1.

2. The gloss 7b clearly derives from vv. 10-11 where the twofold reference to temple treasures is thoroughly appropriate, since the temple liturgy is of much concern in that context.

3. But this concern is not the subject of vv. 1-6 or 8-9 which revolve around the fact that Jerusalem is alone and has no comforter, because her children are dead or exiled, and her friends have abandoned her. Verse 7c, in contrast, is precisely about these same themes of defeat and abandonment.

4. The reason why a glossator glossed the text here is that the speaker in vv. 4, 10 and 11 is not only concerned about Jerusalem, but also about Yahweh's honor, about the proper worship of Yahweh. He does not address Yahweh, but he knows Yahweh will surely overhear this indirect prayer and may help Jerusalem. Jerusalem also shares the

49. So Droin, *Lamentations*, p. 35.

50. Albrektson, *Text and Theology*, pp. 62-63.

51. Albrektson, *Text and Theology*, pp. 62-63.

52. Hillers, *Lamentations*, p. 69.

53. T.J. Meek and W.P. Merrill, *The Book of Lamentations* (IB, 6; Nashville: Abingdon Press, 1956), p. 9.

speaker's sentiments (see v. 18a). But here, in v. 7, without v. 7b, it would seem that Jerusalem only thinks about her own losses, especially her children, who are not around to help her (v. 7c). In order to correct this picture, the glossator brings into the text Jerusalem's concern for the temple treasures, which is ultimately concern for the proper worship of Yahweh. In Exod. 32.11-14, Moses is also concerned about Yahweh's honor when he prays that Yahweh may not destroy his people whom he brought out of Egypt.

The phrase ביד־צר, 'into the hand of the foe', occurs only three other times in MT, and in all three, the verb used is נתן, 'to give over, deliver into', with Yahweh or God as subject (Ezek. 39.23; Ps. 78.61; Neh. 9.27). Thus the implied agent who let the people fall 'into the hand of the foe' in v. 7c is Yahweh. The covenant curse had already warned that there will be no one to help when calamity comes as a result of disobedience (Deut. 28.29, 31). The clause ואין עוזר לה, 'and she had no one to help her', echoes the refrain אין־לה מנחם, 'she has no one to comfort her', in v. 2b. The verb עזר, 'to help', is paired with נחם, 'to comfort', in Ps. 86.17 (NAB):

> Grant me a proof of your favor,
>> that my enemies may see, to their confusion,
>> that you, O LORD, have helped and comforted me.

Jerusalem is utterly alone when disaster strikes. Her children are gone (vv. 4c, 5c, 6bc). Former allies have become foes (v. 2c), therefore they have not sent help (v. 7c). Worst of all, her enemies rejoice at her downfall (v. 7d). One such case of rejoicing by an enemy is recorded in Lam. 4.21 (NAB):

> Though you rejoice and are glad, O daughter Edom,
>> you who dwell in the land of Uz,
> To you also shall the cup be passed;
>> you shall become drunk and naked.

Psalm 137.7 and Obad. 10-14 also relate the treacherous behavior of Edom, a former ally, at the fall of Jerusalem.

The scornful laugh of the enemy is particularly painful to Jerusalem in a society where honor and shame are pivotal values.[54] Yahweh

---

54. B.J. Malina, *The New Testament World: Insights from Cultural Anthropology* (Louisville, KY: Westminster/John Knox Press, 1981), pp. 25-50; L.M. Bechtel, 'Shame as a Sanction of Social Control in Biblical Israel: Judicial, Political, and Social Shaming', *JSOT* 49 (1991), pp. 47-76.

laughs at the wicked (e.g. Ps. 37.13), and the righteous laughs at the evildoer (e.g. Ps. 52.8). However, it is forbidden to rejoice at the downfall of one's enemies: 'Do not rejoice when your enemies fall, and do not let your heart be glad when they stumble' (Prov. 24.17; NRSV).

The memories of these days of defeat, misery and shame are still fresh in Jerusalem's mind. She remembers (זכרה) them. She reflects on them. She can almost see the mocking glance of her enemies and hear their scornful laugh. They wag their heads when they pass by. She has become an object of head-wagging (לנידה היתה, v. 8a) because she חטא חטאה, 'sinned grievously'. The cognate accusative emphasizes the seriousness of the act committed. Sin brings punishment:

זבחי הבהבי יזבחו בשר ויאכלו יהוה לא רצם
עתה יזכר עונם ויפקד חטאותם המה מצרים ישובו:

> Though they offer sacrifice,
>> immolate flesh and eat it,
>> the LORD is not pleased with them.
> He shall still remember their guilt
>> and punish their sins;
>> they shall return to Egypt (Hos. 8.13; NAB).

The prophet Jeremiah warns his people of Yahweh's punishment if they do not return to Yahweh and reform their ways:

לשום ארצם לשמה שריקת עולם
כל עובר עליה ישם ויניד בראשו:

> Their land shall be turned into a desert, an object of lasting ridicule:
> All passers-by will be amazed, will shake their heads (Jer. 18.16; NAB).

Shaking or wagging the head belongs (along with mocking, taunting, hissing, gnashing the teeth, and the like) to the common shaming techniques.[55]

תשימנו חרפה לשכנינו לעג וקלס לסביבותינו:
תשימנו משל בגוים מנוד־ראש בל־אמים:

> You made us the reproach of our neighbors,
>> the mockery and the scorn of those around us.
> You made us a byword among the nations,
>> a laughingstock [lit. 'an object of head-wagging']
>> among the peoples (Ps. 44.14-15; NAB).

---

55. Bechtel, 'Shame as a Sanction', p. 72.

In v. 8b, the pairing of two opposite roots, כבד in the piel, 'to make heavy, to honor', and זלל in the hiphil, 'to make light of, to despise', brings out the contrast characteristic of the dirge, the contrast between past glorification and present abasement. The fact that Jerusalem is despised (הזילוה, '[now] despise her') is shown by her lack of comforters. The primary referents of כל־מכבדיה, 'all those who [once] honored her', are her former allies.[56] They have become disloyal, they have despised her by not sending comforters to this mourning ceremony. The reason for this complete reversal of attitudes is given in the next colon: כי־ראו ערותה, 'for they have seen her nakedness'. The words ערוה and ערום, usually translated 'nakedness' and 'naked', actually refer to two different kinds of nakedness. They can describe a state of complete nakedness (e.g. Gen. 2.25; 3.10; Hos. 2.11), or they can mean 'poorly clothed' (e.g. Deut. 28.48; Isa. 58.7; Ezek. 18.7). In this context, Jerusalem has a skirt on (v. 9a), so she is not completely naked. 'Her nakedness' must refer to her being girt with sackcloth from the hips down, laying bare the chest for beating as part of the mourning practice (e.g. Isa. 32.11-12; 2 Macc. 3.19; Nah. 2.8). Although Lady Jerusalem is in mourning garb, that is, only partly naked, 'her nakedness' may also refer to the shameful experience of her warriors being led into captivity completely naked (see Isa. 20.2-4). 'Her nakedness' thus represents Jerusalem in sackcloth, mourning the defeat and the exile of her people.

The parallelism between the first two bicola in v. 8 follows an a:b::b:a semantic chiastic structure: cause: result::result: cause, Jerusalem sinned: she is an object of head-wagging: she is despised: she was defeated.

Lady Jerusalem remembers the taunts and the jeers of the foes. While she reflects on her sins and the ensuing consequences, she sighs from sorrow and turns back. The phrase שׁוב + אחור denotes defeat in Pss. 9.4; 44.11; 56.10; Isa. 44.25; Lam. 1.13; 2.3. In all the above cases, the agent who causes the turning back in defeat is implicitly or explicitly Yahweh. Here again, Yahweh has brought about the defeat of Jerusalem because of her many sins. Jerusalem turns back because she has been defeated, mocked (v. 8a) and despised (v. 8b). Jerusalem turns back because she is full of shame. The feeling of shame often accompanies the action of turning back, as Isa. 42.17 (NAB) makes clear, although

---

56. Olyan, 'Honor, Shame, and Covenant Relations', p. 216.

the root used with אחור, 'back, backwards', is סוג, 'to turn, move':[57]

> They shall be turned back in utter shame
> 　who trust in idols;
> Who say to molten images,
> 　'You are our gods'.

The verbal phrase סוג אחור, 'to turn back,' is used in parallel with בוש, 'to be ashamed', in Pss. 35.4; 40.15; 70.3.

Jerusalem has been sitting on the ground (implied in v. 1a), therefore טמעתה בשוליה, 'her filth is on her skirt' (v. 9a). The word שולים refers to the skirt, the bottom part of a garment. In Isa. 6.1, the prophet sees Yahweh seated on a lofty throne with his train (שולים) filling the temple. In Nah. 3.5, Yahweh threatens to remove the שולים of Nineveh and expose her nakedness to the nations. Similarly, in Jer. 13.22, 26, Yahweh announces that he will strip off Jerusalem's שולים and expose her shame because of her great guilt.

The common interpretation of טמאתה בשוליה is that Jerusalem's skirt is stained with her menstrual blood.[58] However, menstrual uncleanness is like the uncleanness of childbirth (Lev. 12.2); it is not something to be laughed at or despised. When Laban was searching for his idols in Rachel's tent, Rachel had hidden these idols inside a camel cushion and was sitting on them, but she asked her father to excuse her for not rising in his presence because she was having her period. Then it is stated that Laban could not find his idols (Gen. 31.33-35). It may be inferred from this incident that Laban respected Rachel's request.

In the context of the mourning ceremony, the טמאה, 'uncleanness', on Jerusalem's skirt is the dirt[59] of the ground she is sitting on and which possibly she has sprinkled on her head. The dirt from the ground gets on her skirt and may therefore be called 'her filth, her dirt' (טמאתה). The word טמאה refers generally to ritual uncleanness caused by certain animals, leprosy, death and sexual discharges. It also refers metaphorically to idolatry and sin. In Isa. 6.5-7, טמא, 'unclean', is used in combination with עון, 'iniquity', and חטאת, 'sin'. The prophet sees Yahweh seated on the throne. He fears for his life, calling himself

---

57. J.A. Mayoral, *Sufrimiento y esperanza: La crisis exílica en Lamentaciones* (ISJ, 29; Navarra: EVD, 1994), pp. 55-56.

58. E.g. Provan, *Lamentations*, p. 45; Westermann, *Lamentations*, p. 129.

59. *LHAVT*, pp. 285-86.

אִישׁ טְמֵא־שְׂפָתִים, 'a man of unclean lips'. Then one of the seraphim touches his lips with a live coal, and declares: 'Now that this has touched your lips, your guilt [עֲוֺנֶךָ] has departed and your sin [וְחַטָּאתְךָ] is blotted out' (Isa. 6.7b; NRSV). Thus טֻמְאָתָהּ, 'her filth', may also point to Jerusalem's sins (v. 8a) which are evidenced by her skirt of sack-cloth, for the sackcloth is not only a mourning garb, but also a peniten-tial garb (e.g. 2 Kgs 19.1-2; Neh. 9.1).

When Jerusalem committed her many sins, she did not think of her future (לֹא זָכְרָה אַחֲרִיתָהּ, lit. 'she did not remember her future', v. 9a). Of Babylon's harsh treatment of Yahweh's people subjected to her, a similar comment is made:

לֹא־שַׂמְתְּ אֵלֶּה עַל־לִבֵּךְ לֹא זָכַרְתְּ אַחֲרִיתָהּ:

> You did not lay these things to heart
>   or remember their end (Isa. 47.7b),

this following her boasting about her sovereignty (47.7a). Humankind should 'remember that the days of darkness will be many' (וְיִזְכֹּר אֶת־יְמֵי הַחֹשֶׁךְ כִּי־הַרְבֵּה יִהְיוּ, Qoh. 11.8). 'To remember the future' thus means to remember past events with the view to learning for the future from their consequences.[60] Isaiah 41.22 (NAB) expresses this idea, although from a different perspective:

הָרִאשֹׁנוֹת מָה הֵנָּה הַגִּידוּ וְנָשִׂימָה לִבֵּנוּ
וְנֵדְעָה אַחֲרִיתָן

> What are the things of long ago?
>   Tell us, that we may reflect on them
> And know their outcome.

When Lady Jerusalem sinned, she did not consider the punishment her sins would entail. So, when she fell, it was a great shock: וַתֵּרֶד פְּלָאִים, 'thus she has fallen astoundingly' (v. 9b). From 'princess over the city-states', Jerusalem has become 'forced labor' (v. 1). Jerusalem has descended so low that the difference between her former and her present status is appalling, shocking people who hear of it. The root ירד, 'to come down', is often used in the context of coming down from the throne and sitting on the ground to mourn (e.g. Isa. 47.1; Jer. 48.18; Ezek. 26.16). It is also used of the fall of a besieged city (Deut. 20.20). The word פֶּלֶא, 'wonder, miracle', occurs in MT 12 other times to denote the creative, liberating and redemptive power of Yahweh (Exod.

---

60. H. Eising, 'זכר', *TDOT*, IV, pp. 64-82 (67).

15.11; Isa. 9.5; 25.1; 29.14; Dan. 12.6; Pss. 77.12, 15; 78.12; 88.11, 13; 89.6; 119.129). The wonders performed in Egypt before and at the exodus are redemptive for the Israelites; but for the Egyptians, they are Yahweh's acts of judgment. Ironically, the miraculous, unexpected event here is the fall of Jerusalem, the chosen city of God. Its inhabitants used to think: אלהים בקרבה בל־תמוט, 'God is in its midst; it shall not be moved' (Ps. 46.6). The people expected a mighty deliverance like that of 701 BCE, when Jerusalem was besieged by the Assyrian army of Sennacherib. Even at that time, however, some people did not perceive Yahweh's hand in the deliverance of their city; because of their spiritual blindness, Yahweh will work 'wonders' against them:

לכן הנני יוסף להפליא את־העם־הזה הפלא ופלא
ואבדה חכמת חכמיו ובינת נבניו תסתתר:

> Therefore I will again deal with this people
>   in surprising and wondrous fashion:
> The wisdom of its wise men shall perish
>   and the understanding of its prudent men be hid (Isa. 29.14; NAB).

The wonder, the miracle, in this context, is actually a 'counter-wonder'. Yahweh withdraws his gifts. Those who used to be wise no longer have wisdom. Those who used to have knowledge no longer have understanding. The astounding fall of the city in 587 BCE becomes a counter-wonder, an act of Yahweh's judgment on his people.

At this time of crisis, great upheaval and loss, Lady Jerusalem desperately needs a comforter. Yet she has no מנחם. She is utterly forlorn.

The mourning of Jerusalem (vv. 7-9b) features an *inclusio* with the verb זכר in v. 7a and v. 9a. Jerusalem did not think of the consequences of her sins. Now that she has fallen, she sits on the ground mourning, remembering and reflecting on the horrors of the fall. The cause of Jerusalem's mourning (vv. 3-6) is enclosed within mention of her mourning in vv. 1-2 and 7-9b.

Plea Addressed to Yahweh (Verses 9c-11)
The plea to Yahweh is remarkable in that it is begun by Jerusalem, then continued by the second speaker, and ended again by Jerusalem.

Jerusalem has been sitting on the ground all this time, keeping silent and overhearing what the second speaker says about her sufferings and herself. This is the moment of silence in the mourning ritual. Jerusalem remains silent because she is too overwhelmed by all the terrible things that have befallen her (just as Job's friends sit on the ground with Job for seven days and nights without saying a word [Job 2.13], and Ezekiel sits appalled for seven days among the exiles at Tel-abib [Ezek. 3.15]). This is an apathetic, petrified silence. Moreover, she had better keep silent lest, under the weight of pain, she utter something disrespectful of God, adding to her many sins. Her silence may also be a sign of submission, as in the case of the Servant of Yahweh:

> Though he was harshly treated, he submitted
>   and opened not his mouth;
> Like a lamb led to the slaughter
>   or a sheep before the shearers,
>   he was silent and opened not his mouth (Isa. 53.7; NAB).

Jerusalem's silence means that she acknowledges her sins and accepts Yahweh's well-deserved punishment of her (cf. Lam. 1.18).

Now, Jerusalem as a widow in mourning could appeal to Yahweh to hear her case,[61] since Yahweh is 'the father of the orphans and the defender of widows' (Ps. 68.6). The words of the speaker, by describing exactly her plight and her feelings, have helped somewhat to soothe her pain and arouse her from her lethargic condition. Jerusalem now utters a timid plea to Yahweh. She begs Yahweh to look at her misery, to pay attention to her distress, to take notice of her. She is fully conscious of her faults and she dares not ask for anything else. She may also be aware that in the past Yahweh always acted to save whenever he saw a case of oppression. Yahweh saw the misery of his people in Egypt, he heard their groaning, and decided to deliver them from the Egyptians (Exod. 3.7-8; Deut. 26.7-8). Accordingly, Jerusalem may be confident that once Yahweh sees her affliction, he will act to save. The motivation she gives in urging Yahweh to look at her is that אויב הגדיל, 'the enemy has gone too far' (v. 9c). The hiphil הגדיל without a direct object is loaded with meanings. It may mean 'to boast to the point of blasphemy', as in Jer. 48.26: השכירהו כי על־יהוה הגדיל, 'make him [Moab] drunk, because he boasted against Yahweh'.

Jerusalem's appeal goes something like this: 'It is true that I have sinned, and you, Yahweh, are using the enemy to chastise me. But surely, you did not intend the enemy to treat your people like this! You must have set a limit to what the enemy can do! Moreover, the enemy has no regard for you, Yahweh. He makes his own law and worships

---

61. R.N. Boyce, *The Cry to God in the Old Testament* (SBLDS, 103; Atlanta: Scholars Press, 1988), p. 66.

his own strength!' (See Isa. 47.6; Hab. 1.7, 11.)

The word עֲנִי, 'affliction, misery', comes from the root עֲנה, which is the opposite of the root גדל in הגדיל. Note the near end rhyme in עָנִיי and אוֹיֵב. The appeal sounds like a soft murmur with the alliteration in yod and the assonance in *e* and *i*.

Jerusalem starts the plea to Yahweh in v. 9c and stops there. The memories of all the atrocities committed by the enemy may have been still too fresh in her mind (cf. v. 7); she is too upset to continue. The second speaker now comes to her rescue. Verse 10 shows that the speaker has been present at the mourning ceremony since the very beginning. Actually, it was he who first broke the silence and spoke up, in contrast to Job's friends who spoke only after Job had broken the silence (Job 3).

Not knowing what to say to Jerusalem by way of comfort, he starts by describing her condition and feelings, showing insight and understanding in his speech. He has just heard Jerusalem appeal to Yahweh, so now he tries to expand on what she may have meant by הגדיל. The root פרשׂ with כפים or ידים plus the preposition אל usually denotes an attitude of prayer (e.g. 1 Kgs 8.38; Ezra 9.5; Isa. 1.15; Ps. 143.6; Lam. 1.17). Here, the phrase פרשׂ יד על, 'to stretch the hand over/for', ironically depicts the greed of the foes eager to gather up everything, not leaving anything left over. The nouns מַחְמָד and מַחְמֹד from the root חמד, 'to desire', seem to be used interchangeably (see *qere* and *kethib* in v. 11b) to designate people or things valuable and desirable for their grace and beauty.[62] The temple is called מַחְמַד עֵינֵיכֶם, 'the delight of your eyes' (Ezek. 24.21; NAB). The phrase כלי מחמדיה, 'its precious objects' (2 Chron. 36.19; NAB) probably refers to the temple vessels. In the context of v. 10b, מחמדיה designates the temple vessels.

The הגדיל of the foes consists in their doing what is forbidden them. During the 40 years in the wilderness, whenever the Israelites broke camp, only Aaron and his sons were allowed to cover the sacred objects and the utensils in the meeting tent after which the Kohathites could come in to carry them (see Num. 4.4-15). The priests and the Levites were in charge of the temple and the sacred vessels. Foreign nations were not allowed to enter the sanctuary of Yahweh (cf. Deut. 23.4; Ezek. 44.9). Yet these foes had the insolence to invade the sanctuary and to lay hand on the cultic vessels.

62. G. Wallis, 'חמד', *TDOT*, IV, pp. 452-61 (453-54).

This episode is usually taken to refer to the carrying away of the temple furnishings after the capture of Jerusalem in 587 BCE, as recorded in 2 Kgs 25.13-17. A carrying away of the temple vessels also occurred after the surrender of King Jehoiachin and his officials in 597 BCE (2 Kgs 24.12-13). However, the temple remained standing at that time. There is no mention of the destruction of the temple in Lamentations 1. That is why Rudolph opts for 597 BCE as the historical background of Lamentations 1.[63]

The גוים, the heathen nations with abhorrent religious practices, are already mentioned in v. 3b. They are identified here with the צר, 'the foe', in v. 10a. The verb צויתה, 'you commanded', in the second-person masculine singular and the phrase בקהל לך, 'into your assembly', with the second-person masculine singular suffix, show that the second speaker is addressing Yahweh. The speaker continues Jerusalem's plea on her behalf. The noun מקדש, 'sanctuary', often occurs in the construct state with יהוה or with first- or second-person singular pronominal suffixes referring to Yahweh (e.g. Josh. 24.26; Isa. 60.13; Dan. 9.17). This is the only instance where it occurs with the third-person feminine singular suffix (מקדשה, 'her sanctuary'). The speaker may intentionally use the third-person feminine suffix here and in the previous line with a nuance of reproach: 'Yahweh, you let these things happen as if they were only her sanctuary and her sacred vessels. But they are yours too.' This reproachful tone comes out clearly in v. 10c.

The second speaker continues to explain the הגדיל of the foes in v. 11. The people were dying from a shortage of food during the siege (Jer. 37.21; 38.9; 2 Kgs 25.3). In ancient times, famine could be so severe that people resorted to cannibalism, eating their own children (e.g. 2 Kgs 6.26-30; Lam. 2.20; 4.10). The construct noun מחמדי refers to children in Hos. 9.16 (NRSV): גם כי ילדון והמתי מחמדי בטנם, 'even

---

63. See Chapter 2 n. 1. Other texts also mention the carrying away of the temple vessels by foreigners, by the Egyptians at the time of King Rehoboam (1 Kgs 14.25-26) and by the army of Antiochus IV Epiphanes in 167 BCE (1 Macc. 1.20-24). However, the book of Lamentations as a whole, and Lam. 1 in particular, laments not only the loss of the temple vessels, but also the fall of Jerusalem, the exile of the population, the total loss of nationhood. The event in 1 Kgs 14.25-26 is ruled out because then the kingdom of Judah still continued. The event in 1 Macc. 1.20-24 may also be ruled out since this attack on Jerusalem came a long time after the people had lost their nationhood, been exiled, come back and lived under foreign oppression.

though they give birth, I will kill the cherished offspring of their womb'. That the people had to give up their beloved, treasured children for food (v. 11b) is the most poignant picture and the most degrading situation that can happen to humankind.[64] This is the fulfillment of the covenant curse in Deut. 28.52-57, especially v. 53 (NAB):

> in the distress of the siege to which your enemy subjects you, you will eat the fruit of your womb, the flesh of your own sons and daughters...

When the people of Yahweh are reduced to eating their own children, Yahweh's honor is at stake, as in Moses' prayer when Yahweh wanted to destroy his people following their making of the golden calf (Exod. 32.12; NAB):

> Why should the Egyptians say, 'With evil intent he brought them out, that he might kill them in the mountains and exterminate them from the face of the earth?'

The people groan (נֶאֱנָחִים) in their futile search for food. The root אנח, 'to groan', occurs three times in this first section of the poem (vv. 1-11). First, the priests groan (v. 4b) because the gates are empty of worshipers. Then Jerusalem groans (v. 8c) in shame and sorrow because she has been defeated and become an object of ridicule, of 'head-wagging'. Now the people groan (v. 11a) in hunger. Because of their sins, they are not allowed 'to satisfy their craving or fill their bellies' (Ezek. 7.19). The second speaker brings these groanings to Yahweh's attention in the hope that Yahweh will hear and remember his covenant and act to save (see Exod. 2.23-25; 3.7-8).

Lady Jerusalem closes the prayer with a second appeal to Yahweh to look at her 'despised' condition (v. 11c). The urgency of the request is expressed by the addition of נבט, 'to see', which is another verb from the realm of sight perception. The motivation for Yahweh to look at her in her first supplication (v. 9c) was that the enemy 'has gone too far'. The motivation in this second appeal is the reversed status of Jerusalem in relation to her oppressors. Jerusalem is זוֹלֵלָה, 'despised', from the

---

64. The main concern of the prayer in vv. 9c-11c may revolve around Yahweh's honor and the worship of Yahweh in his temple. So both מַחְמַדֶּיהָ (v. 10a) and מַחְמַדֵּיהֶם (*qere*, v. 11b) refer to the temple vessels. Because of famine during the siege, the people might have put pressure through their elders on King Jehoiachin and his officials to surrender. Yet, after the temple vessels were carried away and the siege lifted, people were still suffering from hunger. This argument would support Rudolph's date of 597 BCE for Lam. 1 (see p. 38).

same root זלל as in v. 8b. This prayer is similar to Nehemiah's appeal: שמע אלהינו כי־היינו בוזה, 'Take note, O our God, how we were mocked!' (Neh. 3.36; NAB). That Jerusalem asks Yahweh to see how she is despised implies a special relationship between Yahweh and her: Yahweh's honor is at stake when Jerusalem is despised. The prayers in the Psalms often bring to God's attention the abject condition of his people (e.g. 44.13-14; 79.4; 80.6). Yahweh will act to save his honor, as he promised in Ezek. 36.22 (NRSV):

> Therefore say to the house of Israel, Thus says the Lord GOD: It is not for your sake, O house of Israel, that I am about to act, but for the sake of my holy name, which you have profaned among the nations to which you came.

In vv. 9c and 11c, Jerusalem is praying that Yahweh take notice of her, yet Yahweh seems distant, indifferent. Jerusalem feels she has been left alone to struggle through her tremendous sufferings. She has no comforter. However, because of her sins, she dares not yet ask for Yahweh's direct intervention on her behalf.

The plea to Yahweh (vv. 9c-11c) is enclosed within two petitions for Yahweh to take notice (v. 9c and v. 11c), both of which start out with the same cry ראה יהוה, 'look, O Yahweh', and end with opposite motive clauses/antithetic parallel cola:

כי הגדיל אויב//כי הייתי זוללה

> For the enemy has gone too far!//How despised I am!

Jerusalem's Address to the Passers-by (Verses 12-16)
Jerusalem begins by describing her mourning, how she feels at being afflicted by Yahweh (vv. 12-14). She gives the cause of her mourning (v. 15), and then goes back to her own feelings of grief and loneliness (v. 16).

Jerusalem has just called on Yahweh to take notice of her. She may have thought that Yahweh would not hear her prayer because of her sins; compare Isa. 59.1-2 (NAB):

> Lo, the hand of the LORD is not too short to save,
>   nor his ear too dull to hear.
> Rather, it is your crimes
>   that separate you from your God,
> It is your sins that make him hide his face
>   so that he will not hear you.

Hence Jerusalem turns to address the passers-by. The scene of the mourning ceremony opens up in both space and time.[65] In space, the call to the passers-by, that is, people from the neighboring countries who pass her by, to witness her grief echoes the call to heavens and earth and people to be witnesses at the divine lawsuit (e.g. Isa. 1.2; Mic. 1.2). This address to the passers-by also recalls the ritual practice of inviting people around to join in mourning (e.g. 2 Sam. 3.31, where David directs Joab and all the people who were with him to mourn over Abner). This call also evokes the summons to professional mourners to lament the dead. In Jer. 9.17-18, a call is issued to the mourning women to come and lament. Their lament helps the bereaved's tears to run down more freely. A similar sequence is found in Jerusalem's address to the passers-by: the call is issued in v. 12, tears flow in v. 16. The indirect question, אִם־יֵשׁ מַכְאוֹב כְּמַכְאֹבִי, 'if there is any pain like my pain' (v. 12b), involves a comparison which naturally springs up in every human mind when faced with something wonderful (e.g. Deut. 4.32-34: the people of Israel heard the voice of God speaking from the midst of fire and still lived) or calamitous (e.g. Judg. 19.30: the concubine of a Levite was raped to death by the Benjaminites at Gibeah). The implied answer is always negative; see, for example, the question suggesting a comparison about the locust plague in the time of Joel, followed by a negative answer (Joel 1.2; 2.2; NAB):

> Has the like of this happened in your days,
>   or in the days of your fathers?

> Their like has not been from of old,
>   nor will it be after them,
>   even to the years of distant generations.

The agent of the polal עוֹלַל from the root עלל, 'to act, to deal severely with', is clearly spelled out in v. 12c: it was Yahweh who brought this incomparable pain on Jerusalem. Here, Yahweh is subject of the same verb as in v. 5b, יָנָה, 'to afflict'. The root עלל is used again in v. 22ab, forming an *inclusio* for this second part of the poem spoken by Lady Jerusalem.

The scene of the mourning ceremony opens up also in time with בְּיוֹם חֲרוֹן אַפּוֹ, 'on the day of his burning wrath'. This phrase is a variation of the prophetic concept יוֹם יְהוָה, 'the day of Yahweh', which had been proclaimed since the time of Amos (e.g. 5.18, 20). It is used to

65. Droin, *Lamentations*, p. 37.

interpret past, imminent or future catastrophic events as Yahweh's judgment for sins.[66] In this context, 'the day of his burning wrath' refers to the momentous event of the fall of Jerusalem in 587 BCE.

The combination חרון אף, 'burning wrath', occurs 33 times in the MT and is used exclusively to express the divine wrath.[67] The motive for Yahweh's wrath is stated in Deut. 29.23-28. Whenever his people break the covenant, that is, fail to obey Yahweh, he reacts to their sin with wrath. The 'wrath' of God is not an attribute of God; it simply denotes the way God reacts to sin and carries out his judgment against sinners.[68]

Verse 13 describes the uniquely terrible pain of Jerusalem with three vivid metaphors: a fire burning inside her, in her bones; an animal caught in a net, with no way of escape; and finally, a woman lonely and sick, on the point of death.

The imagery of fire is often used to describe the manifestation of divine wrath (e.g. Jer. 4.4; 21.12; Lam. 2.4) and follows naturally from the phrase 'burning wrath' in v. 12c. The phrase ממרום, 'from on high', leaves no doubt about the origin of the fire. It is sent by Yahweh who is enthroned 'on high' (מרום, Isa. 33.5). The word עצמות, 'bones', may refer sometimes to the physical body (e.g. Job 21.24), sometimes to the whole person (e.g. Ps. 35.10; Jer. 23.9). It is parallel to ימים, 'days', in Ps. 102.4 and may refer to 'life'. It represents the innermost being of an individual (e.g. Job 4.14; Ps. 42.11). In this context, Yahweh sends his fire deep down into the 'bones' of Jerusalem—her pain is very deep inside her, and cannot be removed easily. Moreover, the fire burns and consumes the bones away: Jerusalem's life is ebbing out of her (cf. דוה, 'sick, in pain', v. 13c). The combined imagery of fire burning in the bones is found also in Jer. 20.9 and Ps. 102.4.

Verse 13b describes Jerusalem's pain in terms of a hunting metaphor. A popular method of hunting is the battue method. The hunters frighten the game by beating the ground, shouting loudly and pounding drums. The game is thus driven before them into a blind canyon, an enclosure of nets, or a prepared pit, where it can be killed easily.[69] Jerusalem's pain is like that of a frightened animal caught in a net, waiting to be killed. This imagery picks up that used in v. 3c where Judah, the game, is overtaken by her hunters in the net of her difficult entanglements.

---

66. A.J. Everson, 'The Days of Yahweh', *JBL* 93 (1974), pp. 329-37.
67. E. Johnson, 'אנף', *TDOT*, I, pp. 348-60 (356).
68. Westermann, *Lamentations*, pp. 149-50.
69. L.E. Toombs, 'Hunting', *IDB*, II, pp. 662-63.

Jerusalem's children are compared to 'antelopes caught in a net' (כתוא מכמר) in Isa. 51.20.

Yahweh has caused Jerusalem to be שׁממה which can mean 'appalled, motionless', or 'forlorn, without a husband, without children' like Tamar, Absalom's sister, after she was raped and sent away by her half-brother Amnon (2 Sam. 13.20). Both meanings pick up the imagery of the lonely widow in v. 1 and apply to Jerusalem in v. 13c. She is called שׁוממה, 'deserted wife', in Isa. 54.1. She is also terrified in her mourning silence. The adjective דוה is used only here and in Lam. 5.17 in the sense of 'sick, faint, in pain'. It is applied twice in Lev. 15.33 and 20.18 to the woman who is having her menstrual flow, and therefore seems to be connected with the weakness that results from 'the outflow of the body's vital fluid'.[70] The masculine biform דוי, 'faint', is always found with the noun לב, 'heart, inner self' (Isa. 1.5; Jer. 8.18; Lam. 1.22), which confirms T. Collins's hypothesis that the heart was seen by the ancient Hebrews as the source of tears, such that the outflow of tears leaves the person weak, exhausted.[71] Jerusalem is worn out from weeping through the night (v. 2a), and all day long (vv. 13c, 16a).

Verse 13 expands on the pain which Yahweh inflicted upon Jerusalem (אשׁר הוגה יהוה, 'with which Yahweh afflicted me', v. 12c; cf. v. 5b, כי יהוה הוגה, 'because Yahweh has afflicted her'). Verse 14 talks about the sins which provoked Yahweh's wrath (ביום חרון אפו, 'on the day of his burning wrath', v. 12c; cf. v. 5b, על רב־פשׁעיה, 'for the multitude of her transgressions'). In the covenant relationship, Yahweh promises blessings for obedience and curses for disobedience (see Deut. 27.16–28.69). The root שׁקד, 'keep watch', is used here in a hostile sense as in Jer. 5.6 (נמר שׁקד על־עריהם, 'leopards keep watch round their cities').[72] Jerusalem's sins have been stored away as in Hos. 13.12 (צפונה חטאתו, 'his sin is stored away') for 'the day of his burning wrath'. Her sins have been fastened, bundled together by Yahweh himself, and laid on her shoulders, around her neck. Jerusalem's strength collapses under the weight of her sins. The psalmist experiences a similar situation (Ps. 38.5; NRSV):

> For my iniquities have gone over my head;
>> they weigh like a burden too heavy for me.

---

70. T. Collins, 'The Physiology of Tears in the Old Testament: Part 1', *CBQ* 33 (1971), pp. 18-38 (31).
71. Collins, 'The Physiology of Tears: Part 1', p. 32.
72. Hillers, *Lamentations*, p. 73.

The first two bicola in v. 14 form a grammatical a:b::b′:a′ chiastic structure: נשקד על פשעי:בידו ישתרגו::עלו על־צוארי:הכשיל כחי, 'A watch was kept over my sins: they were bundled together by his hand::they went up my neck: he caused my strength to fail'. The first and the last cola have a singular verb, and the implied subject is Yahweh. The middle cola have a plural verb with פשעי, 'my sins', as subject.

The last colon presents a picture of sins as 'hands' that close their grip on Jerusalem. This grip is tenacious: she cannot rise up under the weight of her sins. She must bear the consequences of her sins: she is dying. In fact, many of her children have died, as the next verse makes clear.

Both vv. 13c and 14c begin with the same verb: נתנני, lit. 'he gave/made me'. Although Yahweh is not addressed directly, he is the main subject of the discourse in vv. 12-14. It is Yahweh who brought about all this havoc, who caused all these sufferings. This truth is acknowledged by faith. Yet it is so hard to bear, to comprehend. Lady Jerusalem is on the verge of death.

Jerusalem interrupts her lament to state the cause of her mourning, 'an actual event in the siege of Jerusalem',[73] in v. 15. Yahweh, portrayed as the divine warrior, piled up all her strong, choice young men, like sheaves of grain stacked up on the threshing floor. The word בקרבי, 'in my midst', refers not to Jerusalem but to Judah as a whole (v. 15c). This event occurred outside the city (cf. Jer. 34.1, 7; 35.10-11). Then Yahweh summoned a מועד, a gathering of people at an appointed time and place. Usually, the word מועד refers to a festival, a time of celebration and rejoicing (e.g. Lam. 1.4). Here, Yahweh assembled not the people of Judah to a festive celebration, but their enemies to crush them, to celebrate their defeat. Yahweh's judgment on sinners is likened elsewhere to the threshing of wheat or barley after the harvest:

בת־בבל כגרן עת הדריכה

Daughter Babylon is like a threshing floor
at the time it is trodden (Jer. 51.33; NAB).

והמה לא ידעו מחשבות יהוה
ולא הבינו עצתו כי קבצם כעמיר גרנה:

But they know not the thoughts of the LORD,
nor understand his counsel,

---

73. Hillers, *Lamentations*, p. 89; Westermann, *Lamentations*, p. 133.

When he has gathered them
like sheaves on the threshing floor (Mic. 4.12; NAB).

Another image for the divine judgment is the treading of grapes in the winepress (e.g. Isa. 63.3). Both agricultural images are used to express the totality of the slaughter, the severity of the destruction in v. 15, just as in Joel 4.13 (NAB):

שִׁלְחוּ מַגָּל כִּי בָשַׁל קָצִיר
בֹּאוּ רְדוּ כִּי־מָלְאָה גַּת
הֵשִׁיקוּ הַיְקָבִים כִּי רַבָּה רָעָתָם:

Apply the sickle, for the harvest is ripe;
Come and tread, for the wine press is full;
The vats overflow, for great is their malice.

The people of Judah cannot come to the festivals in Jerusalem (v. 4a) because they had been threshed and trodden by a מוֹעֵד, 'an assembly, a gathering', of foes. The active subject, the agent of destruction, is אֲדֹנָי, 'the Lord', mentioned in v. 15a, and repeated in v. 15c, forming an *inclusio* to stress Yahweh's full responsibility for this massacre.

Lady Jerusalem mourns the death of her people and her choice warriors. She weeps (v. 16a). She has no comforter. The phrase רָחַק מִן, 'far from', actually means 'there is not', as the parallelism in Isa. 59.11 (NRSV) shows:

נְקַוֶּה לַמִּשְׁפָּט וָאַיִן לִישׁוּעָה רָחֲקָה מִמֶּנּוּ:

We wait for justice, but there is none;
for salvation, but it is far from us.

The description of weeping followed by the complaint of having no comforter (v. 16ab) is also found in v. 2ab. Lady Jerusalem has no comforter to save her life (מֵשִׁיב נַפְשִׁי, lit. 'one who brings back my life'). One reason why she lacks such a comforter is that her children are שׁוֹמֵמִים, 'appalled, petrified' in silent mourning, away from their homeland, driven into captivity by the conquering foe (כִּי גָבַר אוֹיֵב, 'for the enemy has prevailed').

Jerusalem's address to the passers-by presents an *inclusio* formed by שְׁמָמָה in v. 13c and שׁוֹמֵמִים in v. 16c. The whole address revolves around the pain and sufferings which crush Jerusalem and leave her on the verge of death. She recognizes the hand of Yahweh (הוֹגָה יְהוָה, 'Yahweh afflicted [me]', v. 12c) behind the human enemy (גָבַר אוֹיֵב, 'the enemy has prevailed', v. 16c).

Short Lament by the Second Speaker (Verse 17)
Jerusalem's tears may have caused her to pause temporarily after v. 16. The sympathetic speaker comes in right at the middle of Jerusalem's speech. Her speech has two parts. The preceding five stanzas (a total of 15 bicola, vv. 12-16) are addressed to the passers-by. The second part following the speech of the second speaker also has five stanzas (i.e. 15 bicola, vv. 18-22) which are not equally divided between the two addressees. The first colon (v. 18a) is a comment, a thought spoken out loud for everyone to hear, and addressed to no one in particular. The next five bicola are addressed to all peoples, or nations of the world. The last nine bicola form a prayer addressed to Yahweh.

The second speaker observes that Zion has been begging (פרשׂה בידיה, 'has stretched forth her hands') the passers-by for a comforter. The verbal phrase פרשׂ כפים, 'to stretch forth one's hands', as noted previously in the exegesis of v.10, denotes an attitude of prayer: for example, Exod. 9.29, 33; Ps. 44.21. But her request is not successful. No one agrees to be her מנחם. Yahweh has shut out (שׂתם, 3.8) her prayer. It could not pass through the cloud to him:

סכותה בענן לך מעבור תפלה:

> You have wrapped yourself with a cloud
>   so that no prayer can pass through (3.44; NRSV).

The refrain אין מנחם לה, 'she has no one to comfort her', repeated from vv. 2b and 9b, emphasizes the ineffectiveness of Jerusalem's prayer. Her hands are as useless as Yahweh's hand and the sins' 'hands' are effective (v. 14).[74] She has no comforter because Yahweh has commanded her neighbors to turn against her. The name Jacob is used instead of Israel, because Israel is the one who prevailed in his wrestling with divine and human beings (Gen. 32.29), while Jacob here is defeated by Yahweh through his neighbors. Defeated Jerusalem has become the butt of scorn of her enemies (v. 17c).

Verse 17 picks up the two main motifs which run through the whole poem, namely, the loneliness and the humiliation of Jerusalem, the widow mourner.

Jerusalem's Answer to the Charge in Verse 17b (Verse 18a)
Although the second speaker did not address Jerusalem directly, she overheard the reason he gave in v. 17b for her loneliness and humilia-

---

74. Droin, *Lamentations*, p. 38.

tion: it was Yahweh who commanded her neighbors to turn against her. Jerusalem knows why Yahweh did it. She now tries to clarify Yahweh's action in v. 18a.

The first colon, צדיק הוא יהוה, 'Yahweh is just', is a confession of faith. Yahweh is צדיק because he acts in accordance with who he is and what he says and wills. He is צדיק because he keeps his covenant with his people, blessing obedience and punishing disobedience. The confession of faith requires a corresponding confession of sins: כי פיהו מריתי. 'for I have rebelled against his word'. Jerusalem acknowledges her sins. She deserves to be punished, to be deserted, forlorn and humiliated. She submits to Yahweh's judgment.

A confession of faith is also followed by a confession of sins in the Levites' prayer on behalf of the returned exiles who fast in sackcloth and confess their sins:

ואתה צדיק על כל־הבא עלינו
כי־אמת עשית ואנחנו הרשענו:

> You have been just
> in all that has come upon us,
> For you have dealt faithfully
> and we have acted wickedly (Neh. 9.33; NRSV).

Ezra makes a similar confession of faith and of sins concerning the returned exiles who intermarry with the heathen peoples around them:

> O LORD, God of Israel, you are just [צדיק אתה]; yet we have been spared, the remnant we are today. Here we are before you in our sins. Because of all this, we can no longer stand in your presence (Ezra 9.15; NAB).

Jerusalem knows she deserves her punishment, yet it is so very hard to bear it alone, without a מנחם.

Jerusalem's Address to All Peoples (Verses 18b-19)

From v. 18b on, the scene opens up further to include all peoples in the world. Jerusalem's call to them to listen (שמעו־נא כל־העמים, 'listen, all you peoples') echoes Moses' call to the heavens and earth to hear his teaching (Deut. 32.1). Jerusalem calls to a universal audience because she wants the peoples to hear her story, to learn from her experience. A universal address is associated with universal truths also in Psalm 47 where all the peoples are called to rejoice since Yahweh is king over all the earth, and in Psalm 49 where all the peoples are urged to take heed not to trust in their own riches.

Jerusalem may also be looking for a comforter among the peoples. She appeals to them for sympathy (וראו מכאבי, 'and consider my pain'). The root ראה, 'to look at', in this context has a nuance of look-ing at with kindness and helpfulness, as in the two brief appeals to Yahweh in vv. 9c and 11c. Childless Hannah weeps and prays to Yah-weh to look on her misery (אם־ראה תראה בעני אמתך, 'if only you will look on the misery of your servant', 1 Sam. 1.11). In his flight from Absalom, David is cursed by Shimei. David's men want to kill Shimei, but David tells them to leave Shimei alone. David trusts in Yahweh's intervention: אולי יראה יהוה בעניי, 'perhaps Yahweh will look on my affliction' (2 Sam. 16.12).

In describing her pain beyond all pains to the passers-by, Jerusalem had stopped at the mention of the exile in v. 16c. Now she resumes her description to a different audience. She does not repeat what she has already said concerning her own feelings of anguish and exhaustion (vv. 13-14), and the bloody fighting in Judah (v. 15). She simply picks up where she left off, at the exile.

The pain that Jerusalem wants all peoples to look at with sympathy is the exile of her children (בתולתי ובחורי, 'my young women and my young men'), who constitute the future of the nation. With her children exiled, she has no future.

The pain of exile entails the pain of betrayal, defeat, death, shame and loneliness. In her distress, Jerusalem called for help. In קראתי למאהבי, 'I called to my lovers', the root קרא has the nuance of 'to cry for help':

אז תקרא ויהוה יענה תשוע ויאמר הנני

> Then you shall call, and the LORD will answer,
>> you shall cry for help, and he will say: Here I am! (Isa. 58.9; NAB).

The psalmist is confident of Yahweh's help in Ps. 4.4 (NAB):

ודעו כי הפלה יהוה חסיד לו יהוה ישמע בקראי אליו׃

> Know that the LORD does wonders for his faithful one;
>> the LORD will hear me when I call upon him.

Jerusalem's inconstant lovers did not come to her rescue. Some of these inconstant lovers must be the allies mentioned in Jer. 27.3. They have deceived her, as in Jer. 30.14: כל־מאהביך שכחוך, 'all your lovers have forgotten you'. They are not friends who love at all times and share adversity (Prov. 17.17). They do not keep their pacts and treaties.

The consequence of their deception and betrayal is that her priests, who were authoritative in spiritual and cultic matters, and her elders, who used to render justice at the gates (see Ruth 4.1-12) and to furnish counsel (cf. 1 Kgs 20.7; Jer. 18.18; Ezek. 7.26), have been reduced to searching for food and died of hunger in the midst of the city. When the priests die, there is no one to teach God's law. When the elders die, there is no one to give counsel and administer justice.

The hiphil of שׁוב with the noun נפשׁ, 'to restore life, to revive, refresh', comes back as a refrain for the third time in the poem in v. 19c. In both vv. 11b and 19c, this phrase is used in connection with the search for food. In v. 16b, it is used of the search for a comforter. Life cannot go on without food or without a comforter.

Jerusalem's Plea to Yahweh (Verses 20-22)

The pain of Jerusalem has reached its climax: her children, her priests and elders have died. Jerusalem expected help from her human friends, but she has been bitterly disappointed. She has no other recourse than crying to Yahweh, to him who afflicted her (הוגה יהוה, vv. 5b, 12c).

As she has pleaded before in vv. 9c and 11c, she again pleads with Yahweh to look at her with pity and compassion. She cries out: ראה יהוה כי־צר־לי, 'see, O Yahweh, how distressed I am'. The noun צר, 'distress', harks back to המצרים, 'the straits, difficult situation', in v. 3c and evokes images of being overtaken by hunters (vv. 3c, 6c), caught in a net (v. 13b), with all the ensuing hardships. Jerusalem's pain goes beyond her physical privations and forced labor. She is in a state of inner confusion, inner turmoil. She feels confused like a person under the effects of wine, not knowing what to do or where to turn. She has suffered punishment from Yahweh. Elsewhere, too, Yahweh's punishment is described in terms of his 'making people drunk'; for example, Jer. 48.26: 'Make him [Moab] drunk, because he boasted against Yahweh'; and Ps. 60.5 (NRSV):

הראיתה עמך קשה השקיתנו יין תרעלה:

You have made your people suffer hard things;
  you have given us wine to drink that made us reel.

The root חמר I, 'to ferment, boil, foam up', in מעי חמרמרו, 'my inner parts are in ferment',[75] is used to describe wine, יין חמר, 'foaming wine'

---

75. BDB, p. 330.

(Ps. 75.9), and water, יהמו יחמרו מימיו, 'its waters roar and foam' (Ps. 46.4). Another root חמר II, 'to glow, burn', has also been suggested, yielding the translation 'my inner parts burn'.[76] The first imagery is of chaos and uproar. The second is that of a sensation of burning. Both meanings make sense. They convey the idea of restlessness and anguish. The sensation of something burning inside recalls the imagery of fire burning inside the bones of v. 13a.

The root הפך, 'turn, overthrow, change, transform', has a special meaning in the phrase נהפך לבי, 'my heart is convulsed'. It seems to express 'a surge of emotion and sudden change of heart'.[77] The inner self is not at peace. It is constantly agitated as a result of sin and rebellion ('for I have rebelled stubbornly', כי מרו מריתי). The wicked are compared to the tossing sea and have no peace (Isa. 57.20-21; cf. 48.22).

T. Collins suggests another way of understanding the references to מעי חמרמרו (lit. 'my intestines are in turmoil') and נהפך לבי ('my heart is changed'). The ancient Hebrews viewed the intestines and the heart as the source of tears. An external threat—in this case, the distressing circumstances of the siege and the destruction of the city—provokes a reaction in the intestines, and this reaction in turn changes the physical composition of the heart. The heart then becomes weak and turns to water. This water makes its way through the throat and the eyes and appears as tears on the face.[78] Thus, according to Collins, v. 20a and the first colon of v. 20b describe the weeping of Lady Jerusalem.

Jerusalem must bear the consequences of her sin: death is everywhere, outside the city, in the outlying towns and fields of Judah, and inside the city as well (v. 20c).

In v. 18b, Jerusalem asked the peoples to hear and look. In v. 20, Jerusalem begs Yahweh to look (ראה) at her, to see her distress. In v. 21, she pleads with Yahweh to hear (שמע) her groans. God hears the groaning of the Israelites in Egypt and looks upon them (Exod. 2.24-25). God sees their misery and hears their cry, and decides to deliver them from the Egyptians (Exod. 3.7-8). Yahweh sees and hears that Jacob loves Rachel more than Leah, so Yahweh causes Leah to bear sons for Jacob (Gen. 29.31-33). God sees Jacob's affliction and rebukes Laban (Gen. 31.42). The roots ראה and שמע are often used separately

---

76. H. Ringgren, 'חמר', *TDOT*, V, pp. 1-4 (1-2).
77. K. Seybold, 'הפך', *TDOT*, III, pp. 423-27 (424).
78. Collins, 'The Physiology of Tears: Part 1', pp. 27-31.

or in combination to introduce the motive for divine intervention.

Verse 8c mentions Jerusalem's groans over the shame of her being despised. Here, in v. 21a, her groans encompass everything from suffering under oppression to shame of defeat to pangs of death. Yet through all these heart-rending circumstances, Jerusalem has no comforter. The refrain, 'she has no one to comfort her', אין־לה מנחם, which first appears in the second verse of the poem, now comes back in the second to last verse. She dares not ask Yahweh directly to be her מנחם. She simply confesses her need. She has asked Yahweh to look at her distress and to hear her groaning. She knows that Yahweh is just (צדיק). Because Yahweh is just, he will repay to all according to their works (Ps. 62.13), he will punish the wicked and reward the righteous (Ps. 58.12). Yahweh is אל־צדיק ומושיע, 'a just and saving God' (Isa. 45.21), 'gracious and just' (Ps. 116.5). He will save the oppressed. Jerusalem has no comforter to save her life (משיב נפשי, 'to save my life', v. 16b), so she has brought her need to Yahweh. He is just. He will provide for her need. He will save her from oppression.

Jerusalem's last request in the next four bicola (vv. 21bc, 22ab) concerns her enemies. They rejoice at her downfall (vv. 7d, 21b). They rejoice that Yahweh has done it, has delivered his people into their power (cf. Isa. 47.6). The malice of the enemies and their scornful laugh have aggravated Jerusalem's physical and mental distress. Yahweh has dealt with Jerusalem according to her sins (v. 22b). Now Jerusalem asks Yahweh to deal with her enemies according to their wickedness (vv. 21c, 22a). She begs Yahweh to judge according to his justice, as the psalmist declares:

ישפט־תבל בצדק ועמים במישרים:

He will rule the world with justice
and the peoples with equity (Ps. 98.9; NAB).

Jerusalem pleads with Yahweh to bring on her enemies 'the day' Yahweh has announced, that is, the day of judgment proclaimed by the prophets. That day has come upon Jerusalem through the catastrophe of 587 BCE. Yahweh also has a day, 'the day of his wrath', for each of Jerusalem's enemies: for example, the day for Babylon is announced in Isa. 47.8-11. When that day comes, Babylon will become like Jerusalem (כמוני, 'like me', v. 21c); she will be a widow mourning for her children.

Jerusalem's plea for vindication may sound harsh to Christians who have been taught the spirit of forgiveness, as when Jesus prays on the cross: 'Father, forgive them, they know not what they do' (Lk. 23.34; NAB), or when Stephen cries out before he died: 'Lord, do not hold this sin against them' (Acts 7.60; NAB). Yet Rev. 6.10 records such a prayer for vindication by the martyrs: 'Sovereign Lord, holy and true, how long will it be before you judge and avenge our blood on the inhabitants of the earth?' (NRSV).

Jerusalem's cry for vindication is neatly enclosed within the double mention of her groaning in vv. 21a and 22c. The nominal clause ולבי דוי, 'and my heart is in pain' (v. 22c), harks back to נהפך לב בקרבי, 'my heart is convulsed within me' (v. 20b), and to כל־היום דוה, 'in pain all day long' (v. 13c). Lady Jerusalem is in an extreme state of physical and mental exhaustion. She is on the verge of death. She needs a comforter. She needs Yahweh's deliverance.

The last colon (v. 22c) brings back the picture of Lady Jerusalem in v. 1, a widow lonely and despised, forced to perform hard tasks, mourning her dead, almost succumbing under the weight of her physical and mental sufferings. The whole poem is enclosed within the *inclusio* formed by רבתי in v. 1ab and רבות in v. 22c. A city burgeoning with 'many people' (v. 1a) has become a city dying with 'many groans' (v. 22c).

Conclusion

Lamentations 1 can be understood as an artfully woven tapestry in which ideas and images weave round and round to express the inexpressible sufferings of people who have recently undergone a tragic loss. The ideas and themes in the first 11 verses are repeated and expanded in the second half of the chapter:[79] for example, the themes of loneliness and powerlessness in v. 1 are taken up again in vv. 13c and 14c; the need for a comforter in vv. 2b and 9b is again articulated in vv. 16b, 17a and 21a.

The scene might be depicted as follows: in the aftermath of the fall of Jerusalem, the chosen city of God, a few survivors gather together to mourn the destruction of their beloved city and the death as well as the exile of their loved ones. They sit in sackcloth amid the charred ruins (vv. 1a, 8b, 9ab), they weep (vv. 2a, 16a) and cry out in their suffering. They are fully conscious of the hand of Yahweh, of his chastening rod,

79. Hunter, *Faces*, pp. 88-89.

in what has happened to them (vv. 5b, 9b, 12-15, 17b-18a, 21b, 22b). They recognize their sins (vv. 5b, 8a, 14, 18a, 20b, 22b). Yet it is so hard to bear these terrible losses. Death has claimed so many lives: death through fighting (vv. 15, 20c), death through famine (vv. 6bc, 11b, 19bc, 20c). They suffer so much that they feel as if they are drunk, or in a daze (vv. 13c, 16c, 20ab, 22c). Yahweh seems silent, far away. They may be stupefied by their pains, yet they know one thing: whatever they did then, in the past, and whatever they now feel and say, everything happens *coram Deo*, in the presence of God.[80] So from their laments arise two prayers for Yahweh to intervene to safeguard his honor (vv. 9c-11c) and his justice (vv. 20-22).

---

80. Droin, *Lamentations*, p. 40.

Chapter 3

LAMENTATIONS 2

This poem resembles the first poem, in that its 22 three-line stanzas
begin in the first line of each stanza with the successive letters of the
Hebrew alphabet. However, contrary to the normal ע then פ order in
Lamentations 1, Lamentations 2 exhibits the order פ then ע in vv. 16
and 17. This order also occurs in Lamentations 3 and 4, Psalms 9–10,
and perhaps also originally in Psalm 34, as attested by the flow of
thought in vv. 16-18. It is further reflected in the LXX of Proverbs 31
and in several Hebrew alphabets dated to the eighth century BCE discovered at Kuntilat-Ajrud.[1] It thus seems that the sequence of letters ע
then פ had not yet become normative at the time these poems were put
together.

It has been stated above that, apart from ch. 3, all the chapters of the
book of Lamentations are dated by scholarly consensus to the period
from 587 to 538 BCE. Even Iain Provan, who is extremely cautious
about setting a date for Lamentations and thus proposes a broad span of
time between the sixth and the second centuries BCE, seems quite certain that Lamentations 2 points to the fall of Jerusalem in 587 BCE
because of its reference to the rejection and exile of the king in vv. 6c
and 9b.[2]

וינאץ בזעם־אפו מלך וכהן:

He spurned in his fierce anger
    king and priest (2.6c).

---

1. A. Lemaire, 'Abécédaires et exercices d'écolier en épigraphie nord-ouest
sémitique', *JA* 266 (1978), pp. 221-35. An ostracon dated around the twelfth century BCE discovered at Izbet Sartah also shows the order פ then ע in the Phoenician
alphabet.
2. Provan, *Lamentations*, pp. 7-19.

מלכה ושריה בגוים אין תורה

Her king and princes are among the nations;
   there is no instruction (2.9b).

The first nine verses in Lamentations 2 reflect the course of the Babylonian invasion as recorded in Jer. 35.11 (NAB), through the words of
the Rechabites:

But when Nebuchadnezzar, king of Babylon, invaded this land, we
decided to come into Jerusalem to escape the army of the Chaldeans and
the army of Aram; that is why we are now living in Jerusalem.

See also Jer. 34.6-7 (NAB):

The prophet Jeremiah told all these things to Zedekiah, king of Judah, in
Jerusalem, while the armies of the king of Babylon were attacking
Jerusalem and the remaining cities of Judah, Lachish and Azekah, since
these alone were left of the fortified cities of Judah.

The Babylonian armies first attacked the countryside and the outlying
towns of Judah before they closed in and laid siege to Jerusalem.

Thus the historical background of Lamentations 2 seems to be firmly
established in the events associated with the fall of Jerusalem in 587
BCE.

I will follow the same outline as in the previous chapter: first, I give a
translation of Lamentations 2 with critical notes; then I will treat its
mourning ceremony setting and the problem of poetic structure and
address; the next section will focus on the exegesis. Finally, the conclusion will gather together the new insights derived from a close reading of the poem against the setting of a mourning ceremony.

Translation and Critical Notes

Two voices are heard distinctly in this poem, as in Lamentations 1. One
voice is readily identifiable as that of Lady Jerusalem, the chief mourner, who speaks only in the last three stanzas. The other voice is again
called the 'second speaker' although he speaks first and gives a longer
speech (the first 19 verses). In the following translation, I indicate my
understanding of who is speaking in parentheses before the given
speech.

(The second speaker)

1   Alas! The Lord in his wrath
         abhorred[a] daughter Zion!
      He cast down from heaven to earth
         the glory of Israel.
      He did not remember his footstool
         on the day of his wrath.

2   The Lord consumed without mercy
         Jacob's whole countryside.[a]
      He tore down in his fury
         the fortresses of daughter Judah.
      He brought down to the ground[b] in dishonor
         [c]the kingdom and its princes.[c]

3   He hacked off in burning wrath
         the horn[a] that was Israel's whole strength.
      He turned back [b]his right hand[b]
         before the enemy,
      And blazed against Jacob like a fire[c]
         that consumed all around.

4   [a]He strung his bow[a] like an enemy;
         [b]he aimed with his right hand.[b]
      [c]Like a foe he killed[c]
         [d]all the young warriors who delight the eye.[d]
      In the tent of daughter Zion
         he poured out his fury like fire.

5   The Lord became the enemy,[a]
         he consumed Israel.
      He consumed all his citadels,[b]
         laid in ruin his fortresses,
      And multiplied in daughter Judah
         moaning and mourning.

6   Then he demolished his tent[a] like the garden,[b]
         laid in ruin his place of assembly.

Yahweh caused to be forgotten in Zion
  festival and sabbath,
And spurned in his fierce anger
  king and priest.

7   The Lord rejected his altar,
       abhorred[a] his sanctuary.
     He delivered into the power of the enemy
       the walls of [b]her citadels.[b]
     They shouted in the house of Yahweh
       as on a day of festival.

8   Yahweh was determined to lay in ruin
       the wall[a] of daughter Zion.
     He stretched out the measuring line,
       did not hold back his hand from consuming,
     And caused to mourn[b] [c]the outer and main walls[c];
       together they grieve.

9   Her gates have sunk into the ground,
       he [a]has shattered[a] her bars.[b]
     Her king and princes are among the nations;
       there is no instruction.
     Even her prophets have received
       no vision from Yahweh.

10   They sit[a] on the ground in silence,[b]
       the elders of daughter Zion.
     They have cast dirt on their heads,
       girded themselves with sackcloth.
     They have bowed their heads to the ground,
       the virgins of Jerusalem.

11   My eyes are worn out with tears,
       my inner parts are in ferment.
     My liver has been poured out on the ground
       because of the fall of [a]the daughter of my people,[a]
     When children and nursing infants [b]wasted away[b]
       in the squares of the city.

12   They kept saying to their mothers:
          'Where is grain?'—[a]but there was none[a]—
      As they wasted away like the wounded
          in the squares of the city,
      As their lives expired
          on their mothers' bosom.

13   What [a]can I say to you,[a] to what can I compare you,
          O daughter Jerusalem?
      To what can I liken you, [b]that I may comfort you,[b]
          O virgin daughter Zion?
      For [c]great as the sea's [ruin][c] is your ruin!
          Who can heal you?

14   Your prophets have seen for you
          false and [a]deceptive visions.[a]
      They have not exposed your iniquity
          [b]to restore your fortunes.[b]
      But they have seen for you
          false and misleading[c] oracles.

15   They clapped their hands at you,
          all who passed by.
      They hissed and wagged their heads
          at daughter Jerusalem.
      'Is this the city, [a]the perfection of beauty,
          the joy of all the earth?'[a]

16   They opened their mouths against you,
          all your enemies.
      They hissed and gnashed their teeth;
          they said, 'We have consumed her!
      Ah, this is the day we longed for,
          [a]we have lived to see it!'[a]

17   Yahweh has done what he proposed;
          he has carried out his threat,
      Which[a] he made in days of old;
          he tore down without mercy.

He let the enemy gloat over you;
  he exalted the horn of your foes.

18 ^aCry out from your heart to the Lord,^a
      ^bthe wall of daughter Zion!^b
    Let tears stream down like a torrent
      day and night!
    Give yourself no relief,^c
      ^dyour eyes no respite!^d

19 ^aStart crying^a at night,
      at the beginning of ^bevery watch!^b
    Pour out like water your heart
      in the presence of the Lord!
    Lift up to him your hands
      for the lives of your children!
    ^c[Who waste away from hunger
      at the corner of every street.]^c

(Jerusalem)

20 Look, O Yahweh, and consider
      whom you have dealt with in this way!
    Ought^a women ^bto have eaten^b their offspring,
      ^ctheir carefully reared children?^c
    Ought priests and prophets to have been killed
      in the sanctuary of the Lord?

21 They lay^a on the ground in the streets,
      young and old.
    My young women and men
      fell by the sword.
    You killed on the day of your wrath,
      you slaughtered without mercy!

22 You summoned^a as to a day of festival
      ^bterrors against me from roundabout.^b
    There was on the day of Yahweh's wrath
      neither fugitive nor survivor.
    Those whom I reared and raised
      my enemy has consumed.

1 [a]MT יָעִיב is a *hapax legomenon*. LXX ἐγνόφωσεν, 'darkened, obscured', and Syr
''*yb*, 'overclouded', both connect יָעִיב with עָב, 'dark cloud'. It is still understood
as a denominative verb from עָב by the latest dictionary (*HALOT*, II, p. 794). This
meaning is also accepted here by Albrektson (*Text and Theology*, pp. 85-86) as a
conscious contrast to the image of the cloud as a sign of divine favor elsewhere in
MT. In Exod. 19.9, Yahweh says he will come to Moses in 'a dense cloud' (בְּעַב
הֶעָנָן). At the dedication of the newly built temple, the cloud (הֶעָנָן, 1 Kgs 8.10) filled
the temple. That cloud is identified with Yahweh's glory (כְּבוֹד־יְהוה, 1 Kgs 8.11).
Rudolph (*Klagelieder*, p. 218) suggests a connection with an Arabic root *'yb*, 'to
blame, revile'. But 'to overcloud' or 'to revile' seems too weak in the context of
Jerusalem's destruction (T.F. McDaniel, 'Philological Studies in Lamentations: I',
Bib 49 [1968] pp. 27-53 [34-35]). In addition, the imperfect form followed by the
perfects in the next two lines appears strange. These perfects with a scattering of
wayyiqtols are the tenses used in the speaker's description of what happened to
Jerusalem in vv. 1-9. NAB reads 'has detested', הוֹעִיב (hi. perfect, haplography of ה
after אֵיכָה, 'alas, how') and derives the form from *וֹעֵב, which is the root of תּוֹעֵבָה
(*taqtil*, *HALAT*, p. 1568). Both the meaning and the verb form seem appropriate
here. This understanding of יָעִיב has a close parallel in Ps. 106.40 (NAB): וַיִּחַר־אַף
יְהוה בְּעַמּוֹ וַיְתָעֵב אֶת־נַחֲלָתוֹ, 'And the LORD grew angry with his people, and
abhorred his inheritance.

2 [a]Both נָוֶה and its synonym נָוָה are used to denote the territory on which Israel
lives. In Ps. 83.13 enemies plan to seize Israelite territory, 'the pastures / fields of
God' (נְאוֹת אֱלֹהִים). In Jer. 10.25 the nations leave Jacob's pasture / homeland (נָוֵהוּ)
unpopulated. In Isa. 32.18 Israel will live in a peaceful country (בִּנְוֵה שָׁלוֹם). See
also Ps. 79.7 where נָוֵה means the land of Judah; and Exod. 15.13 where נָוֵה refers
to the land of Canaan. The usage here is similar. Verses 2-9 trace the course of the
enemy invasion. First the countryside is attacked (נְאוֹת יַעֲקֹב, v. 2a); then the fortified towns apart from the capital (מִבְצְרֵי בַת־יְהוּדָה, v. 2b); and finally Jerusalem
itself (vv. 6-9). Thus the phrase נְאוֹת יַעֲקֹב refers to all the areas of Judah where the
Israelites live outside the capital and other fortified towns.
   [b]The masoretic accentuation connects הִגִּיעַ לָאָרֶץ, 'brought down to the ground',
with v. 2b, but the athnach is better transposed to יְהוּדָה in the interest of an accept-
able line structure. See *BHS*; Rudolph (*Klagelieder*, p. 218) and other commentators.
   [c-c]LXX reads βασιλέα αὐτῆς καὶ ἄρχοντας αὐτῆς, 'her king and her rulers'.
McDaniel ('Philological Studies: I', p. 36) suggests repointing מַמְלָכָה, 'the kingdom', to מַלְכָּה, 'her king', on the analogy with v. 9b, and taking the initial מ of
מַמְלָכָה as the final letter of the preceding חִלֵּל, 'he profaned, dishonored'. Conso-
nantal חללם could stand for חֲלָלִם, 'pierced ones', as probably read by Syr with an
explanatory pronoun suffix *qṭylyh*, 'her pierced ones.' However, both *LHAVT*
(p. 445) and *HALOT* (II, p. 595) maintain מַמְלָכָה in the sense of 'king'. Compare
English 'his majesty'. *HALOT* also includes Lam. 2.2 as one of its examples for the
meaning 'king' of מַמְלָכָה. If 'king' is the sense required here, it is unnecessary to
repoint מַמְלָכָה. But that is doubtful. The word מַמְלָכָה is defined by the parallel term
in the preceding line, בַת־יְהוּדָה. In addition, vv. 2-5 describe the invasion of the
kingdom of Judah; vv. 6-9, the subsequent attack on the capital and the exile of

Zion's king and officials living there (מלכה ושריה). In context, the word חלל is appropriate too. For details, see the exegesis, pp. 120-22.

3 [a]The horn (קרן), the dreaded weapon of an enraged bull, is a symbol of military might. Here, it represents Israel's ability to defend itself.

[b-b]The referent of the pronoun suffix in ימינו is ambiguous. It could refer back to the Lord. 'His right hand' would then be the Lord's right hand which was expected to protect Israel. See Ps. 74.11 (reading כלא or תכלא from the root כלא): למה תשיב ידך וימינך מקרב חיקך כלה, 'Why do you hold back your hand, keep your right hand within your cloak?'

But the inter-linear parallelism is against this. Both the preceding and following lines present the Lord actively battling against Israel. The right hand, normally the sword hand (Judg. 3.15-22), like קרן in the preceding line which helps interpret it, is the symbol of Israel's ability to defend itself, and it is this right hand that the Lord defeats. Compare Lam. 1.13b; Ps. 44.11; and especially Ps. 89.44 (reading צר as proposed in *BHS*): אף־תשיב צור חרבו ולא הקימתו במלחמה, 'You turned back his sharp sword, and did not sustain him in the battle'.

See also Hillers, *Lamentations*, p. 98; N.K. Gottwald, *Studies in the Book of Lamentations* (SBT, 14; London: SCM Press, 2nd edn, 1962), p. 10, esp. n. 1.

[c]The opening colon seems too long. Though the sense remains the same, omit להבה. The noun אש was expanded in MT on the basis of the formula אש להבה, 'a fire of flame' (Isa. 4.5; Hos. 7.6; Ps. 105.32). See Hillers, *Lamentations*, p. 98.

4 [a-a]The phrase דרך קשתו means 'he strung his bow'. It designates the action of stringing the bow by using the knee or foot to bend it. In order not to destroy the bow's tension, it was left unstrung till immediately before use. See Y. Yadin, *The Art of Warfare in Biblical Lands* (2 vols.; Jerusalem: International Publishing, 1963), pp. 6, 64; B. Couroyer, '*nḥt*: "Encorder un arc" (?)', *RB* 88 (1981) pp. 13-18, esp. p. 18.

[b-b]Literally, 'he steadied himself as to his right hand'; for the accusative of limitation, see *GHB* §126g (cf., e.g., Gen. 17.11, ונמלתם את בשר ערלתכם, 'You shall circumcise the flesh of your foreskins'; 1 Kgs 15.23, חלה את־רגליו, 'he was diseased in his feet').

[c-c]There is nothing wrong with the Hebrew word order here. Changing the normal word order ויהרג כצר to כצר ויהרג, as MT does, would lay heavy emphasis on כצר. See Carl Brockelmann, *Hebräische Syntax* (Glückstadt: J.J. Augustin; Neukirchen Kreis Moers: Buchhandlung des Erziehungsvereins, 1956), §123f-h; cf., e.g., Exod. 16.6, ערב וידעתם, 'in the evening you shall know'; and Isa. 10.25, כי־עוד מעט מזער וכלה זעם, 'for in a very little while my indignation will come to an end'. The same reversal of normal word order is found in Lam. 1.13, בעצמתי וירדנה, 'he brought it down into my bones'.

[d-d]Lit. 'all the delights of the eye'.

5 [a]The preposition כ in כאויב is the same כ which is used in כאלמנה (Lam. 1.1) and means 'exactly like' (*GHB*, §133g).

[b]The presence of מִבְצָרָיו in the next colon favors the reading אַרְמְנוֹתָו הִשְׁחֵת as proposed in *BHS*. There is a false word division in MT. Note that Lamentations 2 uses the piel (שִׁחֵת, v. 6a) and hiphil (לְהַשְׁחִית, v. 8a) of שחת in more or less the same sense: 'to lay in ruin'.

6 [a]Read שֹכוּ as סֹכּ; שׁ and ס often interchange. See LXX, Vg and Syr. The picture is similar to that in Isa. 1.8. The countryside has been devastated by the invading army (Isa. 1.5-7), and Jerusalem alone is left, a (fragile) hut in a vineyard (at harvest time), a city under siege: ונותרה בת־ציון כסכה בכרם כעיר נצורה (MT has נְצוּרָה, qal pass. part. of נצר, 'to keep, guard, watch').

The word סֹכּ provides an excellent parallel for מועדו, 'his assembly place'. Other occurrences of סֹכ as a designation of Jerusalem / the Jerusalem temple are: כי יצפנני בסכו ביום רעה, 'For he will hide me in his tabernacle in the day of trouble' (Ps. 27.5); and ויהי בשלם סכו ומעונתו בציון, 'His tabernacle has been established in Salem, and his dwelling place in Zion' (Ps. 76.3).

[b]Note the article in כַּגַּן. The גַן here, like the נאות יעקב in v. 2a, designates the countryside of Judah (apart from the capital, Jerusalem) where farming and animal husbandry, the pillars of the economy, were carried out.

7 [a]The root נאר occurs in the piel only here and in Ps. 89.40; its exact meaning is still unknown. LXX reads ἀπετίναξεν, 'he shook off', here, but uses the verb καταστρέφω, 'to overthrow', in Ps. 89.40. Syr renders both occurrences of נאר by *'sly*, 'he rejected, cast away, abhorred'; Syr also translates the root נאץ, 'to despise, spurn', in v. 6c, and six other different Hebrew verbs in the Psalter, apart from נאר and נאץ, by the same root *sl'*. See Albrektson, *Text and Theology*, p. 99.

[b]The referent of the feminine pronoun suffix is ציון in v. 6b. What the word אַרְמוֹן denotes is difficult to pin down, but that it means 'palace' (as rendered by NRSV) here or in v. 5b seems doubtful to me.

The word אַרְמְנוֹתֶיהָ is parallel to מִבְצָרָיו, 'his fortresses', in v. 5b, and to מבצריה in Isa. 34.13. NRSV invariably translates אַרְמְנוֹת by 'strongholds' and NAB by 'castles' in Amos 1.4, 7, 10, 12, 14; 2.2, 5; 3.9, 10, 11; 6.8. The word אַרְמוֹן is connected with בית־המלך, 'palace', in 1 Kgs 16.18 and 2 Kgs 15.25. It is rendered as 'citadel' by NRSV in both texts, and by NAB and Tanakh in the first text. The citadel 'was a replica of the fortified city', with a main wall, a gateway and an outer wall, but smaller in area, and usually included the palace of the king or the governor, the houses of the ministers, and the temple (Yadin, *Art of Warfare*, I, pp. 23-24). In v. 7b, the word אַרְמְנוֹתֶיהָ occurs in proximity to words related to the temple such as מזבחו, 'his altar', מקדשו, 'his sanctuary' (v. 7a), and בית־יהוה, 'house of Yahweh' (v. 7c). Thus the best rendering for אַרְמוֹן seems to be 'citadel'.

8 [a]MT has the singular construct חוֹמַת, used collectively for the walls that enclose the city.

[b]*HALOT*, I, pp. 6-7, identifies a root אבל I, 'to grieve', and a root אבל II, 'to be dry, wither'. For the synonym אמל, *HALOT*, I, p. 63, puts the same meanings under one headword. *LHAVT* (pp. 6, 63) in both cases works with only one root. Perhaps

the demolished outer and main walls are here presented as a lifeless, withered tree. But it seems more likely that the ruins represent a personified mourner sitting on the ground at a mourning ceremony (Lam. 1.1). It is the ruins of these personified walls, as well as the ruins of the rest of the city, that are addressed in vv. 13-19 and that utter the plea in vv. 20-22.

c-cThe rendering 'the outer and main walls' is based on Jewish tradition as represented by LXX τὸ προτείχισμα καὶ τεῖχος and by Vg *antemurale et murus*. The lower outer wall protected the slopes and kept battering rams and scaling parties away from the main wall. See Yadin, *Art of Warfare*, I, p. 20; II, p. 323.

9 a-aThe conflate reading אבד ושבר makes the second colon of v. 9a too long for the *qinah* meter (3 + 2). The original reading was likely שבר since this enhances the *š*, *b* and *r* alliterative pattern: טבעו בארץ שעריה שבר בריחיה, 'Her gates have sunk into the ground, he has shattered her bars'.

bThe antecedent of בריחיה is בת־ציון in v. 8a. The bars are the bolts that held the gate closed. See Yadin, *Art of Warfare*, I, p. 22.

10 aMT treats ישבו as an imperfect qal with the sense of an ongoing present (*GHB*, §113d). The stative present ישבו as in Lam. 1.1 and the *BHS* critical note is also possible.

bMcDaniel ('Philological Studies: I', pp. 38-39), connects ידמו here to דמם II, 'to wail'. See the discussion below, pp. 129-30.

11 a-aHaag ('בת', p. 334) understands בת־עמי to represent the 'national community'. In this way עמי, like ציון in בת־ציון, is an epexegetical / appositional genitive. However, this understanding simply ignores the imagery of the whole poem. The speaker in vv. 1-19 is present at this mourning ceremony with the elders and the young women of Jerusalem who sit on the ground (v. 10). Jerusalem too sits on the ground (vv. 1b, 2c, 8-9a). The speaker addresses Jerusalem (vv. 13-19) and she reacts to that address (vv. 20-22). Nowhere in the poem does the imagery lose sight of the principal mourner at this mourning ceremony, Lady Jerusalem. I thus understand בת־עמי as representing Jerusalem, with בת as an honorific title for a capital city (בת־ציון) or a country (בת־אדום, Lam. 4.21), and עמי as the ordinary genitive of possession. The 'daughter = lady of my people' is Jerusalem as ruler and mother (Lam. 2.22c).

b-bThe word בעטף is actually the niphal infinitive construct בהעטף with syncope of intervocalic ה. The tense of this infinitive is determined by יאמרו (v. 12a), which is probably a past iterative, as is בעטף.

12 a-aRead ואין. See the discussion below, pp. 132-33.

13 a-aThe correctness of MT אעידך has been questioned with some frequency. The note in *BHS* suggests אערך, 'I will / can compare', just as Vg *comparabo*. *HALOT*, II, pp. 795, 884-85, sees this as one possibility among others. But that is hardly right in view of the anaphora of the repeated second feminine singular pronoun suffixes in v. 13ab. R. Gordis (*The Song of Songs and Lamentations* [New York: Ktav, 3rd edn, 1974], p. 164) gives אעידך the sense of the polel of עוד in Pss. 146.9; 147.6 and the hithpolel in Ps. 20.9 (to strengthen, uphold, lift up). But there seems little doubt that the MT form is correct. The fundamental sense of the hiphil of עוד is 'to repeat [words]'. For example, Gen. 43.3 gives, 'The man emphatically instructed / warned [הָעֵד הֵעִד] us: You shall not appear in my presence.' Another instance is Zech. 3.6, 'The angel of Yahweh assured [ויעד] Joshua'. The hiphil of עוד is paired with the hiphil of נגד in 1 Sam. 8.9: כי־העד תעיד בהם והגדת להם, 'You shall solemnly warn them, and inform them'.

A further example of the piel of דבר in: שמעה עמי ואדברה ישראל ואעידה בך, 'Hear, O my people, and I will speak, O Israel, I will testify against you' (Ps. 50.7) and על־מי אדברה ואעידה וישמעו, 'To whom shall I speak? Whom shall I warn, that they may hear?' (Jer. 6.10).

Another example of the qal of אמר in: ואעידה בהם ואמרה אליהם, 'But I warned them and said to them' (Neh. 13.21).

In Sir. 4.11, the hiphil of עוד is paired with the piel of למד, and the person spoken to is introduced by ל: חכמות למדה בניה ותעיד לכל מבינים בה, 'Wisdom teaches her children and admonishes all who can understand her.' (The Hebrew is from M.Z. Segal, ספר בן־סירא השלם [Jerusalem: Bialik Institute, 3rd edn, 1972]. The English translation is from Skehan and Di Lella, *Wisdom*, p. 169.)

The one problem is that in all examples of this type, the person spoken to, when mentioned, is always indicated by ב + the person, whereas in v. 13a, the person spoken to is indicated by the suffixed pronoun. But that the translation above is correct is confirmed by the context. The person who speaks to Jerusalem here is her מנחם who is denying he has any useful advice to give Jerusalem. He later changes his mind and does advise her (vv. 18-19). For the details of the argument, see the exegesis, pp. 140-44.

b-bMT ואנחמך is an indirect volitive after an interrogative clause with the indicative (*GHB*, §116c).

c-cThe usual analysis of כי־גדול כים שברך is 'For vast as the sea is your ruin', or the like. But this makes little sense. The adjective גדול is used to modify שבר seven times in the MT (Jer. 4.6; 6.1; 14.17; 50.22; 51.54; Zeph. 1.10; Lam. 2.13). In the other six instances, the denotation is always 'severe destruction' as opposed to 'light destruction'. An example particularly close to v. 13c is Jer. 14.17: 'The virgin daughter of my people has been struck a [severe destruction] שבר גדול, a very deadly blow'.

Here שבר גדול is defined by its parallel מכה נחלה מאד, 'a very deadly blow'. And that surely is the sense in which Jerusalem's שבר is גדול in v. 13. The sea too can be described as גדול, but in every instance the reference is to the vast breadth of the sea. For example, in Num. 34.6 the Mediterranean sea is called הים הגדול, 'the vast sea'; in Ps. 104.25 it is described as הים גדול ורחב ידים, 'the sea, great and wide'. In the latter example, רחב ידים, 'broad of extent', defines the sense of גדול. Clearly the broadness of the sea is no model for the severity of Jerusalem's destruction.

The obvious solution to the problem is to recognize that it is the severity of the sea's destruction in the primordial battle that is compared with the severity of Jerusalem's destruction. For the pregnant use of כ, see *GHB*, §133h: מָשׁוּה רַגְלַי כָּאַיָּלוֹת, 'He made my feet like [the feet of] does (Ps. 18.34); וְהָיָה כְּאוֹב מֵאֶרֶץ קוֹלֵךְ, 'Your voice shall be like [the voice of] a ghost from the earth' (Isa. 29.4); מַדּוּעַ אָדֹם לִלְבוּשֶׁךָ וּבְגָדֶיךָ כְּדֹרֵךְ בְּגַת, 'Why are your clothes red, and your garments like [the garments of] one who treads the winepress?' (Isa. 63.2)

The speaker here compares Yahweh's devastation of Jerusalem to the devastation of the sea in the primordial battle that was part of the creation process that produced the ordered universe. Compare Isa. 51.9-10 where Jerusalem appeals to Yahweh to act against Babylon by reminding him of the primordial battle against the sea: 'Was it not you that hacked up Rahab, that pierced the dragon? Was it not you that dried up the sea, the waters of the great deep?' For further details, see the exegesis, pp. 133-34.

14 a-aIt is not clear whether תָּפֵל here is תָּפֵל I, 'unsalted, tasteless food', or תָּפֵל II, 'whitewash'. The context seems to require the stronger meaning of תָּפֵל II. Prophets are referred to as 'whitewashers' in Ezek. 13.11 (טָחֵי תָפֵל). See the discussion in *HALOT*, IV, pp. 1775-76.

b-bThe *kethib* is שְׁבִיתֵךְ and the *qere* is שְׁבוּתֵךְ. Scholars hold diferent views about the etymology of these textual variants. J.M. Bracke ('*šûb šebût*: A Reappraisal', *ZAW* 97 [1985], pp. 233-44) summarizes two main ways of deriving שבות and reviews the contextual meaning of the phrase שׁוּב שְׁבוּת in the different texts where it occurs in MT. Both E. Preuschen ('Die Bedeutung von שׁוּב שְׁבוּת im Alten Testamente', *ZAW* 15 [1895], pp. 1-74) and E.L. Baumann ('שׁוּב שְׁבוּת, eine exegetische Untersuchung', *ZAW* 47 [1929], pp. 17-44) derive שבות from שבה, 'to take captive'. Preuschen suggests that the phrase שׁוּב (qal or hiphil) + שְׁבוּת or שְׁבִית means 'to turn the captivity'. Baumann sees no historical or geographic referent for the phrase and thinks it means 'to do away with a sentence of imprisonment'. The suggestion of Preuschen and Baumann is not convincing, especially for Job 42.10: וַיהוָה שָׁב אֶת־שְׁבוּת אִיּוֹב, 'And Yahweh restored the fortunes of Job'. Job was not imprisoned or exiled. He lost his children, his wealth and his health. Yahweh gave him back his children and his wealth, twice as much as he had before. His skin disease (Job 2.7) must have been healed also, otherwise he would not have been able to have children and enjoy company (Job 42.10-17). E.L. Dietrich ('שׁוּב שְׁבוּת: Die endzeitliche Wiederherstellung bei den Propheten', *BZAW* 40 [1925], pp. 32-37) distinguishes two roots. The word שבות is derived originally from שׁוּב, and the phrase שׁוּב שְׁבוּת means 'to render a restoration', that is, to return to an earlier time of prosperity. Later, when the hope for restoration became essentially the hope for return from exile and captivity, שְׁבוּת was confused with שְׁבִית (captivity) which is derived from שבה.

Dietrich's solution seems satisfactory, although scholarly consensus has not been reached about the etymological issue of whether שְׁבוּת and שְׁבִית come from one or two roots. Besides, the grammatical problem of שׁוּב used as a qal transitive in שׁוּב שבות is still unresolved. Bracke ('A Reappraisal', p. 244) concludes that שׁוּב שבות

is a technical phrase indicating a restoration to earlier times of well-being, and this restoration is often characterized by Yahweh's reversal of his previous judgments. See exegesis on p. 136 for the translation 'to restore your fortunes'.

ᶜThe word מדוחים is a *hapax legomenon* from the root נדח which means in the hiphil, 'to banish, compel, seduce'. Both LXX ἐξώσματα and Vg *ejectiones* refer to 'banishments'. The context favors Syr *mt'ynyt'* which means 'seductions'.

15 ᵃ⁻ᵃThis line could possibly be read as a tricolon, which is not the form of the other lines in Lamentations 2. If read as a bicolon, depending on whether כלילת יפי, 'the perfection of beauty', is attached to the first or second colon, one of the cola is too long for the meter of Lamentations 2. This is widely recognized and the line has been variously repaired. *BHS* proposes to delete either שיאמרו, 'about which they used to say', or משוש לכל־הארץ, 'the joy of all the earth'. While certainty is impossible, it seems to me that שיאמרו is a clarifying gloss: 'Is this the city *about which one used to say*...' That is what the line means even without the clarifying gloss.

16 ᵃ⁻ᵃLit. 'we have found, we have seen'.

17 ᵃThe norm for Lamentations 2 is that every line of poetry ends in a full sentence pause. Against this background, the suggestion of Gordis (*Lamentations*, pp. 165-66) has merit: 'What he ordained from days of old [i.e. the temple] he tore down without mercy.'

But there are three exceptions to this 'no *enjambment*' rule: v. 11b where the sentence continues into v. 11c with an adverbial ב + infinitive; and v. 12a where the sentence continues into v. 12b and v. 12c, each opening with an adverbial ב + infinitive. It seems to me more natural to take אמרתו, 'his word / threat', as the antecedent of אשר. The parallelism in v. 17ab is a combination of intralinear parallelism: בצע אמרתו // עשה יהוה אשר זמם, 'Yahweh has done what he proposed; // he has carried out his threat'; and interlinear parallelism: (אמרתו) אשר צוה // אשר זמם מימי־קדם, '...what he proposed // [his threat] which he made in days of old'.

18 ᵃ⁻ᵃThe syntax of the first colon of v. 18a is clear: 'Their heart cried out to the Lord.' Such is the understanding in LXX. In context 'their' can only refer back to צריך, 'your foes', of v. 17c, which makes no sense. For all practical purposes, there is critical unanimity in reading צעקי, 'cry out', for MT צעק, 'cried out' (so the note in *BHS*). The feminine singular imperative with its final *-î* fits an obvious rhetorical pattern tying together vv. 18-19 into a unit where for the first time the speaker decides he has something worthwhile to say to Jerusalem. Each line of vv. 18-19 opens with a feminine singular imperative (or in the case of v. 18c, with its negative equivalent, אל + jussive) with its characteristic final *-î* vowel. The fourth line of v. 19 is an obvious gloss which breaks the three-line pattern of the poem.

There have been various solutions as to what to do with לבם, 'their heart', once it no longer serves as the subject of צעק. T.F. McDaniel ('Philological Studies in Lamentations: II', *Bib* 49 [1968], pp. 199-220 [203-204]), followed by Hillers

(*Lamentations*, p. 101), regards the suffix -*ām* as adverbial, e.g. יוֹמָם, 'by day', רֵיקָם, 'without cause' (*GHB*, §102b). That is possible but not compelling. Parallels are lacking. The correction in *BHS* is common (see *HALOT*, II, p. 515; *HALOT*, IV, p. 1042): צַעֲקִי לָךְ מְלֹא, 'Utter a loud cry for help'. With this may be compared Jer. 12.6, קָרְאוּ אַחֲרֶיךָ מָלֵא: 'they have cried out loudly against you'; and Nah. 1.10: אֻכְּלוּ כְּקַשׁ יָבֵשׁ מָלֵא, 'they have been fully consumed like dry stubble'. For adjectives used as adverbs, see *GHB*, §102c; and for מָלֵא see GesB, p. 424; *LHAVT*, p. 438.

It seems to me the simplest alternative is suggested by Hos. 7.14, וְלֹא־זָעֲקוּ אֵלַי בְּלִבָּם, 'they have not cried out to me from their hearts/sincerely'. For MT לֵב, 'their heart', I read בְּלִבֵּךְ, 'from your heart'. Though, of course, the reading צַעֲקִי בְּלִבֵּךְ, 'cry out from your heart', is conjectural, the corruption of צַעֲקִי בְּלִבֵּךְ to צעק לבם is easily explained: צַעֲקִי was miscopied as צעק and this necessitated the change of בלבך to לבם.

b-bThe phrase חוֹמַת בַּת־צִיּוֹן, 'the wall of daughter Zion', is understood as an appositive of אֲדֹנָי, 'the Lord', in the first colon of v. 18a. See exegesis, pp. 140-42.

cThe poet uses פוּגַת, 'relief', a feminine noun in the archaic absolute state in ת for the sake of *t* alliteration in v. 18c: אַל־תִּתְּנִי פוּגַת לָךְ אַל־תִּדֹּם בַּת־עֵינֵךְ, 'Give yourself no relief, your eyes no respite'.

d-dLit. 'Let not the daughter = pupil of your eye be still!' Compare Gk κόρη, 'girl, daughter, pupil'; Vg *pupilla*, 'an orphan girl, pupil'; and Eng. 'pupil' (of the eye, and 'pupil' as schoolchild). Two other occurrences of דמה II in the sense of דמם I, 'to be silent, to cease (weeping)' are: תֵּרַדְנָה עֵינִי דִּמְעָה לַיְלָה וְיוֹמָם וְאַל־תִּדְמֶינָה, 'Let my eyes run down with tears night and day, and let them not cease' (Jer. 14.17); and עֵינִי נִגְּרָה וְלֹא תִדְמֶה מֵאֵין הֲפֻגוֹת, 'My eyes flow without ceasing, there is no respite' (Lam. 3.49).

19   a-aThis translation takes קוּמִי רֹנִּי as a case of coordination of complementary verbs where both the aspectual and main verbs appear in identical finite forms. See *GHB* §177e; GKC §120g; and exegesis, pp. 142-43.

b-bGordis (*Lamentations*, p. 168) notes that this is the distributive use of the plural (see GKC, §124o).

c-cThis is the only line in the unit of vv. 18-19 that does not open with a second person volitive. It is generally recognized as a scribal expansion, composed of bits and pieces from vv. 11c, 12b and 4.1b, and the only bicolon which can be omitted without causing difficulties in the unit (Hillers, *Lamentations*, p. 101).

20   aAnother illustration of the double rhetorical question, both halves of which are introduced by אִם, and both requiring the answer 'No', is found in Job 6.12: אִם־כֹּחַ אֲבָנִים כֹּחִי אִם־בְּשָׂרִי נָחוּשׁ, 'Is my strength the strength of stones, is my flesh bronze?'

b-bThe imperfect תֹּאכַלְנָה could be rendered as a present modal (must eat) describing the situation after the fall of Jerusalem. But its companion יֵהָרֵג (ought to have been killed) clearly refers to events at the time of the fall of the city. This understanding is reinforced by the past tenses in vv. 21-22. Jerusalem's address to the Lord ignores the difficult situation in Judah during the occupation, the literary setting of the poem, and concentrates on the horrors during the fall of the city.

ᶜ⁻ᶜThe word טפחים is a *hapax legomenon*. Fortunately, its sense in context can be defined with some precision. The parallel for עללי טפחים in v. 20b is פרים, 'their offspring'. The root recurs in v. 22c in the verb form טפחתי which is paired with ורביתי, 'and I raised'. Here טפחתי ought to mean something like 'I reared'. In addition there is the rhyming wordplay between טפחתי (v. 22c) and טבחת, 'you slaughtered' (v. 21c). In this context טפחתי ought to mean something like 'I carefully reared', and עללי טפחים something like 'children of careful rearing'. With this קטולים noun formation may be compared שכלים, 'childlessness', הלולים, 'jubilation'. Traditionally, טפחים has been connected to Heb. / Aram. טפה, 'to spread out, extend'. From this root is derived טפה, 'palm/ hand', while from that noun comes the denominative verbal root טפה, 'to handle / raise children'. The noun טפחים, 'careful rearing', is derived from that denominative verb. See BDB, p. 381, and *LHAVT*, p. 287. This derivation has the advantage of being based on an inner-Hebrew analysis. Contrast *HALOT*, II, p. 378.

21 ᵃNote the past meaning of the *yiqtol*s in v. 20b and c. Theoretically, שכבו, 'lie, lay', can denote a stative past or present, but in context it can only be past. Note too that נפלו, 'fell', an action verb, can only be a past tense. This also indicates the past state of שכבו, 'lay'.

22 ᵃThe imperfect here is the old narrative *yiqtol* without ו (i.e. *wayyiqtol*; GKB, II, §7h). The opening ת was needed for the ת strophe. Some examples of the old narrative *yiqtol* are: יאבד יום אולד בו, 'Perish the day on which I was born!' (Job 3.3); and הביטו אל־אברהם אביכם ואל־שרה תחוללכם, 'Look to Abraham, your father, and to Sarah, who gave you birth' (Isa. 51.2).

ᵇ⁻ᵇThe expression מגורי מסביב cannot be separated from מגור מסביב, 'terror round about' (Jer. 6.25; 46.5; 49.29). In each of those texts מגור is the sum of those aspects of a military attack that inspire terror in the weaker of the two opponents. The plural מגורים appears only here. It denotes the enemy army, hunger during a siege, scenes of destruction and bloodshed, or the like.

The Mourning Ceremony Setting

Lamentations 2 describes the mourning ceremony in fuller detail than Lamentations 1. Present at the ceremony are the elders of Jerusalem in typical mourning posture (v. 10). They are seated on the ground. They have strewn dust on their heads, and girded themselves with sackcloth. They grieve silently. They have entered the second phase of mourning, the moment of silence.

Present also are the virgins of Jerusalem, who keep their heads bowed to the ground (v. 10). The chief mourner is Lady Jerusalem, 'cast down from heaven to earth' (v. 1b). She is represented by the grieving collapsed wall (v. 8c), the gates sunk into the ground, and the broken bars (v. 9a).

An essential presence at the mourning ceremony is that of the מנחם, 'comforter', who is represented here by the speaker of the second voice, since he[3] expresses a sincere desire to comfort Jerusalem:

מה אשוה־לך ואנחמך בתולת בת־ציון

> To what can I liken you, that I may comfort you,
> O virgin daughter Zion? (2.13b)

The task of the מנחם is to comfort the mourner by mourning with him or her, speaking reassuring words (e.g. Gen. 50.21; Isa. 40.1-2), giving him or her advice as to what to do. Job's friends come a long way to comfort Job, but they fail in their task. Job calls them מנחמי עמל, 'woeful, miserable comforters' (16.2).

The speaker of the second voice begins by lamenting the ravages suffered by Judah and Jerusalem (vv. 2-9). He speaks as if he is voicing Jerusalem's thinking and feelings. He knows that the first cause, the primary agent of this terrible devastation is no other than Yahweh himself. He speaks with empathy. He freely expresses his emotions in v. 11ab:

כלו בדמעות עיני חמרמרו מעי
נשפך לארץ כבדי על־שבר בת־עמי

> My eyes are worn out with tears,
>   my inner parts are in ferment.
> My liver is poured out on the ground
>   because of the fall of the daughter of my people.

This lament must have been soothing to Jerusalem's ears.

Lamentations 1 describes Jerusalem weeping (vv. 2a, 16a, 20ab). Here, the second speaker, the מנחם, weeps (v. 11ab) just as Job's friends do (Job 2.12). Then he turns to address Jerusalem directly. He states his foremost desire is to comfort her, but confesses his inability to do so (v. 13) in face of the overwhelming disaster that has befallen her. He honestly acknowledges her sins (v. 14) and reflects on Yahweh's chastisement called forth by Jerusalem's breach of the covenant:

3.   As in my exegesis of Lam. 1 in Chapter 2 above, I assume the 'comforter' here is male, since Job's comforters are male and David's envoys to comfort King Hanun are also male. Also, to refer to the comforter as 'he' avoids undue confusion since Jerusalem is represented as the female mourner.

עשׂה יהוה אשׁר זמם בצע אמרתו
אשׁר צוה מימי־קדם הרס ולא חמל

Yahweh has done what he proposed;
   he has carried out his threat,
Which he made in days of old;
   he tore down without mercy (v. 17ab).

Jerusalem has suffered greatly from Yahweh's hand because of her sins. No human help is available: the passers-by show no more sympathy than the enemies (vv. 15-16). The מנחם finally advises Jerusalem to call upon Yahweh for help (vv. 18-19).

Jerusalem knows that the מנחם truly cares for her. She gives heed to his advice and cries out to Yahweh (vv. 20-22). Yet she does not formulate any clear or direct petition. She pours out the bitterness in her heart; she reminds Yahweh of the atrocities he did in her midst: he killed all her people, young and old, women and men, priests and prophets.

Poetic Structure and Address

Like Lamentations 1, Lamentations 2 is an alphabetic acrostic poem with 22 verses of three bicola each. The difference from the first poem is that here, the letters ע and פ are reversed, that, the stanza with ע comes in v. 17, after the stanza with פ in v. 16. The reason for this reversal, as stated earlier, may be that the alphabetic order ע then פ had not yet become the norm at the time the poem was composed. Droin offers a rather convoluted explanation. The original order of Lamentations 2 was ע then פ. Verse 17, which is a theological statement summarizing the first ten stanzas of the poem, would then have functioned to divide the speech addressed to Jerusalem (vv. 13-19) into two equal parts of three stanzas vv. 13-15, and vv. 16, 18-19. However, the scorn of the enemy weighs so heavily upon the remaining survivors that the mocking remark in v. 15c slips easily into the boastful exclamations of the enemy in v. 16. The extant order thus became פ before ע.[4]

Another difference with the first poem lies in the unequal length of the speeches. Dramatic tension is built up when the second speaker first talks about Jerusalem in the third person (vv. 1-10), then breaks down and reveals his own emotions in the first person (vv. 11-12), and finally addresses Jerusalem in the second person (vv. 13-19). Jerusalem utters a final cry in the last three stanzas (vv. 20-22).

4.   Droin, *Lamentations*, pp. 24-26.

Poetic Structure

Lamentations 2 is composed of three sections: (1) lament of the second speaker (vv. 1-12); (2) the second speaker's address to Jerusalem (vv. 13-19); (3) Jerusalem's prayer to Yahweh (vv. 20-22). The components of each section are treated in detail below.

Verses 1-12. The lament (vv. 1-12) is structured as follows:

(1)   vv. 1-10: The mourning ceremony
    (a)   v. 1: Jerusalem's mourning (she is cast down to earth)
    (b) vv. 2-9: cause of her mourning
          vv. 2-5: devastation of Judah
          vv. 6-9: devastation of Jerusalem
    (c)   v. 10: people present at the ceremony, elders and virgins

1. *Verses 1-10.* This unit is clearly marked by the *inclusio* of בת־ציון (vv. 1a, 10a), and ארץ (vv. 1b, 10ac). In addition, the first verse contains an *inclusio* with אפו in the first and the last lines. Verse 1b is marked by a liquid and sibilant alliteration and *e* assonance:

השליך משמים ארץ תפארת ישׂראל

He cast down from heaven to earth
   the glory of Israel.

There is also a near end rhyme in באפו and בת־ציון (v. 1a) and ארץ and ישׂראל (v. 1b). Verses 2 to 5, which describe the invasion of Judah, are tied together by the *inclusio* of בלע (vv. 2a, 5ab), אדני (vv. 2a, 5a), מבצרי בת־יהודה (v. 2b) and מבצריו (v. 5b), and בת־יהודה (v. 5c), and by the repetition of key words such as יעקב (vv. 2a, 3c), ישׂראל (vv. 3a, 5a). There is a labial and liquid alliteration in v. 2b:

הרס בעברתו מבצרי בת־יהודה

He tore down in his fury
   the fortresses of daughter Judah.

Verse 3c (emended) is marked by alliteration in yod, *b*, ע and א:

ויבער ביעקב כאשׁ אכלה סביב:

He blazed against Jacob like a fire
   that consumed all around.

Verse 5c has a labial and yod alliteration, and an end rhyme in יהודה and ואניה:

וירב בבת־יהודה תאניה ואניה:

He multiplied in daughter Judah
   moaning and mourning.

Verses 6 to 9 likewise form a tight literary unit around the destruction of Jerusalem with the *inclusio* of יהוה (vv. 6b, 9c) which is also repeated in vv. 7c, 8a and מלך (v. 6c), מלכה (v. 9b). Verse 7a has an end rhyme in מזבחו and מקדשו. There is a guttural and sibilant alliteration as well as an *a* assonance in v. 8a:

חשב יהוה להשחית חומת בת־ציון

Yahweh was determined to lay in ruin
   the wall of daughter Zion.

Verse 9a has an end rhyme in שעריה and בריחיה.

The mourning ceremony in vv. 1-10, besides the outermost *inclusio* with v. 1 and v. 10, has other layers of *inclusio* like concentric circles converging at the center, vv. 5 and 6:

(a) ושׂריה in vv. 2c and 9b
(b) השׁיב in vv. 3b and 8b
(c) אויב in vv. 4a and 7b
(d) שׁחת in vv. 5b and 6a

2. *Verses 11-12*: grief of the second speaker over the destruction of Jerusalem. These two verses form a self-contained unit with the repetition of the roots שׁפך (vv. 11b, 12c), עטף (vv. 11c, 12b), and the phrases ברחבות (vv. 11c, 12b) and אמתם (vv. 12a, 12c). Verse 11a has an end rhyme in עיני and מעי. The end rhyme in כבדי and בת־עמי characterizes v. 11b. Verse 12c is marked by the end rhyme in נפשם and אמתם.

Verses 13-19. The address to Jerusalem is composed of:

1. *Verses 13-14: possible* מנחמים, *'comforters'*:

   v. 13—the speaker is overwhelmed by the destruction and has nothing to say in order to comfort Jerusalem
   v. 14—her prophets could not comfort her because they failed to expose her sins so as to restore her fortunes

Verse 13 is characterized by a series of second-person feminine singular suffixes. Verse 14 has an *inclusio* with שׂוא in vv. 14a and 14c, and an end rhyme in עונך and שבותך in v. 14b.

2. *Verses 15-16: scorn and derision from passers-by and enemies*:

v. 15—no sympathy from passers-by
v. 16—malicious boasting of enemies

This unit has an *inclusio* with עליך in vv. 15a and 16a, and שׁרקו in vv. 15b and 16b. Verse 16c has an end rhyme in שׁקּוינהו and ראינו.

3. *Verse 17: a reflection on Yahweh's act of punishment*. This verse is marked by *a* and *e* assonance.

4. *Verses 18-19: advice to Jerusalem to pray to the Lord*: These verses are tied together by a series of feminine singular imperatives at the beginning of every line, except v. 18a where the correction to צעקי is called for, and v. 19d which is a gloss.[5] Besides, there are *inclusiones* with אדני (vv. 18a, 19b), לבך (vv. 18a emended, 19b), and לילה (vv. 18b, 19a). Verse 18b has an end rhyme in דמעה and ולילה. Verse 19c also has an end rhyme in כפיך and עולליך.

Verses 20-22. Jerusalem's prayer to Yahweh also reveals a tight structure with the *inclusio* of יהוה (vv. 20a, 22b) and the root טפח (vv. 20b, 22c), the repetition of the root הרג (vv. 20c, 21c) and the phrase ביום אף (vv. 21c, 22b). Verse 21ab follows a predicate: subject::subject: predicate chiastic pattern: שׁכבו לארץ חוצות:נער וזקן::בתולתי ובחורי:נפלו בחרב, 'they lay on the ground in the streets: young and old::my young women and men: fell by the sword'.

Verse 21c has an end rhyme in אפך and חמלת. The paired words פּליט ושׂריד have *a* and *î* assonance. Verse 22c is marked by *i* and *î* assonance.

Address
Verses 1-12: Lament of the Second Speaker (vv. 1-12).
1. The main verbs in the unit of vv. 1-10 are in the third person. The second speaker speaks of אדני and יהוה in the third person. He laments the downfall of daughter Zion 'from heaven to earth' (משׁמים ארץ, v. 1b). He goes on to describe the ravages done to the whole land of Judah (v. 2a), to Jerusalem and the temple (vv. 6-9a), the slaughter of the warriors (vv. 3a, 4b), the destruction of the strongholds and citadels (vv. 2b, 5b, 7b), and the exile of the leaders (king, priests, princes,

5. See critical note 19[c-c] above.

vv. 2c, 6c, 9b). He finally comes back to the scene present before his eyes, the mourning ceremony with the elders and the young women in the midst of the ruins of Jerusalem, personified as a mother (vv. 21b, 22c).

From the very beginning (v. 1a), he has already identified Yahweh as the divine agent of destruction. He does not address Yahweh directly. He simply enumerates Yahweh's destructive acts, yet his statements seem to be charged with silent questions: 'How could you do that, why did you do that to Jerusalem, O Yahweh?' Westermann calls vv. 1-9a 'an accusation against God'.[6]

2. In the unit on the grief over the destruction of Jerusalem (vv. 11-12), the first person singular pronominal suffixes in כְּבֵדִי, מֵעַי, עֵינַי and עַמִּי show that the speaker is also in mourning. He is deeply distressed at the sight of the ruins, especially as he recalls the scene of starving young children dying on their mothers' laps.

Verses 13-19. The unit of vv. 13-19 is marked by the presence of second person feminine singular pronominal suffixes in words such as אֲעִידֵךְ, לָךְ, the vocative הבת ירושלם, and especially the second person feminine singular imperatives such as הורידי (v. 18b), קומי (v. 19a), which prove that the second speaker is now addressing Lady Jerusalem, the chief mourner at this mourning ceremony.

1. In vv. 13-17, the speaker eliminates himself as a possible מנחם by confessing his inability to find appropriate words of comfort (v. 13). He enumerates two other kinds of people who could have acted as מנחמים: Jerusalem's prophets and her neighbors (the passers-by). But her prophets are found unfit for the task because they gave her false hopes instead of exposing her sins and warning her of the coming disaster (v. 14). Her neighbors, far from sympathizing with her in her misfortune, mock her with shaming or apotropaic gestures (v. 15). They have sided with her enemies who, of course, rejoice blatantly at her defeat and destruction (v. 16). The main agent who caused all this pain and shame is Yahweh, her covenant partner (v. 17).

2. As the second speaker reflects on the cause of Jerusalem's misfortune, he finally comes up with some advice to give to Jerusalem (vv. 18-19): call to the Lord for help. With this timely advice, he fulfills his role of מנחם.

---

6.   Westermann, *Lamentations*, p. 147.

Verses 20-22. Lady Jerusalem, the chief mourner, follows his advice and prays to Yahweh (vv. 20-22). Her prayer starts with the familiar plea ראה יהוה as in Lam. 1.9c, 11c, 20a. She has been listening to the speaker's lament in vv. 1-12, and she also identifies Yahweh as the divine agent behind all her sufferings (vv. 20a, 21c, 22a). She asks Yahweh to remember her as Yahweh's covenant partner:

> Look, O Yahweh, and consider
>> whom you have dealt with in this way! (v. 20a)

She is full of bitter reproach as she describes her misery.

Her beloved children, that she had carefully raised, have been consumed by the enemy summoned by Yahweh. She does not offer any specific or explicit petition. She brings to Yahweh her whole situation, her devastation, her agony, her questions, her reproach. Because her sufferings are so severe, and beyond human comprehension, her prayer becomes a direct 'accusation against God'.

Exegesis

Lament of the Second Speaker (Verses 1-12)
The Mourning Ceremony (Verses 1-10). As was stated earlier, this section is clearly marked off by the *inclusiones* of בת־ציון, 'daughter Zion', in vv. 1a and 10a, and ארץ, 'earth, ground, dirt', in vv. 1b and 10ac. Although the subsections divided according to content are also marked off by *inclusiones* (see 'Poetic Structure', pp. 113-15), the literary interlocking of the whole passage is remarkable. There are *mots crochets* (catchwords) throughout, connecting each verse with the preceding one. The words אדני, 'the Lord', in v. 2a and ארץ, 'ground', in v. 2c are linked with אדני in v. 1a and ארץ in v. 1b; the name יעקב, 'Jacob', in v. 3c with יעקב in v. 2a; the phrase ימינו, 'his right hand', in v. 4a with ימינו in v. 3b; the phrase כאויב translated literally 'like an enemy' in v. 5a with כאויב in v. 4a; the verb שחת, 'laid in ruin', in v. 6a with שחת in v. 5b; the words יהוה and מועד, 'festival', in v. 7c with יהוה and מועד in v. 6b; the construct noun חומת, 'wall of', in v. 8a, the phrase ידו, 'his hand', in v. 8b, and the noun חומה in v. 8c with יד and חומת, 'walls', in v. 7b; the name יהוה in v. 9c with יהוה in v. 8a; the phrase לארץ, 'on/to the ground', in vv. 10a and 10c with בארץ, 'into the ground', in v. 9a.

The second speaker is present at this mourning ceremony along with Jerusalem, the chief mourner (vv. 1b, 8c, 9a), and the elders and virgins of the city (v. 10). Everyone at the ceremony is silent (v. 10a), overcome with grief. The second speaker is the מנחם; he is supposed to speak, to say something to comfort the mourners (v. 13). He is one with the mourners. He knows their thoughts and feelings. He intones a lament. He portrays Jerusalem as a woman cast on the ground in mourning.

1. *The mourning of Jerusalem (v. 1)*. The מנחם begins by stating that 'the Lord abhorred daughter Zion'. If the suggested emendation to הועיב is correct, the root ועב implies that daughter Zion had become an abomination to the Lord for her worshiping of non-gods. (The derived noun תועבה, 'abomination', often occurs in such contexts: e.g. Jer. 44.2-6, 22-23; Ezek. 5.5-13.) She had failed to live up to her covenant responsibilities and incurred the Lord's wrath. This reason for the divine anger is clearly stated in Deut. 29.23-24 (NAB):

> They and all the nations will ask, 'Why has the LORD dealt thus with this land? Why this fierce outburst of wrath?' And the answer will be, 'Because they forsook the covenant which the LORD, the God of their fathers, had made with them when he brought them out of the land of Egypt...'

The Lord's wrath caused him to bring upon Zion the calamity of 587 BCE. References to Yahweh's 'wrath, anger'[7] occur in vv. 1a, 1c, 2b, 3a, 3c, 4c, 6c, 21c and 22b. The whole chapter revolves around this dominant theme. The mourners experience the wrath of Yahweh through the destruction of their city and temple, and the death of their loved ones.

The phrase בת־ציון, 'daughter Zion', occurs in synonymous parallelism with תפארת ישראל, 'the glory of Israel', and הדם־רגליו, 'his footstool'. All three expressions must then designate one and the same object, Jerusalem, the beloved capital city. That object is enclosed within the wrath of the Lord, the *inclusio* formed by אפו in the first colon of v. 1a and the last colon of v. 1c.

The severity of the catastrophe, the effect of the Lord's anger, is expressed through the imagery of 'the glory of Israel' cast down from heaven (משמים), the traditional height limit (e.g. Deut. 1.28, 'the cities are large and fortified up to heaven', ערים גדלת ובצורת בשמים; see also Jer. 51.53), to earth, the traditional limit for depth.[8] 'The glory of Israel'

---

7. See my comment on Lam. 1.12 above, p. 83.
8. D.R. Hillers, 'History and Poetry in Lamentations', *CurTM* 10 (1983), pp. 155-61 (159).

(תפארת ישׂראל) in Lam. 2.1b is parallel to 'daughter Zion' (בת־ציון) in
v. 1a. Daughter Zion was 'the glory of Israel' because she housed the
temple of Yahweh. The word תפארה, 'glory, splendor, beauty', designates the temple in Ezek. 24.25, משׂושׂ תפארתם, 'their glorious joy', and
in Isa. 64.10, בית קדשׁנו ותפארתנו, 'our holy and glorious temple'. Elsewhere, she is called the 'city of God' (עיר־אלהים, Pss. 46.5; 48.2, 9;
87.3); 'the city of Yahweh' (עיר־יהוה, Pss. 48.9; 101.8), 'the mountain
where God chooses to reign' (ההר חמד אלהים לשׁבתו, Ps. 68.17).
Daughter Zion was thought to be invincible because of the presence of
the temple and of God within the city:

אלהים בקרבה בל־תמוט

God is in the midst of it [the city];
it shall not be moved (Ps. 46.6).

But now the 'city of God', the 'glory of Israel', has been cast down
from heaven to earth. She cannot fall any further down. Similar imagery
of being cast down to earth for sinful haughtiness is used for the king of
Babylon (Isa. 14.12-15) and the king of Tyre (Ezek. 28.16-17). The
contrast between the glorious past and the humiliated present is a motif
typical of the dirge.

The phrase הדם־רגלים, 'the footstool', occurs six times in the MT. It
is used figuratively for the ark in Pss. 99.5; 132.7; 1 Chron. 28.2; for the
earth in Isa. 66.1; and for Zion in Lam. 2.1; in the last instance, Ps.
110.1, it refers to the defeated enemies as the footstool of the king. The
footstool occurs in connection with כסא, 'throne' (Isa. 66.1), and kingship (Pss. 99.5; 110.1). In fact, it was part of the throne or an accessory
for the throne in Mesopotamia and Egypt as far back as 3000 BCE.[9]
Here הדם־רגליו, 'his [own] footstool', represents Zion, the chosen city,
which also stands for the chosen people (cf. Isa. 51.16, 'who said to
Zion, "You are my people" '). The verb root זכר, 'to remember', with
God as subject, usually implies life and hope.[10] When God remembered
Noah in the ark, he made a wind blow and caused the waters of the
flood to subside (Gen. 8.1). Yahweh remembered Hannah who was
childless, and in due time Hannah conceived and bore a son (1 Sam.
1.19-20). The root זכר is also used in connection with the divine
covenant.[11] God promises to remember the covenant he makes with

9. H.-J. Fabry, 'הדם', *TDOT*, III, pp. 325-34 (326-29).
10. Droin, *Lamentations*, p. 48.
11. Eising, 'זכר', pp. 70-71.

Noah (Gen. 9.15). When the Israelites were oppressed in Egypt, God heard their groaning; he remembered his covenant with the patriarchs, and acted to save the Israelites (Exod. 2.24; 6.5). In anticipation of the coming disaster, Jeremiah prays that Yahweh remember his covenant and not dishonor his 'glorious throne' (Jer. 14.21). The 'glorious throne' may refer to the temple of Yahweh and the cult of Yahweh.[12] It may also refer to Zion as the city where the temple is, and to Zion as the people of God. Here, Zion is the footstool of Yahweh. If to remember implies salvation, life and posterity, 'not to remember' means the reverse—destruction and death. When 'the Lord did not remember his footstool', Zion, 'the glory of Israel', was 'cast down from heaven to earth'. The chosen city has been discarded. Note the liquid alliteration in *r* and the *e* assonance in ארץ and תפארת (v. 1b).

'The day of his wrath', ביום אפו, refers to the horrible disaster which befell Jerusalem and Judah in 587 BCE.[13] Although daughter Zion housed Yahweh's temple, although she was his footstool, she had broken the covenant with Yahweh and must incur his wrath, for Yahweh is just (Lam. 1.18) and shows no partiality (e.g. Deut. 10.17). The movement of descent from heaven to earth is symbolic of mourning. Therefore, since daughter Zion experiences the wrath of Yahweh, she is now in mourning. The consequences of the divine wrath, described in the following verses, are the direct cause of her mourning.

2. *The cause of Jerusalem's mourning (vv. 2-9).* The second speaker describes the cause of Jerusalem's mourning in two stages. First, he laments the destruction of the whole land of Judah, its countryside and its fortified towns (vv. 2-5). Then he bemoans the destruction of Jerusalem, the city and the temple (vv. 6-9).

a. *Devastation of Judah (vv. 2-5).* Verses 2-5 depict the effects of Yahweh's wrath on the land of Judah in swift sweeping strokes. The fundamental meaning of the root בלע (vv. 2a, 5ab) is to swallow food, 'eagerly and quickly, before anyone else can get to it'.[14] It implies a swift and total act of destruction. The object being swallowed disappears out of sight, it is no more. The earth opened its mouth and swallowed up Korah, Dathan and Abiram, together with their households and their goods (Num. 16.32). A large fish swallowed up Jonah when

---

12. Holladay, *Jeremiah 1*, p. 438.
13. See my comment on Lam. 1.12 above, p. 83.
14. J. Schüpphaus, 'בלע', *TDOT*, II, pp. 136-39 (137).

he was thrown into the sea (Jon. 2.1). The word כל, 'all', occurs in
every verse of the unit. The 'whole countryside of Jacob', 'the whole
horn [strength] of Israel', 'all [the young warriors] who delight the eye',
'all its citadels'—all is destroyed.

The Lord who is רחום וחנון, 'merciful and gracious' (Ps. 103.8), now
destroys 'without mercy', ולא חמל. The negative of חמל is used three
times in this poem (vv. 2a, 17b, 21c) as a reversal motif common in
laments.[15] The root הרס, 'to tear down', occurs as the opposite of בנה,
'to build up' in several texts (e.g. Jer. 45.4; Ezek. 36.36). It represents
the Lord's act of judgment. Again, the mention of the divine wrath,
בעברתו, 'in his fury', is a reminder that God's destroying acts represent
his reaction to the sin of the people in Judah. From the root עבר, 'to
pass over prescribed boundaries', the scope of meaning for the noun
עברה ranges from 'pride' and 'exaltation' to 'destructive anger'.[16] The
phrase הגיע לארץ, 'he brought down to the ground' (v. 2c), recalls the
clause in v. 1b, השליך משמים ארץ, 'he cast down from heaven to earth',
and evokes the concrete picture of razed fortifications as well as the
ceremonial posture of mourning—seated on the ground. The verb הרס
and the verbal phrase הגיע לארץ are concrete acts which explain the
metaphor of בלע, 'to swallow up', when the object is not food but land,
fortresses and people.

The root חלל is ambiguous. BDB distinguishes three different roots:
the first means 'to pierce, slay, wound'; the second is a denominative
verb meaning 'to play the pipe'; and the third means 'to pollute, defile,
profane'. Most commentators adopt the third root here[17] which also
implies the shame of defeat. It is used in parallel with the hiphil of קלל,
'to make light, dishonor, shame', in Isa. 23.9 (NRSV):

---

15. Dobbs-Allsopp, *Weep*, pp. 38-41.

16. J. Bergman and E. Johnson, 'אנף', *TDOT*, I, pp. 348-60 (353).

17. E.g. Hillers, *Lamentations*, p. 97; Westermann, *Lamentations*, pp. 141, 144.
D.N. Freedman (*Pottery, Poetry, and Prophecy* [Winona Lake, IN: Eisenbrauns,
1980], pp. 27-28) derives חלל from the first root 'to slay' and follows the masoretic
punctuation, with a pause after הגיע לארץ, thus making מבצרי בת-יהודה the object
of הגיע:

> the fortresses of Daughter-Judah
>> he brought down to the earth—
> He slew her king and her princes.

יהוה צבאות יעצה לחלל גאון
כל־צבי להקל כל־נכבדי־ארץ:

The LORD of hosts has planned it—
  to defile the pride of all glory,
  to shame all the honored of the earth.

This root is also used with לארץ without the hiphil of נגע to convey the same sense of being brought to the ground in dishonor:

שלחו באש מקדשך לארץ חללו משכן־שמך:

They set your sanctuary on fire;
  they desecrated the dwelling place of your name, bringing it to the
  ground (Ps. 74.7; NRSV).

נארתה ברית עבדך חללת לארץ נזרו:

You have renounced the covenant with your servant;
  you have defiled his crown in the dust (Ps. 89.40; NRSV).

'The kingdom and its princes' have been defeated, and are now mourning on the ground.

The wrath of the Lord is stressed again in v. 3a with the phrase בחרי־אף, 'in burning wrath'. The root חרה means originally 'to glow, to burn'.[18] This imagery of burning continues through this verse and the next. The 'horn', קרן, is the symbol of the strength and/or power of a person (e.g. Ps. 75.11, קרני רשעים, 'the horns of the wicked', and קרנות צדיק, 'the horns of the righteous') or a country (e.g. Jer. 48.25, קרן מואב, 'the horn of Moab'). The fortresses (v. 2b) and the princes (v. 2c) are part of the 'horn' of Israel. Again ישראל (v. 3a) and יעקב (v. 3c) emphasize the extent of the devastation: the whole land.

The verbal phrase שוב אחור denotes defeat as in Lam. 1.13b; Ps. 44.11. The Lord turns back in defeat the right hand or the power of Israel to defend itself. This fulfills the covenant curse in Deut. 28.25, 'Yahweh will cause you to be defeated before your enemies'. Although the enemy is mentioned (מפני אויב, 'before the enemy'), the real cause of defeat is the Lord.

The imagery of burning in בחרי־אף is picked up by the root בער, 'to burn', which usually denotes a function of fire, but is now boldly applied to the Lord himself. The Lord's destructive acts are compared to a blazing fire.

The key to the interpretation of נצב ימינו in v. 4a is to note the sequence:

18. Bergman and Johnson, 'אנף', p. 353.

(1) he strung his bow;

(2) נצב ימינו, 'he aimed [lit. steadied] with his right hand';

(3) like a foe he killed = he shot.

What we have here is the set series of steps taken by the archer: ready, aim, fire! Thus נצב ימינו in the sequence means 'he aimed with his right hand'. Ezekiel 39.3 makes clear that the left hand holds the bow while the right hand holds the arrows and the string:

והכיתי קשתך מיד שמאולך וחציך מיד ימינך אפיל:

I will strike your bow from your left hand, and will make your arrows drop out of your right hand (NRSV).

It is the right hand that draws the bow, that is, the archer must aim with his right hand.

Lamentations 3.12-13 displays a similar sequence:

(1)　he strung his bow (דרך קשתו);

(2)　he stationed me as the target of his arrow, that is, he set me in his line of fire, he aimed at me (ויציבני). Note that the root נצב is used here too.

(3)　he brought (= shot) his arrows into my kidneys.

Psalm 11.2 also evidences the series:

(1)　the wicked string their bows;

(2)　they set their arrows on the bowstring;

(3)　in order to shoot...

The Lord acts as an enemy (כאויב in v. 4a, and כצר in v. 4b) and no longer as a covenant partner. He kills all the troops outside the capital trying to halt the invasion.

The 'tent of daughter Zion' (v. 4c) refers first of all to Jerusalem where daughter Zion lives. But this section (vv. 2-5) is about the attack on the countryside, and Jerusalem is affected as a sorrowing observer of the scene. The countryside and its inhabitants (Jerusalem's sons and daughters) are the ones physically harmed, and they too are the referents of אהל בת־ציון.

The Levite in Judg. 19.9 goes to his tent (לאהלך); this is not a reference to the area circumscribed by the boundaries of his tent, but to the area where the tent is located. The tents of Jacob or Judah in Jer. 4.20; 30.18; Zech. 12.7; Mal. 2.12 are a reference to the whole of Judah.

But אהל can also refer to the family or tribe. In Prov. 14.11, בית is parallel to אֹהֶל, and both words mean 'family'. In Ps. 78.67, אֹהֶל is parallel to שֵׁבֶט and means 'tribe'.

The 'tent of daughter Zion' refers both to the people and the territory of Judah. Both suffer from the wrath of God which is described by the imagery of fire in vv. 3c and 4c. The root שָׁפַךְ, 'to pour out', which normally goes with water, or something liquid, is now used for wrath compared to fire. Wrath is compared to water in Hos. 5.10 (NRSV):

עֲלֵיהֶם אֶשְׁפּוֹךְ כַּמַּיִם עֶבְרָתִי:

> On them I will pour out
>   my wrath like water.

The imagery of wrath being poured out occurs also in Isa. 42.25 וַיִּשְׁפֹּךְ עָלָיו חֵמָה אַפּוֹ, 'so he poured upon him the heat of his anger'; and in Ezek. 20.34, וּבְחֵמָה שְׁפוּכָה, 'and with wrath poured out'. It is interesting to note that the noun חֵמָה, 'anger, fury', in v. 4c is also used in the Isaiah and Ezekiel texts. It comes from the root יָחַם, 'to be hot'. The person who is angry feels hot, and the effects of anger are devastating like those of fire. In this context, anger is poured out because it comes from above, from God (cf. Rev. 16 which describes the pouring out of the seven bowls of the wrath of God).

The repetition of בלע in vv. 5a and 5b reinforces the identification of the Lord with the enemy. This identification is not a dogmatic affirmation; it is only the expression of intense suffering. The first colon of v. 5a, הָיָה אֲדֹנָי כְּאוֹיֵב, 'the Lord became the enemy', is a bitter cry out of the depths of suffering. Verses 2-5 are nicely demarcated as a literary unit about the destruction of Judah by the *inclusio* formed with בלע and מבצרי בת־יהודה in v. 2ab and בלע, מבצריו and בת־יהודה in vv. 5a, 5b and 5c. Citadels and fortresses are places where people come for refuge in times of war. The destruction of the citadels and fortresses thus implies the destruction of the people. Another motif of reversal is found in v. 5c. Instead of multiplying the people through the covenantal blessing (Deut. 28.4, 11), the Lord multiplies the sound of lament through the increasing number of the dead. The root אנה in תַאֲנִיָּה וַאֲנִיָּה belongs to a group of words which register 'undirected and inarticulate cries of pain'.[19] In a context involving covenantal partners, an undirected cry of pain may function as a cry for help (Exod. 6.5; Judg. 2.18). Here, however, the wrath of the Lord was so great that 'he did not remember his

---

19. Boyce, *Cry to God*, pp. 17, 62-65.

footstool' (v. 1c), that 'he destroyed without mercy' (v. 2a), that he did not respond to the cry of pain by alleviating it. Instead, he let it intensify. Note the plaintive melody formed by the alliteration of *n* and yod, and the *a* and *i* assonance in תאניה ואניה. The whole land is in mourning. The prophecy in Isa. 29.2 has been fulfilled:

והציקותי לאריאל והיתה תאניה ואניה

Yet I will bring distress to Ariel,
and there shall be moaning and mourning.

Another cause of mourning for Jerusalem is the devastation of the capital city and temple described in the next subsection.

b. *Devastation of Jerusalem (vv. 6-9)*. After a general overview of the effects of destruction on the whole land, the מנחם now gives a close-up on Jerusalem and the temple. Verse 6 describes the swallowing up (root בלע in v. 8b) of Zion in three dimensions: spatial (שכו, 'his tent', and מועדו, 'his place of assembly' in v. 6a), temporal (מועד ושבת, 'festival and sabbath' in v. 6b), and ministerial (מלך וכהן, 'king and priest' in v. 6c).[20] The root חמס denotes lawlessness. Of the eight occurrences of the verb in the MT (seven in the qal: Job 15.33; 21.27; Prov. 8.36; Jer. 22.3; Lam. 2.6; Ezek. 22.26; Zeph. 3.4; and one in the niphal: Jer. 13.22), only one has Yahweh as subject (Lam. 2.6). The word שכו is an orthographic variation of סכו which designates Jerusalem and / or the Jerusalem temple (e.g. Pss. 27.5; 76.3). In his wrath, Yahweh even acted against the law by destroying his own temple! He destroyed his temple as he destroyed the 'garden', that is, the pastures of Jacob (v. 2a), the land of Judah. The fact that Yahweh destroyed his own temple is deplored as a lawless act because Yahweh specifically required his people to assemble before him there to keep his sabbaths (e.g. Lev. 19.30; 26.2) and to celebrate the three yearly festivals, namely, Passover, the Feast of Weeks, and the Feast of Booths (cf. Exod. 23.14-17 = Deut. 16.1-17). After the destruction of the temple and the exile of the majority of the population, festivals and sabbaths must have fallen slowly into oblivion, especially after the incident recorded in Jer. 41.4-9 about 80 men in mourning garb who had come to worship at the house of the Lord but were murdered by Ishmael and his men. Festivals and sabbaths are no longer celebrated in Zion (v. 6b). The root שכח, 'to forget' (v. 6b), harks back to לא־יזכר, 'not to remem-

---

20. Droin, *Lamentations*, p. 48.

ber' (v. 1c). The reversal motif in v. 6b makes an implicit contrast with the past where Zion used to be called קרית מועדנו, 'the city of our festivals' (Isa. 33.20).

Yahweh destroyed his own temple, the place which he chose as the dwelling place for his name (cf. Deut. 12.11). Yahweh also rejected the king whom he chose to lead his people (cf. Deut. 17.14-15) and the priest whom he chose to minister in his name (cf. Deut. 18.5). Temple, king and priest, once objects of Yahweh's choice, have now come under his curse. This is implied in the phrase בזעם־אפו, 'in his fierce anger', since the root זעם means both 'to be angry' and 'to curse'.[21] All that the people had so far relied upon for safety and order, instruction and direction, Yahweh has destroyed.[22]

Verse 7 continues with the destruction of the temple. The root זנח also implies the wrath of God, for it is parallel to אנף, 'be angry' (Ps. 60.3); to יעשן אפך, 'your anger smokes' (Ps. 74.1); and to hithpael עבר, 'be full of wrath' (Ps. 89.39). In his wrath, the Lord rejected his altar where his people offered sacrifices to him. Likewise, he rejected his sanctuary, where his name dwelt (cf. Ps. 74.7). The enemies were able to invade the temple and destroy it because the Lord allowed the defense system of Jerusalem to be broken (v. 7b): the walls of Jerusalem were breached in the fourth month (2 Kgs 25.3-4). Verse 7c prolongs the reversal motif in v. 6b. In the past, God's people would throng to the temple on festival days with 'shouts of joy and songs of thanksgiving', בקול־רנה ותודה (Ps. 42.5c). Now the shouts of joy are heard in the temple, but not on a feast day, nor are they shouts by God's people. These are cries of victory by the enemy armies.

Verses 6 and 7 have focused on the destruction of the temple. Now v. 8 shifts the focus to the destruction of the city, daughter Zion. First, the protective walls must come down. And Yahweh 'was determined' to make it happen. Inherent in the root חשב is the notion of rational scientific calculation.[23] The destruction of Jerusalem was not something whimsical or unexpected. It had been implied in the Mosaic covenant whereby the people of Israel would enjoy blessings or incur curses according to whether they obey and observe Yahweh's commandments or not (cf. Deut. 27.9–28.68). The 'measuring line', קו, is used to divide into portions (e.g. Isa. 34.17), for building purposes (e.g. Jer. 31.39;

---

21. B. Wiklander, 'זעם', *TDOT*, IV, pp. 106-11 (107-108).

22. Westermann, *Lamentations*, p. 152.

23. K. Seybold, 'חשב', *TDOT*, V, pp. 228-45.

Zech. 1.16), or to mark the limits for destruction (e.g. 2 Kgs 21.13; Isa. 34.11). Here it is stretched out obviously for the purpose of destruction. The clause לא־השיב ידו מבלע, 'he did not hold back his hand from consuming', recalls the opposite action: השיב אחור ימינו, 'he turned back his [Israel's] right hand', in v. 3b. Yahweh held back his hand and did not destroy his people when they rebelled in the wilderness (Ezek. 20.22). But now, Yahweh did not draw back his hand. This complete sovereignty of Yahweh is expressed fully in Isa. 14.27 (NAB):

כי־יהוה צבאות יעץ ומי יפר וידו הנטויה ומי ישיבנה:

> The Lord of hosts has planned; who can thwart him?
> His hand is stretched out; who can turn it back?

The outer and main walls are personified by the roots אבל and אמל. They too are grieving, because they failed in their purpose of protecting the city and the people within it.[24] The demolished outer and main walls are now heaps of ruins sitting on the ground, like people in mourning.

As a result of the demolishing process, the walls fell on top of one another, sinking the base and foundations deeper into the ground, and thereby sinking the gates attached to the lower part of the walls. Once the bars, which provided an additional strengthening device for the closed gates, were shattered, the enemy could easily break through the gates and capture the city. The picture of gates with shattered bars sunk into the earth reflects the mourning posture. A similar personification of the gates and of Zion in mourning is depicted in Isa. 3.26 (NRSV):

ואנו ואבלו פתחיה ונקתה לארץ תשב:

> And her gates shall lament and mourn;
> ravaged, she shall sit upon the ground.

Her king and princes, her secular leaders, are now in exile among the nations. The nominal phrase אין תורה, 'there is no instruction', refers to the absence of the priests whose function is to teach the law, as reflected in the following texts: כי לא־תאבד תורה מכהן, 'for instruction will not perish from the priest' (Jer. 18.18), and ותורה תאבד מכהן, 'instruction will perish from the priest' (Ezek. 7.26). Right after the capture of Jerusalem in 587/586 BCE, the priests Seraiah and Zephaniah were taken to the king of Babylon at Riblah who put them to death (2 Kgs 25.18-21). The other priests must have already been in exile (cf. Jer. 29.1).

---

24. Westermann, *Lamentations*, p. 152.

A list of secular and religious leaders for the people in Jerusalem and Judah is found in Jer. 2.26:

כבשת גנב כי ימצא כן הבישו בית ישראל
המה מלכיהם שריהם וכהניהם ונביאיהם:

> As a thief is ashamed when he is caught,
>> so the house of Israel will feel ashamed,
> They, their kings, their princes,
>> their priests, and their prophets.

Similar lists are found in Jer. 4.9; 8.1; 32.32.

There is no one around to advise Jerusalem in her hour of need, no מנחם. Even the prophets, whose primary task was to speak the words of Yahweh to his people (cf. Deut. 18.18), to confront them with Yahweh in history,[25] have not received any 'vision' from Yahweh. A vision (חזון) may refer to a word from Yahweh (cf. 1 Sam. 3.1; Ps. 89.20; Job 33.14-16) and not necessarily to something seen. These prophets have not received visions from Yahweh; consequently, they cannot advise the survivors of the catastrophe on how to deal with their grief; they have no oracles of salvation with which to comfort the mourners. This situation echoes the lament in Ps. 74.9:

אותתינו לא ראינו אין־עוד נביא ולא־אתנו ידע עד־מה:

> Signs for us, we do not see;
>> there is no longer any prophet,
>> and none of us knows how long.

The absence of the prophetic word is a curse pronounced against Israel by the prophet Amos (8.12):

ונעו מים עד־ים ומצפון ועד־מזרח ישוטטו
לבקש את־דבר־יהוה ולא ימצאו:

> They will wander from sea to sea,
>> they will range from north to east,
> In search of the word of Yahweh,
>> but they will not find it.

The occurrence of the divine name יהוה in every verse of vv. 6-9, and the repetition of catchwords such as מועד, 'appointed place, or festival' (vv. 6ab, 7c), ציון (vv. 6b, 8a), מלך (vv. 6c, 9b), חומת and חומה (vv. 7b, 8ac), bind vv. 6-9 together into a literary unit on the destruction of Jerusalem and the temple.

---

25. B.D. Napier, 'Prophet, Prophetism', *IDB*, III, pp. 905-906.

3. *People present at the ceremony (v. 10).* Verse 10 is the counterpart of v. 1. It closes the section on the causes of mourning with a portrayal of the mourning ceremony.

On the basis of Akkadian *damamu* (to mourn, moan; *CAD*, III, pp. 59-61), BDB (p. 199) tentatively identifies a דמם II, 'to wail', in Isa. 23.2. This suggestion has been taken up more recently in the case of דמם in Lam. 2.10.[26] *HALOT* (I, p. 226) accepts this suggestion, and it is possible. Wailing was part of the mourning ceremony. But the problem is that silence is also part of the mourning ceremony, as Lohfink has argued.[27] When the three friends come to comfort Job, they first wail, weep, tear their garments, sprinkle dust on their heads, and then sit with him on the ground for seven days and nights in silence. They evidently do this because they are so overwhelmed by Job's misfortune that they do not think they have anything useful to say.

While I admit the possible appropriateness of דמם II, 'to mourn, moan', in context here, it seems to me that the traditional דמם I, 'to be silent', has a better claim. Verse 9b notes that the former secular and religious leadership is in exile and thus is in no position to solve Jerusalem's problems. Verse 9c notes that Jerusalem's prophets, presumably still in Jerusalem, have had no visions and consequently have nothing to say to Jerusalem to help her either.

The new leaders of the Jerusalem community are the 'elders of daughter Zion' (v. 10a) whom the Babylonians did not think it worth their while to bring to Babylon as slaves. Although the biblical sources do not associate the 'elders' as a collective body of leadership with a specific age group, it is safe to assume a general link between 'elders' and the older age group.[28] These 'elders of daughter Zion' were probably too old to be thought capable of surviving the march into exile.[29]

---

26. McDaniel, 'Philological Studies: I', pp. 38-40.

27. See Chapter 1, pp. 29-31.

28. The 'elders' are drawn from the 'heads' or fathers of the בית, 'house', which was the basic social and economic unit in Israelite patriarchal tribal society. The 'house' included the father, his wives, their children and their children's children, up to four generations, and also other relatives, guests (גרים) and slaves. See Hanoch Reviv, *The Elders in Ancient Israel* (Jerusalem: The Hebrew University, 1989), p. 11.

29. There were other elders who might have been relatively younger and stronger among the exiles (cf. Jer. 29.1; Ezek. 8.1; 20.3).

Elders usually had life experience; they were highly regarded in Israelite society and often provided advice and guidance (cf. 1 Kgs 12.6-7). But now they have nothing to say to Jerusalem.

Their position is the same as that of the speaker of vv. 1-19. Though he ultimately decides otherwise (vv. 18-19), he admits in v. 13 he has no advice to give to Jerusalem. The elders and the speaker are in the same situation as Job's friends, who are so overwhelmed by his sad plight that they are unable to say anything to him for seven days and nights. Finally, after Job speaks in ch. 3, they object to his theology and set out to correct him.

The typical mourning rites are observed: the elders sit on the ground, girded with sackcloth; they have cast dust on their heads. The virgins have bowed their heads to the ground. All these acts of self-abasement express grief and repentance in the face of sin and death,[30] and serve as reminders of one's own mortality.[31] The elders or old men and the virgins or young women represent the two opposite poles of the population in terms of age, sex and experience. They form a merism to denote the whole surviving community: all survivors of the catastrophe are mourning.[32] A poetic contrast between זְקֵנִים, 'elders', and בְּתוּלֹת, 'virgins', is made through the use of different action verbs: the elders הֶעֱלוּ, 'cause [dirt] to go up', and the virgins הוֹרִידוּ, 'cause [their heads] to go down'. Actually, all the mourners at this mourning ceremony are sitting on the ground in silence, have cast dirt on their heads, are girded with sackcloth and have bowed their heads to the ground.

In the face of such total devastation, what else could the survivors of the catastrophe do but begin a mourning ceremony? The wrath of Yahweh in v. 1 has led to the mourning rites in v. 10. Daughter Zion has indeed become an abomination to the Lord.

The מְנַחֵם's Own Grief (Verses 11-12). The מְנַחֵם or the poet and speaker is temporarily interrupted in the course of his lament by his own uncontrollable emotions. He cannot hold back his grief any longer. He pours it out. His vision becomes blurred through his tears, and so the tears are said to weaken or wear out the eyes, to deprive them of 'their vital substance which runs out in the form of water'.[33] The connection between

---

30. Ferris, *Genre of Communal Lament*, pp. 79-107.
31. Hillers, *Lamentations*, pp. 105-106.
32. Hillers, *Lamentations*, p. 106; Westermann, *Lamentations*, p. 153.
33. Collins, 'Physiology of Tears: Part 1', p. 21.

the inner parts (or bowels) and the tears is that sorrow causes a strong disturbance in the inner parts of a person, causing them to break down and thereby to lose their vital fluid, which comes out through the eyes as tears. The second colon of v. 11a, חמרמרו מעי, 'my inner parts are in ferment', is reminiscent of the anguished cry of Lady Jerusalem in 1.20. I noted there that the root חמר I, 'to ferment, boil', describes pains as the effects of drunkenness. It may be added here that the word מעים, 'inner parts', refers to the womb in Gen. 25.23, Isa. 49.1, Ps. 71.6 and Ruth 1.11.[34] Thus מעים is evocative of childbirth pangs. People are seized with anguish and 'pain as of a woman in labor' (חיל כיולדה) when they hear news of war and destruction (e.g. Jer. 6.24; 50.43). The first colon in v. 11b resumes and compresses the two cola in v. 11a: the liver represents the inner parts, it is poured out on the ground in the form of tears.[35]

The phrase בת־עמי stands for Jerusalem.[36] The word בת is used preponderantly as an honorific title for a capital city, and עמי cannot be an epexegetical/appositional genitive like ציון in בת־ציון since עם is a masculine noun and never referred to as בת. Verses 11 and 12 are primarily directed toward the events in Jerusalem ('in the squares of the city', ברחבות קריה, v. 11c; ברחבות עיר, v. 12b). Moreover, vv. 8-9 describe the destruction of Jerusalem, v. 10 the mourning ceremony taking place in Jerusalem, while the following vv. 13-19 are addressed to Jerusalem.[37]

The מנחם is greatly distressed over the fall of Jerusalem, the destruction of the temple, royal palace and other important buildings in the city, and the death of his people. But the definitive event which causes him to break down completely is a particularly poignant scene: innocent children dying on their mothers' breasts. The same verbal root שפך, 'to pour out', is used to describe the psychological collapse of the speaker (נשפך לארץ כבדי, 'my liver has been poured out on the ground', v. 11b) and the death of the starving children (בהשתפך נפשם, 'as their lives expired', lit. 'were poured out', v. 12c). This verbal link reinforces

---

34. B.B. Kaiser, 'Poet as "Female Impersonator": The Image of Daughter Zion as Speaker in Biblical Poems of Suffering', *JR* 67 (1987), pp. 164-82 (169).

35. Kaiser, 'Poet', p. 23.

36. See p. 105 above.

37. Fitzgerald, 'BTWLT and BT', pp. 172-77.

the notion that it is the terminal fate of the children that triggers the מנחם's emotional breakdown.[38]

The tense of the infinitive בעטף is determined by יאמרו in v. 12a. It is not clear whether the reference to hunger here is to hunger during the siege or hunger at the time when the מנחם speaks, that is, in the period after the siege, during the mourning ceremony which is the literary setting of the poem. If the reference is to hunger during the siege, יאמרו and בעטף are past iteratives (*GHB*, §113e). Two reasons incline me to think that the reference is to starvation during the siege: first, dead children lay in the city squares in vv. 11c and 12b because there was no place to bury the corpses within the city (Jer. 33.5); these city squares presumably were filled with rubble and unoccupied after the siege; secondly, the reference to hunger in v. 20b is paired with the killing of priests and prophets in the sanctuary (v. 20c) that clearly took place at the time of Jerusalem's fall.

The difference between עוֹלֵל/עוֹלָל and יונק is that יונק is the 'unweaned child' (cf. Joel 2.16), while עולל is the 'boy', presumably the next stage of life, the upper limits of which I would not want to set. The 'unweaned child' and the 'boy' are also distinguished in 1 Sam. 15.3; 22.19; Jer. 44.7. These three texts give a similar list: (1) male and female adults; (2) male and female children (taking the word עולל as a collective noun, inclusive of both sexes); (3) again, both male and female unweaned children (*LHAVT*, p. 579).

The יונק in v. 12a could talk and ask for grain because women in the ancient Near East nursed children longer than is the custom now: for example, the mother in 2 Macc. 7.27 nursed her youngest child for three years; the young Samuel goes to live at the shrine away from home when he is weaned (1 Sam. 1.22).

I favor reading וְאֵין, 'but there was none', for the following reasons: first, if children are dying of hunger, they do not ask for wine; secondly, the combination דגן ויין, 'grain and wine', occurs only here, the standard phrase being either דגן ותירש, 'grain and new wine' (e.g. Gen. 27.37; Deut. 33.28; Isa. 36.17), or לחם ויין, 'bread and wine' (e.g. Gen. 14.18; Judg. 19.19; Neh. 5.15); thirdly, the clause ואין very frequently continues sentences with verbs of seeking, hoping for, and the like (e.g. Isa. 41.17; 59.11; Ps. 69.21; Job 3.9; Ezek. 7.25); see BDB, p. 34; and

---

38. A. Mintz, 'The Rhetoric of Lamentations and the Representation of Catastrophe', *Prooftexts* 2 (1982), pp. 1-17 (6).

finally, the mistake presumed could have occurred easily enough: the א being misread as a י.

However, we cannot be certain without versional evidence. In addition, Palestine is a Mediterranean country, and even today, wine is drunk by children younger than those in America.

According to Collins,[39] v. 12c simply says that the children are weeping from hunger. Their life force or the substance of their throats is being poured out in the form of tears. This explanation seems too weak, since the children are said to 'waste away like the wounded' (בהתעטפם כחלל, v. 12b). Moreover, the siege of 588–587 BCE, apart from a brief interlude when the Egyptian army forced the Babylonians to withdraw temporarily during the spring or summer of 588 (Jer. 37.5-11), lasted at least a year and a half.[40] Food ran low (Jer. 37.21), and it is not surprising if people, especially children, were dying of hunger at that time.

Verses 11 and 12 are tightly bound together by the repetition of the phrase ברחבות, 'in the squares/streets' (vv. 11c, 12b), of the verb roots שפך and עטף (vv. 11bc, 12bc), and by the a:b::b:a chiastic pattern formed with these verbs: נשפך:בעטף::בהתעטפם:בהשתפך, 'has been poured out (v. 11b): wasted away (v. 11c)::wasted away (v. 12b): expired (v. 12c)'. Note that the first two verbs are in the niphal while the last two are in the hithpael.

Address to Jerusalem (Verses 13-19)

After pouring out his own grief, the מנחם addresses Lady Jerusalem with a series of rhetorical questions expressing his own unmitigated grief. He tries to think of who could really comfort her and heal (רפא, v. 13c) her, in the sense of assuaging her pain and restoring her loss.

Possible מנחמים, *'Comforters' (Verses 13-14).* The speaker now turns to address Jerusalem in the second person feminine singular. He clearly expresses his own desire to comfort Jerusalem (ואנחמך, v. 13b) but confesses his inability to do so. To give comfort in this context seems to require the ability to say something useful, to give an advice or a warning (מה-אעידך, 'what can I say to you?'). It has already been noted in Chapter 1 that 'to comfort' means 'to speak kindly, tenderly, to the mourner or distressed person' (e.g. Gen. 50.21; Ruth 2.13). To comfort

---

39. Collins, 'Physiology of Tears: Part 1', p. 25.

40. J. Bright, *A History of Israel* (Philadelphia: Westminster Press, 3rd edn, 1981), pp. 329-30.

also involves finding an adequate comparison for the misery of Zion. The root דמה, 'to be like, look like', is present in the noun דמות, 'likeness', which is used in Gen. 1.26 to express the likeness (or solidarity) between God and human beings. The root שׁוה, 'to be like, resemble', has the nuance of 'to be equal to'.[41] These two roots are used in Isa. 40.18, 25 to affirm the incomparability of Yahweh.[42] Here also, they serve to express the incommensurability of Zion's sufferings. The מנחם despairs of being able to find an adequate comparison for her pains. Hillers is not clear as to why finding a comparison for Zion would comfort her.[43] Comparisons or metaphors from the finite and known world of experiences could, however, comfort by giving some anchorage and orientation in the maze of sufferings.[44] A precedent case of similar suffering—however inadequate the metaphor is—could give comfort by the example it shows or the lesson one can learn from the way the people who suffer come out of suffering, how they go beyond their wretchedness toward wholeness.

The devastation of Lady Jerusalem is unprecedented in history. The speaker was able to find a comparison after all, but it is a comparison with the cosmic destruction of the sea monster Rahab / Leviathan by Yahweh, in the primordial battle at creation, when Yahweh's victory established order out of watery chaos (Job 9.13; 26.12; Pss. 74.13-14; 89.10-11; 104.5-9; Isa. 27.1; 51.9).[45] This destruction of the sea monster is a faint reminiscence of the Babylonian creation myth *Enūma elish* in which Marduk, the victorious god of order, split in two the corpse of Tiamat, the goddess of chaos, and created the heavens by spreading out one half like a roof.[46] The sea suffered a total definitive defeat. So did Jerusalem. The situation is really bleak. There seems to be no answer to the desperate question מי ירפא־לך, 'who can heal you?' Yahweh himself declares:

אנוש לשברך נחלה מכתך:

> Incurable is your wound,
>> grievous your bruise (Jer. 30.12; NAB).

41. BDB, p. 1000. LXX renders by the verb ἰσόω, 'to make equal'.
42. H.D. Preuss, 'רמה', *TDOT*, III, pp. 250-60 (255-57).
43. Hillers, *Lamentations*, p. 106.
44. Mintz, 'Rhetoric of Lamentations', p. 7.
45. F.R. McCurley, *Ancient Myths and Biblical Faith* (Philadelphia: Fortress Press, 1983), p. 47.
46. *ANET*, p. 67.

Implied in the מנחם's question—'who can heal you?'—is the answer that only Yahweh is able to heal such an incurable wound, as he affirms in Deut. 32.39 (NAB):

> Learn then that I, I alone, am God,
> and there is no god besides me.
> It is I who bring both death and life,
> I who inflict wounds and heal them [ארפא],
> and from my hand there is no rescue.

The speaker now tries to find a מנחם for Jerusalem among her own prophets. The verb root חזה (v. 14a), an Aramaic loan word, refers to a special form of revelation, the perception of the divine voice during a deep sleep (cf. Job 4.13-21; 33.14-18), distinct from a dream. Before the fall of Jerusalem, prophets claimed to have received a word from Yahweh and declared it to the people, while in fact Yahweh did not send them. They were only telling lies, empty words (שוא) which have no substance, which cannot be fulfilled (cf. Ezek. 13.6; Jer. 29.21-23). They smeared whitewash (תפל) over the dark grim condition of the people (Ezek. 13.10-16). An illustration is the prophet Hananiah who prophesied in the fourth year of King Zedekiah that King Jeconiah and all the vessels in the Lord's house and all the exiles would be brought back to Jerusalem within two years (Jer. 28.1-4). But Yahweh did not send him, and he died in the same year (Jer. 28.15-17).

There were also false prophets living among the exiles of the first deportation to Babylon like Ahab, son of Kolaiah, and Zedekiah, son of Maaseiah, who received their due punishment from King Nebuchadnezzar of Babylon (Jer. 29.20-23). The phrase נביאיך, 'your prophets', is a sweeping generalization in retrospect since the prophet Jeremiah was also active during that time. People did not want to listen to his lone voice of impending judgment for sin. They preferred the soothing false promises of peace and prosperity.

ולא־גלו על־עונך להשיב שבותך

> They did not expose your iniquity
> to restore your fortunes (v. 14b).

Verse 14b gives the definition of true prophecy. Jerusalem's prophets should have exposed the sins of her people, warned them of the coming judgment, and called them to repentance (e.g. Jer. 3.12, 14, 22; 23.22). The goal of 'exposing iniquity' is להשיב שבותך. NAB renders this phrase 'to avert your fate', NIV 'to ward off your captivity'. The implication is that if the pre-exilic prophets had denounced the people's sins and called them to repentance, the people might have repented and so would have been spared this terrible devastation and exile. Bracke holds that the phrase occurs in a context of great sufferings inflicted by Yahweh's judgment; so the phrase להשיב שבותך would mean a reversal of Yahweh's judgment,[47] that is, a coming out of the present situation of loss, bereavement and privations, and a return to times of abundance and joy. Provan prefers the translation 'to restore your fortunes' (RSV) and explains v. 14 as concerning false prophecy in the present time, after the fall of Jerusalem.[48] The prophets should have exhorted the survivors of the catastrophe to repent so that Yahweh could heal them and bring them back to earlier times of prosperity.

My translation is the same as that in RSV (and NRSV). Lady Jerusalem has suffered destruction on an unprecedented scale. The speaker does not know how to comfort her. He is searching for comforters who would know what to say to help her out of her dreadful misery. He is searching for someone who could heal her wounds (v. 13). 'To restore your fortunes' is what Jerusalem needs. She needs healing and restoration. The prophets could have offered a means of healing and restoration by pointing her back to Yahweh through repentance. They could have been her comforters if they had exhorted her to repentance. The wonderful promise of restoration and blessing in Jer. 33.6-13 follows Yahweh's command to call on him (33.3). The promise of healing in Jer. 3.22 depends upon the prior condition of a return to Yahweh:

שובו בנים שובבים ארפה משובתיכם

Return, rebellious children,
and I will cure you of your rebelling (NAB).

Verse 14c is a virtual repetition of v. 14a. The meaning of true prophecy (v. 14b) is enclosed between two lines about the harmful effects of false prophecy. The word מַשְׂאוֹת / מַשְׂאֹת (oracles) has the connotation of 'threats against the foreign nations'.[49] Jerusalem's prophets not only prophesied lies to the people, promising peace when there was no peace (e.g. Jer. 14.13-14; Ezek. 13.16), but they also misled the people by giving them false hopes about the imminent destruction of the foreign enemy nations (cf. Jer. 27.9-10). These lying prophets must bear the

47. Bracke, 'A Reappraisal', p. 242.
48. Provan, *Lamentations*, p. 74.
49. A. Jepsen, 'חזה', *TDOT*, IV, pp. 280-90 (283).

responsibility for their words before Yahweh (cf. Jer. 23.30-32). They 'have seen false and deceptive visions' because they were not sent by Yahweh, and Yahweh did not speak to them (cf. Jer. 23.21). They 'have received no vision from Yahweh' (v. 9c). Jerusalem's prophets cannot act as her מנחמים.

Verse 14 reveals an *inclusio* with the root חזה and the word שוא in vv. 14a and 14c. Verses 13 and 14 are linked together by the repetition of לך (vv. 13abc, 14ac) and the close association of ideas in the clauses ואנחמך, 'that I may comfort you' (v. 13b), מי ירפא־לך, 'who can heal you?' (v. 13c), and להשיב שבותך, 'to restore your fortunes' (v. 14b), which revolve around the theme of comfort, healing and restoration.

Reactions of Passers-by and Enemies (Verses 15-16).

1. *No sympathy from passers-by (v. 15).* Clapping the hands (here with the root ספק),[50] hissing, wagging the head—all these acts belong to the list of common shaming techniques that belittle a defeated enemy.[51] They may also be apotropaic acts which are believed to ward off evil or bad luck. The phrase ספק כף denotes a gesture of anger. Balak asked Balaam to curse the Israelites, but Balaam blessed them at Yahweh's command. Balak became angry and clapped his hands (ויספק את־כפיו, Num. 24.10). The phrase ספק כף is used in parallel with שרק, 'to hiss, whistle', in Job 27.23 and here to express hostility.[52] The presence of the root שמם in connection with the roots שרק and נוע in several texts shows that these verbs express fear as well as mockery (cf. Jer. 18.16; 19.8; 49.17; 50.13; Ezek. 27.35-36; Zeph. 2.15). The עברי דרך (passers-by) are the neighboring countries of Judah. They fear the same fate for themselves, yet instead of showing compassion, they deride Jerusalem. Their seemingly incredulous question echoes in a sarcastic tone the same expressions of praise that the people of Israel used to sing about their beloved city: כלילת יפי, 'the perfection of beauty' (Ps. 50.2); משוש לכל־הארץ, 'the joy of all the earth' (Ps. 48.3).

---

50. Nili S. Fox ('Clapping Hands as a Gesture of Anguish and Anger in Mesopotamia and in Israel', *JANESCU* 23 [1995], pp. 49-60 [51]) distinguishes four verbal roots used with יד, 'hand', or כף, 'hand, palm': the roots מחה, 'to clap', and תקע, 'to clap, strike', express triumph, approval and rejoicing; the roots ספק or שפק, and the hiphil of נכה, 'to strike', express anger, hostility or anguish.

51. Bechtel, 'Shame as a Sanction', p. 72.

52. P.R. Ackroyd, 'יד', *TDOT*, V, pp. 393-426 (414).

Jerusalem's neighbors should instead have followed the injunction given to Moab's neighbors at its downfall:

נדו לו כל־סביביו

Console him, all you his neighbors! (Jer. 48.17)

The usual translation of this verse (e.g. NIV, NRSV) is 'mourn over him, bewail him'. However, the semantic range of the root נוד covers the meanings 'to comfort, console, take pity' (cf. Jer. 15.5; Ps. 69.21; Job 2.11; 42.11).[53] There might be a touch of irony in this summons to comfort Moab; nevertheless, the concept is there that neighbors are expected to offer comfort at times of calamities. But Jerusalem's neighbors show her no pity.

2. *Malicious boasting of enemies (v. 16)*. To open the mouth (פָּצָה פֶּה) may by itself denote a hostile and mocking gesture (cf. Ps. 22.14; Lam. 3.46), or may be the initial act preparatory to hissing and gnashing the teeth (here, and in v. 15). Gnashing the teeth expresses anger (cf. Job 16.9), hostility (cf. Pss. 37.12; 112.10), scorn (cf. Ps. 35.16). It must be an unbearable pain for Jerusalem to hear her enemies boasting ruthlessly over her ruin (cf. Ps. 35.21, 25). The same root בלע that is previously applied to Yahweh as the agent of destruction (vv. 2, 5) is now used by the enemies. They have attained their long-awaited goal: they have succeeded at last in destroying Jerusalem, the city that 'God has firmly founded forever' (אלהים יכוננה עד־עולם, Ps. 48.9). The root קוה, 'to wait, long for', implies endurance.[54] To capture Jerusalem was a long, arduous task.

Verses 15 and 16 are bound together by a very similar structure. They both begin with a perfect tense verb (סָפְקוּ, 'clapped', and פָּצוּ, 'opened'), plus a prepositional phrase (עָלַיִךְ, 'at/against you'), plus a direct object (כַּפַּיִם, 'their hands', and פִּיהֶם, 'their mouths'), plus a subject introduced by כֹּל־, 'all'. The second line in both verses starts with the same perfect verb שָׁרְקוּ, 'hissed', after which follow a *wayyiqtol* and a direct object. Both third lines are direct quotations. Verse 15c is composed of three nominal clauses (i.e. if one omits שֶׁיֹּאמְרוּ, 'about which they used to say', as a gloss) making up an incredulous question on the part of the passers-by, implicitly contrasting the past glory of Jerusalem with her present ruins: הֲזֹאת הָעִיר, 'is this the city', כְּלִילַת יֹפִי, 'the per-

53. Hillers, *Lamentations*, p. 38; Dobbs-Allsopp, *Weep*, p. 107.
54. BDB, p. 875.

fection of beauty', and מָשׂוֹשׂ לְכָל־הָאָרֶץ, 'the joy of all the earth'. Verse 16c comprises three short verbal clauses which spell out the intense craving and the triumphant cries of her enemies: שֶׁקִּוִּינֻהוּ, 'which we longed for', מָצָאנוּ, 'we have found [it]', and רָאִינוּ, 'we have seen [it]'.

Jerusalem's neighbors and enemies did not follow the advice given in Prov. 24.17 (NRSV),

> Do not rejoice when your enemies fall,
>   and do not let your heart be glad when they stumble.

A Reflection on Yahweh's Action (Verse 17). In v. 17 the speaker reflects on the gross boasting of the enemies (בִּלָּעֲנוּ, 'we have consumed her!', v. 16b). What he has already stated in his description of the catastrophe (vv. 1-9), he now reaffirms: עָשָׂה יְהוָה אֲשֶׁר זָמָם, 'Yahweh has done what he proposed' (v. 17a). The cry בִּלָּעֲנוּ sounds hollow alongside בִּלַּע אֲדֹנָי (v. 2a), בִּלַּע יִשְׂרָאֵל (v. 5a), בִּלַּע כָּל־אַרְמְנוֹתֶיהָ (v. 5b; see pp. 103-104 above), לֹא־הֵשִׁיב יָדוֹ מִבַּלֵּעַ (v. 8b). The day for which the enemies had waited so long (זֶה הַיּוֹם) was the day of Yahweh's wrath (יוֹם אַף־יְהוָה, vv. 1c, 21c, 22b).

The verb זָמַם repeats the idea expressed in חָשַׁב יְהוָה (v. 8a). The root בצע has the original meaning of 'to cut off' with reference to the weaver cutting off the last thread of a finished piece of woven cloth.[55] The word אִמְרָתוֹ refers to the word of God which may signify 'pledge, promise, protection, support and comfort' (Ps. 119.38, 41, 58, 76, 82, 116, 170). In Isa. 28.23 and 32.9, the word אִמְרָה / אֶמְרָה, refers to the prophetic announcement of calamity, which is the sense here.[56] When the circumstances were ripe for punishment, Yahweh 'cut off the thread' and let disaster fall on Jerusalem and her people. This word of calamity had been announced by the prophet Jeremiah (e.g. Jer. 4.3-4) long before it happened. In fact, it had already been proclaimed in the covenant curses (Deut. 28.15-69). The destruction carried out by Yahweh in vv. 1-9 is summarized in a colon of three words: הָרַס וְלֹא חָמָל, 'he tore down without mercy' (v. 17b). Yahweh 'became the enemy' (v. 5a). He caused the enemy to rejoice (v. 17c) but Jerusalem to mourn (v. 8c). He gave strength to her foes while he shattered her own might (v. 3a). The covenant curses were fulfilled because Yahweh's people failed to obey him.

---

55. D. Kellermann, 'בצע', *TDOT*, II, pp. 205-208 (206-207).
56. S. Wagner, 'אמר', *TDOT*, I, pp. 328-45 (345).

The second speaker, in his address to Jerusalem, expresses first his deep sympathy and sincere desire to comfort her. However, he finds himself inadequate for the task, and so thinks of the prophets. They might be able to comfort her if they had a word from Yahweh, for example, Isa. 40.1:

נחמו נחמו עמי יאמר אלהיכם

> Comfort, O comfort my people,
>   says your God.

But Jerusalem's prophets gave the people false hopes and led them astray in the past, so now they have not heard from Yahweh. They have no advice to give Jerusalem. They cannot comfort her. They do not qualify for the task of מנחמים.

The speaker goes down the list. What about the neighbors? They passed by and saw Jerusalem in great distress. Yet they showed no sympathy, they acted like her enemies. They clapped their hands and hissed. They rejoiced over her downfall. They can only aggravate the pain of Jerusalem.

The speaker pauses to reflect on the catastrophe. This is Yahweh's punishment for sin. His people have not kept the covenant, they have not been faithful to Yahweh. As a result, they are bearing the consequences of their disobedience. The speaker finally comes up with some advice to give Jerusalem. He can now fulfill his part as the מנחם.

Advice to Jerusalem (Verses 18-19). Jerusalem is advised to appeal to the Lord for help. The root צעק means the loud and agonized cry of a person in distress calling for deliverance.[57] The emended phrase בלבך, 'from your heart, sincerely', denotes genuine repentance and humility, qualities that are also implied in the profuse weeping and shedding of tears.

The word חומת is emended with some frequency to המי or נהי: 'Lament/wail, O daughter Zion!'[58] However, this emendation may not be necessary. The phrase חומת בת־ציון could well be meant to recall the same phrase in v. 8a where the Lord is presented as tearing down the wall of Jerusalem. The paradox involved would have to do with the speaker's shift in thought revealed through his speech to Jerusalem. Throughout vv. 1-16, and specifically in his speech addressed to

---

57. G. Hasel, 'זעק', *TDOT*, IV, pp. 112-22 (115).
58. See *HALOT*, I, p. 298.

Jerusalem (vv. 13-16), the speaker insists that Yahweh has destroyed Jerusalem and that he himself has nothing to say to comfort her (v. 13). The reflection in v. 17 brings about a shift in the speaker's thinking. He has come to recognize that Yahweh acted like 'an enemy' because he was faithful to his covenant while his people were not. So he advises Jerusalem to appeal to this same Lord who was behind all that destruction (vv. 18-19).

Syntactically, there are two ways in which the phrase חומת בת־ציון can be fitted into v. 18a, with the first word emended to צעקי.

First, it could be the vocative, 'O wall of daughter Zion!', with the implied meaning of 'O devastated daughter Zion!' With this may be compared Isa. 52.9. The unit Isa. 52.7-10 is addressed to Jerusalem. See 52.8a:

> Listen, your watchmen [צפיך] have raised a cry,
> together they shout for joy.

Then v. 9a continues:

> Break out in joyful song,
> you ruins of Jerusalem [חרבות ירושלם]!

The ruins of Jerusalem are devastated Jerusalem, the personified city addressed in the unit. If חומת בת־ציון in Lam. 2.18 is interpreted this way, the paradox becomes: the one hope for the devastated wall of Jerusalem is the Lord who destroyed that wall (v. 8).

The other possibility is to take חומת בת־ציון as an appositive for אדני of the first colon. Then the paradox is: the Lord destroyed Jerusalem's wall, but the possibility exists for the future that he personally will be her wall.[59] The implication is that no wall built by human hands will be needed.

I favor this second analysis of the syntax of חומת בת־ציון as an appositive. It presents a sharper contrast just as it highlights the covenant theology which is then immediately picked up in v. 20a where Jerusalem begins to speak:

> Look, O Yahweh, and consider
> whom you have dealt with in this way!

Yahweh is often called משגב, 'stronghold', in the Psalms (e.g. Pss. 9.10; 18.3 = 2 Sam. 22.3; 46.8, 12; 48.4; 59.10, 17, 18) or מעוז, 'fort-

---

59. Gottwald (*Studies*, p. 11) and Provan (*Lamentations*, p. 76) also think that 'the wall of daughter Zion' is a description of God.

ress, refuge' (e.g. 2 Sam. 22.3; Pss. 27.1; 28.8; Isa. 25.4; Jer. 16.9). These words belong with חומה (Lam. 2.18) to the word group for defensive fortifications. Yahweh gets called a חומה because of the wordplay with חומה in v. 8a. Yahweh is called a חומה also in Zech. 2.9, though not in the sense of city wall:

> I will be for her [Jerusalem]—oracle of Yahweh—
> a wall of fire roundabout [חומת אש סביב].

In 1QH 3.37, the worshiper praises Yahweh who has proved to be his 'strong wall', לחומת עוז. Yahweh is referred to as חומה in 1QS 8.7 and 1QH 7.8 as well.

In Egypt, the epithet 'wall' was used of both gods and kings.[60] The same thing occurs in Akkadian:[61] the personal name *Nabû-dūri* means 'the god Nabû is my wall'; *dūr makî šarru* means 'the king is the protecting wall of the weak'.

Weeping profusely and continuously, day and night (v. 18bc), expresses one's deep sorrow as well as one's own acknowledgment of sin (vv. 18bc, 19b).[62] Yahweh calls his people to repentance in Joel 2.12:

> שבו עדי בכל־לבבכם ובצום ובבכי ובמספד:

> Return to me wholeheartedly,
> with fasting, weeping and mourning.

Weeping in repentance is found also in Ezra 10.1; Neh. 1.4; and Mk 14.72.

The imperative קומי may be interpreted in two ways:[63] first, it could mean the physical act of getting up from a lying or sitting position. The translation would be 'arise'. In that case, the command shows that Jerusalem has been sitting on the ground, in mourning. Standing seems to have been the normal posture for prayer (cf. 1 Sam. 1.26; 1 Kgs 8.22; Mt. 6.5; Mk 11.25; Lk. 18.11).

Secondly, it could be used as a complement to the main verb to indicate an inceptive or ingressive action, 'start crying'. This understanding is supported by the temporal adverbial clause לראש אשמרות (lit. 'at the head of watches', i.e. 'at the beginning of every watch').

I prefer the second interpretation. All the mourners have been sitting

---

60. A. Alt, '*Hic murus aheneus esto*', *ZDMG* 86 (1932), pp. 33-48 (38-43).
61. See *CAD*, III, p. 194.
62. V. Hamp, 'בכה', *TDOT*, II, pp. 116-20 (119).
63. Dobbs-Allsopp, *Weep*, p. 35 n. 18.

on the ground, girded in sackcloth, with heads bowed. They are already in the posture which seems to characterize especially intense prayer, for example, Josh. 7.6; 1 Kgs 18.42; Ezra 10.1; Jdt. 9.1; Mk 14.35.[64]

The root רנן is used for cries of joy more often than for cries of distress (there are only two occurrences, as far as I know, i.e. in Ps. 17.1 and here). Jerusalem is to cry aloud, to make a public confession of her sins and needs. This loud cry for help is the counterpart of the enemies' cry of triumph in vv. 7c and 16bc. The night is divided into three watches (cf. Judg. 7.19; 1 Sam. 11.11). Jerusalem is to weep continuously, without ceasing (v. 18bc) and to cry out to the Lord even at night, with renewed effort at the beginning of each watch (cf. Ps. 63.7).

The speaker repeats his advice to weep profusely before the Lord (v. 19b), to show sincere repentance so as to gain Yahweh's attention (cf. Lam. 3.49-50). The imagery behind the clause שׁפכי כמים לבך, 'pour out like water your heart', is that of a heart broken from grief and turned to water which is then poured out in the form of tears.[65] The phrase שׁפך...לב occurs once more in Ps. 62.9 (NAB):

> Trust in him at all times, O my people!
> Pour out your hearts before him [שׁפכו־לפניו לבבכם];
> God is our refuge!

Jerusalem is asked to intercede for her children. The word עולליך, 'your children', recalls those weak and helpless little children who moved the speaker to tears in vv. 11-12. It may also refer generally to the inhabitants of Jerusalem. The hands are usually lifted up in prayer (cf. Pss. 28.2; 63.5; 134.2). Verse 19d is a gloss prompted probably by the association of עולליך of v. 19c with עולל of v. 11c.

The exhortation given in vv. 18-19 concentrates on praying earnestly to the Lord (vv. 18a, 19ac), with much weeping (vv. 18bc, 19b) in sincere repentance. It was Yahweh who destroyed the land, the cities and the people. 'Human help is worthless' (Ps. 60.13) since Jerusalem's wound is incurable (cf. Jer. 10.19; 14.17; 15.18; 30.12, 15). Only Yahweh can bring healing and restoration. The only course of action for Jerusalem now is to pray earnestly to Yahweh, to follow the decision spoken of in Hos. 6.1 (NAB):

---

64. C.W.F. Smith, 'Prayer', *IDB*, III, pp. 857-67 (866).
65. Collins, 'Physiology of Tears: Part 1', pp. 33-35.

לכו ונשובה אל־יהוה
כי הוא טרף וירפאנו יך ויחבשנו:

Come, let us return to the LORD,
For it is he who has rent, but he will heal us;
He has struck us, but he will bind our wounds.

The summons to weep and pray is characterized by alliteration with *t* in v. 18c, with *r* and *š* in v. 19a, and with *k* in v. 19b.

Jerusalem's Prayer (Verses 20-22)

Jerusalem follows the מנחם's advice and prays to Yahweh. She starts with a plea for Yahweh to take notice of her: ראה יהוה והביטה, 'Look, O Yahweh, and consider' (v. 20a). This same plea occurs in 1.11c. This is an implicit prayer for Yahweh to show compassion. The next colon למי עוללת כה, 'whom you have dealt with in this way!', seems to be voiced in a reproachful tone. It conveys two ideas. Jerusalem asks Yahweh to consider, to look at who she is (למי, 'whom'). Yahweh destroyed and killed like an enemy. But Jerusalem is no enemy. She is the elect of God (e.g. Deut. 7.7; Ps. 78.68). In the same clause Jerusalem asks Yahweh to consider, to look at what he did to her (כה, 'in this way').

Jerusalem proceeds to describe the atrocities that happened during the siege (v. 20b, mothers eating their own children, as predicted in the covenant curse in Deut. 28.53-57) and at the fall of the city, when the enemies invaded the temple and killed Yahweh's ministers right there, defiling the sanctuary with bloodshed (cf. Num. 35.33). The law states that anyone who defiles Yahweh's temple is punishable by death (cf. Lev. 15.31; 20.3). Priests are appointed by Yahweh to serve him (cf. Deut. 18.5) and prophets to speak his words to the people (cf. Deut. 18.18). Yet they were killed right in their place of service.

The two rhetorical questions in v. 20bc demand a negative answer, yet they describe events that actually took place. The questions express sufferings which are incomprehensible. The description of Jerusalem's bitterness is sharpened by the use of paronomasia. The root עלל, 'to act, deal, severely with', in עוללת (v. 20a) has the same consonants as the word for children in עללי טפחים, 'carefully reared children' (v. 20b). The wordplay reminds Yahweh that those toward whom he acted so harshly are Zion's children, that is, his own children.[66] In other words, Yahweh is responsible for the horrible cannibalism described in v. 20b:

66. Kaiser, 'Poet', p. 181.

אִם־תֹּאכַלְנָה נָשִׁים פִּרְיָם, 'ought women to have eaten their offspring?'
The *n* alliteration and *a* and *i* assonance seem to bring back the cruel
realities of the siege.

Jerusalem continues the description of her misery in v. 21. Her streets
are littered with unburied dead (cf. Jer. 16.6; 33.5; Ps. 79.2-3). Death is
rapacious, it took everyone: young and old, male and female (cf. Jer.
6.11; Ezek. 9.6). The sword (v. 21b) may be wielded by a human hand,
but the true killer is Yahweh. Yahweh is responsible for all these dead
(הָרַגְתָּ, 'you killed', and טָבַחְתָּ, 'you slaughtered'; note the opening
rhyme of these two verbs in the two cola of v. 21c). Jerusalem bursts
out into an 'accusation against God'. Her sufferings are beyond human
comprehension. How could Yahweh have done this to her?

The root טבח is used mainly for the killing of animals for a banquet:
Joseph orders an animal to be slaughtered for the meal he will share
with his brothers (Gen. 43.16); Nabal has meat 'slaughtered' for his
sheepshearers (1 Sam. 25.11). When טבח is used with human beings as
object, it refers to ruthless, massive killing. It is more expressive of a
bloody massacre than הרג.[67] The young men of Moab go down to
slaughter (Jer. 48.15); the people of Edom will be slaughtered for Yahweh's sacrifice in Bozrah (Isa. 34.5-6). The root טבח, 'to slaughter'
(v. 21c), sounds similar to טפח, 'to rear carefully' (vv. 20b, 22c). The
paronomasia brings together the agent responsible for the slaughter,
Yahweh and the victims of the slaughter, the children of Zion's careful
rearing.

The threefold repetition of לֹא חָמַל (vv. 2a, 17b, 21c) emphasizes the
great extent of the destruction brought on the land, the fortifications and
the people. Note the *a* assonance in v. 21c.

The 'accusation against God' continues in the next stanza. Although
the root טבח is limited in the MT to secular usage, the first line in v. 22
turns the slaughter in v. 21 into a sacrifice (cf. Isa. 34.6-7; Jer. 46.10;
Ezek. 39.17; Zeph. 1.7). The guests invited to this day of festival / religious assembly (יוֹם מוֹעֵד) are the 'terrors from round about', that is, the
enemy army, hunger under siege, pain and death, and the like. It was
Yahweh who invited those guests. Note the grim irony in the mention
of this sacrificial feast alongside the previous verses which state that
Yahweh rejected his temple and assembly place (v. 6a), brought feasts
and sabbaths to an end (v. 6b), rejected king and priest (v. 6c), rejected

---

67. V. Hamp, 'טבח', *TDOT*, V, pp. 283-87 (286).

his altar and sanctuary (v. 7a) where priests and prophets were killed (v. 20c).

The phrase כיום מועד in v. 22a echoes that in v. 7c: part of the 'terrors from round about' are the enemies who shouted in the temple. That יום מועד was actually the יום אף־יהוה, 'the day of Yahweh's wrath' (vv. 1c, 21c, 22b), the dominant theme of the poem. On that day, no one could escape the slaughter (cf. Jer. 50.29). This hyperbolic statement is not fully consistent with the presence of mourners in v. 10, and the children who are still alive in v. 19c. However, it is a feature of poetry and is meant to stress the magnitude of the disaster.

Besides the assonance in *i* and *î*, v. 22c has a *casus pendens* structure: אשר־טפחתי ורביתי איבי כלם, 'those whom I reared and raised, my enemy has consumed'. This structure emphasizes the object of כלה, 'has consumed', that is, the children whom Zion has carefully and lovingly brought up. In light of the context, where Yahweh has been accused of slaughtering without mercy (v. 21c) and of summoning the terrors from round about (v. 22a), the word איבי, 'my enemy', can only refer to Yahweh.[68] Lady Jerusalem as the grieving mother is fully aware that the real author who planned and carried out this terrible slaughter against her is Yahweh.

In summary, Jerusalem heeds the מנחם's advice and appeals to Yahweh to take notice of her. She pours out the bitterness of her heart. She describes the cannibalistic killing of the little children by their own mothers (v. 20b), the killing of priests and prophets—Yahweh's anointed—in his own sanctuary (v. 20c), the killing of young people in battle (v. 21b), the death of people of all age groups (v. 21a). She boldly accuses Yahweh of this massive massacre (v. 21c) which is grimly compared to the slaughter on a feast day (v. 22a). But this feast day is the day of Yahweh's wrath (v. 22b), and the human sacrifices are her own children (v. 22c). The mention of Yahweh's wrath is an indirect acknowledgment of sin, for Yahweh reacts in anger only when his people commit sin. Jerusalem recognizes her sins. However, her questions (v. 20bc) and her direct accusations (vv. 21c, 22a) seem to imply that she thinks her punishment was too severe. She still holds Yahweh responsible for her unbearable sufferings. Her bitterness is revealed through the indirect, low-keyed accusation: איבי כלם, 'my enemy has consumed'. Yahweh is referred to here in the third person, 'my enemy'.

Jerusalem does not voice any particular petition. Her prayer is a

68. Kaiser, 'Poet', p. 182.

vehement cry out of the agony and bitterness of her heart. The wonder is that Jerusalem can still cry out to Yahweh against him. Yahweh allows for this cry of accusation because he knows the depths of human suffering.

Conclusion

Lamentations 2 begins with daughter Zion cast on the ground by Yahweh's wrath (v. 1). It ends with the portrayal of daughter Zion bereaved of her children by Yahweh's wrath (v. 22b), and crying out to Yahweh from the depths of her incomprehensible sufferings.

At the mourning ceremony in Lamentations 2 (v. 10), in the aftermath of the fall of Jerusalem, the mourners are still deeply engrossed in the atrocious sufferings they have just undergone. Even the charred walls, the gates and the broken bars look like people in mourning. Scenes of killing and death are still fresh in their minds (vv. 4b, 12c, 21c). Yahweh is perceived as the enemy (כאויב in vv. 4a, 5a; כצר in v. 4b; איבי in v. 22c) relentlessly destroying pastures and fortifications (vv. 2-8), killing people of all strata and age groups (vv. 20b-21b). Some sufferings, like the derision of the enemy (vv. 15-16), are not over in a week or two. They may last for a long time, probably until Jerusalem is restored or the enemy is punished. Famine may still be raging after the fall, for Jerusalem is urged to pray for the lives of her children (v. 19c). The sufferings coming from Yahweh are so incomprehensible that, when Jerusalem prays, she can only cry out an accusation against Yahweh himself.

This complaint against God has a dimension of protest.[69] The protest lays out before God what the community of mourners cannot understand. How could Yahweh have inflicted such severe sufferings upon his people? I have noted that Jerusalem does not offer any petition. Actually, the petition is inherent in her protest. Yahweh will have to solve her problem. The prayer in vv. 20-22 is the bitter outcry of mourners who have no one else to turn to when their world is shattered, and who 'cling to God against God'.[70]

---

69. C. Westermann, *Praise and Lament in the Psalms* (Atlanta: John Knox Press, 1981), p. 270.

70. Westermann, *Praise*, p. 273.

Chapter 4

ISAIAH 51.9–52.2

The poem in Isa. 51.9–52.2 is part of the collection of chs. 40–55 in the book of Isaiah that is assigned to Second Isaiah by the vast majority of scholars today. The prophet Second Isaiah is assumed to have lived in Babylon and to have been active some time during the period between the destruction of Jerusalem in 587 BCE and the fall of the Babylonian empire in 539 BCE. His message is addressed to the exiled Jewish communities of the time, urging them to join him in a new exodus, out of Babylon, and back to the homeland, to Jerusalem, 'the holy city' (52.1). His speeches hail Cyrus as the shepherd who will carry out Yahweh's purpose (44.28) as Yahweh's anointed (45.1), who will build Yahweh's city and set his exiles free (45.13). Second Isaiah must have delivered these oracles some time after 550 BCE, when Cyrus, King of Persia, deposed his sovereign Astyages and incorporated Media into the Persian empire. Lydia, on the west frontier of Media, was conquered in 546 BCE. Cyrus continued to extend the borders of his territory until the entire Babylonian empire came under his sovereignty in 539 BCE.[1]

As with Lamentations 1 and 2, the translation of Isa. 51.9–52.2 is followed by critical notes. The mourning ceremony setting will be established for the poem before dealing with the problem of its delimitation in conjunction with the question of poetic structure and address. Finally, the exegesis will be given in light of the mourning ceremony setting and the conclusion will summarize the chapter's contributions to the appreciation of the poem's flow of thought and contextual meaning of terms.

---

1. R.J. Clifford, 'Second Isaiah', *ABD*, III, pp. 490-501 (492-93); C. Westermann, *Isaiah 40–66* (OTL; Philadelphia: Westminster Press, 1969), pp. 3-4.

Translation and Critical Notes

Like the two poems in Lamentations 1 and 2, this Isaian poem cites speeches without narrative introductions. I indicate my understanding of who is speaking in parentheses before the appropriate speeches. The speaker who responds to the first speech is clearly Yahweh, who introduces himself in 51.15. Another speaker addresses Jerusalem (51.17; 52.1) and proclaims Yahweh's word to her (51.22). He[2] is the prophet. The speaker of the lament in the very first stanza must then be dejected Jerusalem, who needs to hear the comforting words of Yahweh and the prophet.

(Jerusalem)

9   Awake, awake, put on strength,
        O arm of Yahweh!
    Awake as in the days of old,
        as in generations long past!
    Was it not you that [a]hacked up[a] Rahab,
        that pierced the dragon?

10   Was it not you that dried up the sea,
        the waters of the great deep?
    That made[a] the depths of the sea into a road
        for the redeemed to cross over?

11   [ab]'Those ransomed[b] by Yahweh will return,
        they will enter Zion with a joyful cry.
    Eternal joy will be upon their heads,
        gladness and joy will meet them,
        sorrow and sighing [c]will have fled.'[ca]

(Yahweh)

12   I, even I, am he who comforts you.[a]
        Who are you, [b]that you fear[b] human beings [c]who die,[c]
        mortals [d]who ought to be considered[d] as grass'?

---

2.   As in the other two poems, for the sake of clarity, I have assumed the voice to be that of a male prophet, so as to avoid confusion with Jerusalem personified as a female mourner.

13   [Who are you,] ^athat you forget^a Yahweh your maker,
    who stretched out the heavens,
    who laid the foundations of the earth,
  ^aThat you dread^a continually, all day long,
    the fury of the oppressor?
  But though he has planned to destroy,
    of what account now is the oppressor's fury?

14   ^aThose stooping down^a will soon be released:
    ^bthey will not die, going down to the pit,^b
    nor will they lack bread.^c

15   For I am Yahweh your God,
    who ^astirred up^a the sea, so that its waves roared,^b
    whose name is Yahweh of hosts.

16   I have put my words in your mouth,
    and in the shadow of my hand covered you,
  I ^bwho ^astretched out^{ab} the heavens,
    ^bwho laid the foundations^b of the earth,
    ^bwho said^b to Zion: 'You are my people!'

(Prophet)
17   Rouse yourself, rouse yourself,
    get up, O Jerusalem!
  You who have drunk from Yahweh's hand
    the cup of his wrath,
  Who have drunk and drained
    the chalice, the cup^a ^bthat causes staggering!^b

18   There is no ^aone to lead^a you
    from all the children ^byou bore;^b
  No one to take your hand
    from all the children ^byou raised^b.

19   Two things have happened to you:
    who can grieve with you?
  Devastation and destruction, famine and the sword—
    who ^acan comfort^a you?

20   Your children lay unconscious,
         at the corner of every street,
         like antelopes in a net,
      Filled with the wrath of Yahweh,
         with the blast of your God.

21   Therefore, listen to this, O afflicted one,
         drunk[a] but not with wine.

22   Thus says your Lord Yahweh,
         your God who contends for his people:
      'Look, I have taken from your hand
         the cup that causes staggering,
      The chalice, the cup of my wrath,
         you will no longer drink.

23   I will put it into the hand of your tormentors
         who said to you:
         'Bow down that we might walk over!'
      So you made your back like the ground,
         like the street for them to walk on.'

(Prophet)
52.1 Awake, awake,
         put on your strength, O Zion!
      Put on your glorious garments,
         O Jerusalem, holy city!
      For there will no longer enter you
         the uncircumcised or the unclean.

52.2 Shake the dirt off yourself, get up,
         [a]sit enthroned,[a] O Jerusalem!
      Cast[b] [c]the fetters[c] off your neck,
         O captive daughter Zion!

9 [a-a]The MT root חצב, 'to hew, cleave, hack up', is used commonly for quarrying stones (e.g. 1 Chron. 22.2; Isa. 22.16). *BHS* suggests reading with 1QIsa^a המחצת, 'the one smiting, wounding severely' (cf. Job 26.12). E.Y. Kutscher (*The Language and Linguistic Background of the Isaiah Scroll (1QIsa^a)* [STDJ, 6; Leiden: E.J. Brill, 1974], pp. 33, 255) notes that both roots חצב and מחץ occur in parallel three times in Ugaritic, but that חצב to denote 'kill/slay' is less common in Hebrew (only here and probably Hos. 6.5, compared to 14 occurrences of מחץ) and therefore is more likely to be original. The omission of v. 9c in LXX is probably due to *homoioarcton*. Aq, Sym and Theod. support MT by reading the aorist participle of λατομέω, 'to quarry, hew out'. The Syr root *psq* is used to translate both חצב and מחץ (cf. Ps. 110.6; Isa. 10.15).

10 [a]The MT accentuation suggests taking the article as the relative pronoun with qal perfect, third person feminine singular, but the context requires a qal participle, with accent on the last syllable, as read by LXX ἡ θεῖσα (GKC, §138k; *GHB*, §145e).

11 [a-a]This is an implicit quotation from 35.10. See exegesis, pp. 168-70.

[b-b]1QIsa^a reads ופזורי, 'and the scattered ones of'. Kutscher (*Isaiah Scroll*, p. 275) notes that the scribe of 1QIsa^a first wrote פדוי, 'the ransomed ones of', as in MT and then erased it. LXX and Theod. read the perfect participle of λυτρόω, 'to redeem'. Syr *prÿqwhy*, 'the ransomed of', and Vg *redempti*, 'redeemed', also support MT.

[c-c]*BHS* suggests reading with many Hebrew MSS, Syr and 35.10 ונסו, 'will flee' (*weqataltí = yiqtol*, *GHB*, §119c). The ו at the end of ישׂיגון may be a misplaced ו due to a problem of word division. MT נסו is also defensible as a future perfect, 'will have fled' (*GHB*, §112i; D. Dempsey, 'The Verb Syntax of Second Isaiah and Deuteronomy Compared' [PhD dissertation, Washington, The Catholic University of America [1988], p. 185). 1QIsa^a ונס and Tg ויסוף have ו, but the verb is singular. LXX and Vg have no copulative. I read MT.

12 [a]The addressee is identified as second person masculine plural in מנחמכם (v. 12a), second person feminine singular in את ותיראי (v. 12b), and second person masculine singular in ותשׁכח and ותפחד (v. 13), and the four ך suffixes (vv. 13, 15, 16). *BHS* suggests correcting to second person masculine singular throughout. The text could be corrected just as easily to second person feminine singular address: מנחמך (v. 12a, dittography of מ); ותשׁכחי (v. 13a, haplography of י); ותפחדי (v. 13b); and the four ך suffixes could be repointed as feminine singular suffixes (Dempsey, 'Verb Syntax', pp. 185-86). The shifting singular/ plural and masculine/feminine address of MT may be justified on the basis that the addressee Jerusalem/Zion (fem.) represents the national community, the people (masculine sing./plur.; cf. עמי־אתה, v. 16b).

[b-b]The *wayyiqtol*, ותירא, 'that you fear', expresses a logical consequence in the stative present of the preceding nominal clause (GKC, §111m; *GHB*, §118h, n. 1).

[c-c]The asyndetic verbal clause ימות, 'who dies', expresses the timeless present of truths of experience and functions as an attributive adjective.

d-dThe *yiqtol*, יִנָּתֵן, represents the timeless present of truths of experience, with a modal nuance, 'who ought to be given, considered' (*GHB*, §113c, m).

13 a-aThe *wayyiqtol*s, וַתִּשְׁכַּח, 'that you forget', and וַתְּפַחֵד, 'that you dread', function in much the same way as וַתִּירָא in v. 12b. They introduce consecutive clauses in the stative present after the implied nominal interrogative clause מִי־אַתְּ, 'who are you?'

14 a-aThis is the inclusive plural. MT צֹעֶה, 'the one stooping down', is singular.
b-bLit. 'he will not die to the pit'. This is a pregnant construction with לְ (GKC, §119ee, gg).
cBHS suggests reading לֵחוֹ or לֵחָמוֹ, 'his freshness, vigor', for MT לַחְמוֹ, 'his bread'. Cf. Deut. 34.7 וְלֹא־נָס לֵחֹה, 'and his vigor had not abated'. Theod., Syr and Vg support MT. Both readings make sense. There is no need to emend MT.

15 a-a BHS suggests גְּעַר, 'rebuke', for MT רֹגַע, 'stir up'. The root רגע is also used with הַיָּם, 'the sea', in Jer. 31.35 and Job 26.12. I read MT.
bוַיֶּהֱמוּ, a *wayyiqtol* past tense, determines the tense of the participle רֹגַע, despite *GHB*, §118r (Ferrie, *Meteorological Imagery*, pp. 165, 198). See exegesis (p. 179 n. 32).

16 a-aRead לִנְטֹת, 'to stretch out' (cf. v. 13 נֹטֶה שָׁמַיִם and Syr *mth* in both vv. 13 and 16).
b-bThe three infinitive constructs לִנְטֹעַ (emended to לִנְטֹת 'who stretched out'), וְלִיסֹד, 'who laid the foundations', and וְלֵאמֹר, 'who said', function as attributive relative clauses, like רֹגַע in v. 15 (*GHB*, §124p; GKB II, §11p). Dempsey ('Verb Syntax', p. 192) points to a comparable case in Ps. 104.10-15 where a series of three attributive participles functioning as relative clauses is continued by two infinitive constructs: הַמְשַׁלֵּחַ, 'who sends forth' (v. 10); מַשְׁקֶה, 'who waters' (v. 13); מַצְמִיחַ, 'who makes sprout' (v. 14); לְהוֹצִיא, 'who makes grow' (v. 14); and לְהַצְהִיל, 'who makes shine' (v. 15).

17 a BHS proposes to delete the word כּוֹס, 'cup', in both vv. 17c and 22c, because it is missing in either Sym or LXX and Syr. This proposal overlooks the chiastic structure in these verses. See below, p. 160.
b-bThe noun תַּרְעֵלָה functions as a genitive of purpose, 'that causes staggering' (GKC, §128q).

18 a-aLXX παρακαλῶν and Syr *mby'*, both meaning 'one who comforts', probably misread MT מְנַהֵל, 'one who leads', as מְנַחֵם.
b-bHebrew allows the use of the third person (גִּדְּלָה, בְּיָדָהּ, יִלָּדָה, לָהּ) in a relative clause instead of the expected second person (*GHB*, §158n; Brockelmann, *Syntax*, pp. 149, 153).

19 a-aRead the third person singular יְנַחֲמֵךְ with 1QIsaa and LXX, Vg and Syr.

21   [a]The word שכרת may be a case of a noun with an old feminine ending, in order to avoid the hiatus הָ ו, rather than a construct state (GKC, §130b).

52.2   [a-a]Read שְׁבִי from ישׁב, 'sit', with 1QIsa[a] and LXX, Vg and Syr. Many Hebrew MSS omit *dagesh* to allow for the meaning 'captivity'. *BHS* suggests שְׁביה, 'captive', as in v. 2b.

[b]Read *qere*, התפתחי, imperative feminine singular with LXX, Aq, Sym, Theod., Syr and Vg. The following pronoun in צואָרֵך, 'your neck', is feminine singular.

[c-c]There is no need to add the preposition מִן, 'from', as suggested by *BHS*, since the hithpael in this case indicates an action performed 'with regard to, for' oneself, and can take an accusative (GKC, §54f).

The Mourning Ceremony Setting

The principal characters in a mourning ceremony and the mourning rites described in Chapter 1 above are readily identified in the Zion poem in Isa. 51.9–52.2.

The Chief Mourner

The bereaved at this mourning ceremony is Lady Jerusalem, just as in Lamentations 1 and 2. She can be recognized as such for at the end of the Isaian passage (52.1-2), she is told to end her mourning and to take her seat on the throne:

לבשי בגדי תפארתך ירושלם עיר הקדש
התנערי מעפר קומי שבי ירושלם

> Put on your glorious garments,
>   O Jerusalem, holy city!...
> Shake the dirt off yourself, get up,
>   sit enthroned, O Jerusalem! (52.1b, 2a)

The fact that Jerusalem is told to shake the dirt off herself, to get up and to put on her glorious clothes shows that she has been mourning, seated on the ground, girded in sackcloth, with dirt strewn on her head. Lady Jerusalem mourns the loss of her children (51.18) who either died during the siege (51.20) or were taken into exile (51.14; 52.2b).

That the text of Isa. 52.1-2 was read as above in antiquity is indicated by Bar. 4.20 and 5.1. In the course of mourning her exiled children, Jerusalem says in Bar. 4.20:

> I have taken off the garment of peace [τὴν στολὴν τῆς εἰρήνης],
>   have put on sackcloth for my prayer of supplication
> [σάκκον τῆς δεήσεώς μου].

In Bar. 5.1, the Lord assures Jerusalem that her exiled children will return and tells her:

> Jerusalem, take off your robe of mourning and misery [τὴν στολὴν τοῦ πένθους καὶ τῆς κακώσεώς σου];
>> put on the splendor of glory from God [τὴν εὐπρέπειαν τῆς παρὰ τοῦ θεοῦ δόξης] forever.

This ritual ending of the mourning ceremony recalls the end of mourning of El for Baal in *Poems about Baal and Anath*, and the end of the period of supplication of Danil for a child in *The Tale of Aqhat*: both El and Danil laughed, put their feet on a stool, and shouted, 'I now take my seat and rest'.[3]

These verses in Isa. 52.1-2 form a striking contrast with 47.1-2 where Lady Babylon is told to begin her mourning:

רדי ושבי על־עפר בתולת בת־בבל
שבי־לערץ אין־כסא בת־כשדים
כי לא תוסיפי יקראו־לך רכה וענגה׃
קחי רחים וטחני קמח גלי צמתך
חשפי־שבל גלי־שוק עברי נהרות׃

Come down and sit on the dirt,
  virgin daughter Babylon!
Sit on the ground without a throne,
  daughter Chaldea!
For no longer shall you be called
  tender and delicate.
Take the millstones and grind meal,
  remove your veil,
Strip off your robe, uncover your legs,
  pass through the rivers.

A passage in Ezek. 26.16-17a describes the ritual beginning of a mourning ceremony in similar terms: the maritime partners of Tyre step down from their thrones, remove their embroidered robes and sit on the ground. They keep a moment of silence before they intone a lament over Tyre.

The moment of silence is not mentioned in this Isaian passage. It may be presumed to have been kept before Lady Jerusalem addresses her prayer lament to 'the arm of Yahweh'. The significant difference between the laments in Lamentations 1 and 2 and this lament is the

---

3. See Chapter 1.

absence of a contrast motif between Jerusalem's glorious past and her present sorry state in the latter. The contrast is drawn instead between Yahweh's apparent present inactivity and his mighty workings in the past (51.9-10).

The Comforter

With regard to the indispensable role of the מנחם, 'comforter', at mourning ceremonies, there seems to be a progression from the apparent absence of the comforter in Lamentations 1 to his tentative presence in Lamentations 2, to his affirmative presence in Isa. 51.9–52.2. Indeed, both the bereaved Jerusalem and the second voice bewail the need and the lack of a comforter in the first poem: אין־לה מנחם, 'she has no one to comfort her' (Lam. 1.2, 9, 17); רחק ממני מנחם, 'far from me is any comforter' (1.16); אין מנחם לי, 'I have no one to comfort me' (1.21). In Lamentations 2, the poet sincerely desires to comfort daughter Zion, but does not think himself up to the task:

מה־אעידך מה אדמה־לך הבת ירושלם
מה אשוה־לך ואנחמך בתולת בת־ציון

> What can I say to you, to what can I compare you,
>   O daughter Jerusalem?
> To what can I liken you, that I may comfort you,
>   O virgin daughter Zion? (2.13ab)

In the Isaian poem, Yahweh introduces himself to Jerusalem as her comforter:

אנכי אנכי הוא מנחמכם

> I, even I, am he who comforts you (51.12a)

When Yahweh assumes the task of comforting, he does it effectively, for he is the creator of heaven and earth. He has the power to set the prisoners free (Isa. 51.14), and to render justice by punishing Jerusalem's oppressors (51.23), which is what she asked for directly in Lam. 1.21-22, and indirectly in Lam. 2.20-22. Yahweh also protects his people (51.16). Yahweh's comfort brings about the positive result of ending the mourning process (Isa. 52.1-2).

The Chief Lamentation Singer

The prophet is the chief lamentation singer who conveys Yahweh's message to Jerusalem, sometimes verbatim, sometimes in his own words. His address to Jerusalem vividly describes the tremendous sufferings she went through and her present sad and lonely state (51.17-20). Her unbearable pains defy any human comfort (v. 19). His lament ends, however, on a hopeful note: he delivers the promise of salvation from Yahweh (vv. 22-23) and Yahweh's command to terminate the mourning ceremony (52.1-2).

The presence of the chief mourner (bereaved Jerusalem seated on the ground in mourning garb), of Yahweh the comforter, and of the prophet as the chief lamentation singer, points to the mourning ceremony as the literary setting of this Isaian poem. Further, the roots נוד, 'to grieve, console', and נחם (piel), 'to comfort', in 51.19 often appear in contexts of mourning (e.g. Job 2.11; 42.11; Jer. 16.5, 7).

Poetic Structure and Address

The pattern of the mourning ceremony in Isa. 51.9–52.2 helps to define the limits of the poem and enables a proper understanding of its sub-units and their interrelationships.

This section will deal with the delimitation of the poem in conjunction with the question of structure and the identification of speakers and addressee.

Poetic Structure
Delimitation of the Unit.

1. *Stylistic features.* Verses 51.9 and 52.1 begin with almost exactly the same words: עורי עורי לבשי־עז (עורי עורי לבשי עזך in 52.1) which serve to mark off the first and the final stanzas of the poem. The final stanza is in turn defined by a pattern of *inclusio* with ציון at the end of vv. 1a and 2b, and by the chiastic occurrence of the vocatives ציון (1a)::ירושלם (1b)::ירושלם (2a)::ציון (2b).

The verses making up 51.9–52.2 are further bound together by the repetition of important words and phrases throughout the unit. The root עור, 'awake', occurs at the beginning of 51.9, 17, and 52.1, setting off a new stanza each time. The root לבש, 'to put on, clothe oneself', in v. 9a is repeated in 52.1ab. The word ים, 'sea' (v. 10a) is repeated in vv. 10b and 15a. The root שום, 'to make, place, put', is used four times with a different object each time (v. 10b, 'a road'; v. 16a, 'my words'; v. 23a, 'the cup that causes staggering'; v. 23c, 'your back'). The verb עבר, 'to cross, pass over', occurs three times with two different subjects: 'the redeemed' (v. 10b) and 'the tormentors' (v. 23bc). The phrase בא ציון, 'enter Zion', occurs in v. 11a and 52.1c (בך for ציון). The word ראש,

'head', occurs in vv. 11b and 20a. The root נחם (piel), 'to comfort', is used in vv. 12a and 19b. The noun חמה, 'fury, rage', occurs in vv. 13c (twice), 17b, 20b, 22c. The root פתח, 'to open, release', in v. 14 occurs again in 52.2b. The root קום, 'to get up', is used twice as a command addressed to Jerusalem (v. 17a; 52.2a). The negative verb לא יסף in v. 22c is repeated in 52.1c.

These repetitions show the close interrelationship between the verses of 51.9–52.2 and validate my thesis that 51.9 is the beginning and 52.2 the end of the poem.

2. *Consistent imagery.* Jerusalem (51.17; 52.1b, 2a) is also called Zion interchangeably (51.11, 16; 52.1a, 2b), and is personified as a woman bereaved of children (51.18, 20) who has been sitting on the ground (52.2a), apparently in a mourning garment, for she is commanded to end her mourning and to put on her glorious clothes (52.1b).

Jerusalem / Zion represents not only the buildings (temple, palaces, houses, and the like) that suffered destruction, but also the inhabitants who died from famine and the sword (51.19b), and those who were taken captive to the land of their oppressors (51.14; 52.2b, 'captive daughter Zion').

At the beginning of the poem, the bereaved Zion cries out to 'the arm of Yahweh' and reminisces about Yahweh's mighty acts in creation and in the exodus from Egypt. She receives consolation from Yahweh her comforter and from the prophet who proclaims Yahweh's promise of salvation to her.

3. *Unity of the Zion poem.* R.J. Clifford recognizes the unity of 51.9–52.2, but ends the passage at 52.12, saying that Zion's chief suffering had been the lack of her children (51.18-20) and that Zion could be comforted only with the restoration of her children (52.1-2, 7-10).[4]

C. Westermann includes 52.3 (but without the prophetic formula כה אמר יהוה, 'Thus says Yahweh'), which would supply 52.2 with a כי clause corresponding to 52.1c.[5] However, the stanza 52.1-2 is addressed to Zion / Jerusalem in the second person feminine singular throughout, while the addressee in v. 3 is second person masculine plural. It thus seems more appropriate to leave v. 3 with the unit 52.3-6, which is neatly composed of three pairs of statements: in the first, each is

4.   Clifford, *Fair Spoken*, p. 170.
5.   Westermann, *Isaiah 40–66*, p. 247.

introduced by 'for thus says Yahweh', כי כה אמר יהוה (vv. 3, 4); in the second, each includes נאם־יהוה, 'oracle of Yahweh' (v. 5); and in the third, each begins with לכן, 'therefore' (v. 6).[6]

Both suggestions by Clifford and Westermann add extra pictures of redemption, joy and gladness, and a triumphant processional return to Zion, which are all related to the divine answer to the prayer lament of Jerusalem in 51.9-11. Nevertheless, both the stylistic features and the unifying imagery of mourning call for ending the poem at 52.2.

J. Alec Motyer takes 51.1–52.12 as a whole made up of three parts: 51.1-8; 51.9-16; and 51.17–52.12.[7] It is true that there are important vocabulary connections between the Zion poem in 51.9–52.2 and the preceding (51.1-8) and following verses (52.3-12). The root חצב, 'to hew', in 51.1 occurs again in 51.9. The phrase ששׂון ושׂמחה, 'joy and rejoicing', in 51.3 recurs in 51.11. The themes of comfort (piel of נחם 51.3, 12, 19 and 52.9) and redemption (root גאל in 51.10; 52.3, 9) run through the whole section. The anthropomorphic imagery of 'the arm of Yahweh' is used throughout (51.5, 9; 52.10). However, the particular stylistic features and the mourning imagery in 51.9–52.2 set this passage off as a poem in its own right.

Other commentators, however, distinguish two poems: 51.1-16 and 51.17–52.12.[8] This division does not account for the mourning ceremony evidenced by the command to end the mourning process at 52.1-2 and the interplay of words and themes that bind the verses in 51.9–52.2 into a distinct poem.

Division into Sub-Units or Stanzas. The Zion poem in 51.9–52.2 is composed of four clearly delimited stanzas:

(1) a prayer lament (51.9-11)
(2) the divine comfort (51.12-16)

---

6. J.A. Motyer, *The Prophecy of Isaiah* (Downers Grove, IL: InterVarsity Press, 1993), p. 417.

7. Motyer, *Prophecy*, pp. 402-22.

8. E.g. C.C. Torrey, *The Second Isaiah: A New Interpretation* (New York: Charles Scribner's Sons, 1928), pp. 394-409; J. Muilenberg, 'The Book of Isaiah, Chapters 40–66', *IB*, V, pp. 381-773 (588-613); J.K. Kuntz, 'The Contribution of Rhetorical Criticism to Understanding Isaiah 51.1-16', in D.J.A. Clines, D.M. Gunn and A.J. Hauser (eds.), *Art and Meaning: Rhetoric in Biblical Literature* (JSOTSup, 19; Sheffield: JSOT Press, 1982), pp. 140-71.

(3)   the prophet's comfort (51.17-23)

(4)   end of Zion's mourning (52.1-2)

The first, the third and the fourth stanzas each begin with the double imperative of עור, while the second begins with the double assertion אנכי אנכי (51.12).

1. *First stanza: A prayer lament (51.9-11).* The first stanza is characterized by an *inclusio* based on יהוה (v. 9a) and עולמים (v. 9b) and יהוה (v. 11a) and עולם (v. 11b).

a. Invocation: Appeal to 'the arm of Yahweh' (v. 9ab). The first two lines of v. 9 begin with the imperative call עורי, 'awake', which is repeated twice in v. 9a.

b. Lament proper: Recollecting the past (vv. 9c-10). All three lines in this section start with הֲ, הֲ and הַ, the first two being the interrogative particle, the last one, a definite article.

c. Petition: Mourning turned to joy (v. 11). Verse 11b ends with an *a:b::b':a'* chiastic pattern of subjects and verbs ששׂון ושׂמחה::יגון ואנחה ישׂיגון::נסו, 'gladness and joy: will meet [them]::will have fled: sorrow and sighing'.

2. *Second Stanza: The divine comfort (vv. 12-16).*

(a)   Assurance and reproof (vv. 12-13)

(b)   Promise of salvation (v. 14)

(c)   Assurance and affirmation (vv. 15-16)

The whole stanza is marked off by the *inclusio* based on נוטה שׁמים ויסד ארץ in v. 13 and לנטת שׁמים וליסד ארץ (emended) in v. 16.

3. *Third Stanza: The prophet's comfort (vv. 17-23).*

(a)   First command to get up (v. 17a)

(b)   The reasons for Zion's mourning (vv. 17b-20)
        Yahweh's cup of wrath (v. 17bc)
        Loss of children (vv. 18-20)

(c)   Punishment of Zion's oppressors (vv. 21-23)

An *a:b::b:a* chiastic pattern holds the verses in this stanza together: כוס חמתו:כוס התרעלה::כוס התרעלה:כוס חמתי, 'the cup of his wrath: the cup that causes staggering::the cup that causes staggering: the cup of my wrath'.

4. *Fourth Stanza: End of Zion's mourning (52.1-2).*

   (i)   Command to change garments (v. 1)

   (ii)   Second command to get up (v. 2)

Besides the chiastic pattern in the names of Zion and Jerusalem, ציון:ירושלם::ירושלם:ציון, this final stanza rounds off the poem by returning to the image of awaking and getting ready for the new task. Whereas the first stanza stresses the act of awaking with the triple repetition of the imperative עורי, 'awake' (v. 9ab), the last stanza gives equal emphasis to the acts of awaking and putting on new clothes. Both imperatives, עורי and לבשי, are used twice in 52.1ab.

Address

First Stanza: A Prayer Lament (Verses 9-11). This prayer lament is addressed to זרוע יהוה, 'the arm of Yahweh', which stands for Yahweh himself,[9] since Yahweh responds in the next stanza (vv. 12-16). The speaker of the first stanza is not readily identified. The prayer appeals to Yahweh to 'awake and put on strength', as he did in the past, then recalls Yahweh's mighty deeds at creation and at the exodus, and finally cites Yahweh's earlier oracle in 35.10 so as to urge Yahweh to fulfill his promise to bring the exiles back to Zion. Therefore, we may conclude that this prayer was offered by Jerusalem / Zion, representing the Jewish exiled community.

Second Stanza: The Divine Comfort (Verses 12-16). The speaker of this stanza introduces himself as 'Yahweh your God' (v. 15). Yahweh's reply to the prayer lament begins with the double reassuring assertion, אנכי אנכי, 'I, even I' (v. 12a). Yahweh offers to become Zion's comforter. His reply is framed by the question–answer form מי־את (v. 12b) and עמי־אתה (v. 16b), and by the double clause stressing the creative activity of Yahweh: נוטה שמים ויסד ארץ, 'who stretched out the heavens and laid the foundations of the earth' (v. 13ab), and לנטע שמים וליסד ארץ (v. 16b; see p. 153 above). The addressee is someone being oppressed and fearful of the oppressor (vv. 12b, 13bc). The oppressed in this context are the captives, the exiles, who are promised deliverance in the very near future (v. 14). Zion is addressed as שביה בת־ציון, 'captive daughter Zion', in 52.2b. It follows that the feminine address in

9.   Cf. Isa. 51.5; J.D. Smart, *History and Theology in Second Isaiah: A Commentary on Isaiah 35, 40–66* (Philadelphia: Westminster Press, 1965), p. 182.

מִי־אַתְּ וַתִּירְאִי, 'who are you that you fear?', refers to Zion. At the end of Yahweh's speech, Zion is addressed as second masculine singular in agreement with עַם, 'people' (וַלֵּאמֹר לְצִיּוֹן עַמִּי־אָתָּה, 'who said to Zion: You are my people!', v. 16b). I have already drawn attention to the fact that Zion / Jerusalem represents the city of God as well as the people of God. This explains the apparent confusion in the address, which switches from masculine plural (מְנַחֶמְכֶם, v. 12a) to feminine singular (אַתְּ וַתִּירְאִי, v. 12b) to masculine singular (וַתִּשְׁכַּח, v. 13a; וַתְּפַחֵד, v. 13b; and the four ךְ suffixes in vv. 13a, 15a, 16a). In summary, the addressee in Yahweh's speech is Zion (Jerusalem), who utters the lament prayer to Yahweh in the first stanza.

Third Stanza: The Prophet's Comfort (Verses 17-23). The third stanza begins with the double hithpolel imperative of עוּר and is clearly addressed to Jerusalem (v. 17a). The speaker not only knows what sufferings Jerusalem is going through (vv. 18-20), but also why all these calamities have come upon her (v. 17). He sympathizes with her (v. 19). He mentions Yahweh in the third person (vv. 17b, 20b, 22a). He proclaims Yahweh's word to Jerusalem (vv. 22-23). He speaks for Yahweh. Hence, he is the prophet who comforts Zion by announcing the good news of Yahweh's coming deliverance.

Fourth Stanza: End of Zion's Mourning (52.1-2). The fourth and final stanza of the poem also begins with the double imperative of עוּר and is addressed to Zion (Jerusalem). The speaker could be Yahweh continuing his speech from v. 22b and now commanding Zion to end her mourning. Most probably, however, it is the prophet who speaks and gives orders on behalf of Yahweh.

Exegesis

First Stanza: Zion's Prayer Lament (Verses 9-11)
It may be reasonably presumed that the moment of silence in the mourning context—the silence of consternation, dismay and confusion—is over, and Zion now utters a prayer lament to Yahweh. According to Westermann,[10] the basic structural components of the lament are: invocation, lament, petition. In this lament prayer of Zion, the invocation is the call on the 'arm of Yahweh' to 'awake and put on

---

10. Westermann, *Praise*, p. 170.

strength' (v. 9ab). The lament proper (vv. 9c-10), by recollecting Yah-weh's mighty deeds at creation, and especially at the exodus, makes an implied contrast between Yahweh's working in the past and his present non-intervention. The petition (v. 11) is veiled under a quotation of Yahweh's former promise in Isa. 35.10.

Invocation: Appeal to 'the Arm of Yahweh' (Verse 9ab). The double imperative עורי עורי, 'awake, awake', denotes the urgency of the times and the restlessness of Zion, the chief mourner. She has been suffering too much and for too long. She has waited and waited for Yahweh's deliverance. Now she calls on the 'arm of Yahweh' to intervene, to act on her behalf. It seems as if Yahweh has forgotten his people.

ותאמר ציון עזבני יהוה ואדני שכחני:

> But Zion said: 'Yahweh has forsaken me;
> my Lord has forgotten me' (Isa. 49.14).

Calling on the 'arm of Yahweh' to awake sounds less irreverent than calling on Yahweh himself. By contrast, the psalmist puts matters very bluntly in Ps. 44.24-25 (NAB):

עורה למה תישן אדני הקיצה אל־תזנח לנצח:
למה־פניך תסתיר תשכח ענינו ולחצנו:

> Awake! Why are you asleep, O Lord?
> Arise! Cast us not off forever!
> Why do you hide your face,
> forgetting our woe and our oppression?

It must be noted that the sleep imagery, inherent in the call to awake used here as an appeal to Yahweh for his help, does not allude in any way to the Canaanite nature cult of the dying and rising fertility god Baal (cf. 1 Kgs 18.27).[11]

הנה לא־ינום ולא יישן שומר ישראל:

> Indeed he neither slumbers nor sleeps,
> the guardian of Israel (Ps. 121.4; NAB)

Zion knows full well that her God does not sleep, yet she is so over-whelmed by the intensity of her sufferings that the reality of Yahweh's care and protection is momentarily blurred.

The parallelism in Isa. 51.5b makes clear that the 'arm of Yahweh' is no other than Yahweh himself:

11. H.-J. Kraus, *Psalms 1–59* (Minneapolis: Augsburg, 1988), p. 171.

אלי איים יקוו ואל־זרעי ייחלון׃

In me shall the coastlands hope,
and my arm they shall await (NAB).

The 'arm' of Yahweh is an exodus motif (e.g. Exod. 6.6; 15.16; Deut. 4.34; 5.15; Ps. 136.12) as well as a creation motif (e.g. Jer. 27.5; 32.17). It connotes might (e.g. Exod. 15.16), kingship (Isa. 40.10; 51.5; Ezek. 20.33), victory (e.g. Isa. 59.16; 63.5). It evokes the image of Yahweh the victorious warrior (e.g. Isa. 42.13).

The 'arm of Yahweh', that is, Yahweh, is urged to 'put on strength', a strength that is already an attribute of Yahweh himself:

יהוה בעזך ישמח־מלך ובישועתך מה־יגיל מאד׃

O Yahweh, in your strength the king rejoices;
in your victory how greatly he exults! (Ps. 21.2)

רומה יהוה בעזך נשירה ונזמרה גבורתך׃

Be exalted, O Yahweh, in your strength!
We will sing and praise your might (Ps. 21.14).

מצאתי דוד עבדי בשמן קדשי משחתיו׃
אשר ידי תכון עמו אף־זרועי תאמצנו׃

I have found my servant David;
    with my holy oil I have anointed him;
My hand shall always remain with him;
    my arm also shall strengthen him (Ps. 89.21-22; NRSV).

Strength is inherent in the arm of Yahweh. Therefore, calling on the arm of Yahweh 'to put on strength' has the sense of beseeching Yahweh to reveal his intrinsic strength through action, as the following verse shows:

חשׂף יהוה את־זרוע קדשו לעיני כל־הגוים
וראו כל־אפסי־ארץ את ישועת אלהינו׃

Yahweh has bared his holy arm
    before the eyes of all the nations;
And all the ends of the earth shall see
    the salvation of our God (Isa. 52.10).

Yahweh 'has bared his holy arm', that is, he has rolled up his sleeves for action, and has accomplished salvation for all people to see.

The repetition of עורי at the beginning of v. 9b, followed by the recollection of Yahweh's mighty deeds in the past, adds urgency to Zion's appeal and makes clear Zion's intention in calling upon Yahweh to awake: Zion implores Yahweh to come to her rescue by acting mightily against her oppressors. Her wish may be expressed through the words of the psalmist:

עורה לקראתי וראה:
ואתה יהוה־אלהים צבאות אלהי ישראל
הקיצה לפקד כל־הגוים אל־תחן כל־בגדי   און סלה:

Awake, come to my help and see!
You are Yahweh, God of hosts, the God of Israel.
Arise to punish all the nations,
Have no pity on any of those who treacherously plot evil.   Selah
(Ps. 59.5b, 6).

When the expression כימי קדם, 'as in the days of old', refers to the time of the beginning, the time of creation, it is usually connected with the primordial battle,[12] for example, Ps. 74.12-13:

ואלהים מלכי מקדם פעל ישועות בקרב הארץ:
אתה פוררת בעוזך ים שברת ראשי תנינים על־המים:

Yet, O God, my king from of old,
    working saving deeds on earth,
You divided the sea by your might,
    you smashed the heads of the dragons in the waters.

The expression can also refer to historical time, such as at the making of the covenant,[13] for example, Mic. 7.20:

תתן אמת ליעקב חסד לאברהם
אשר־נשבעת לאבתינו מימי קדם:

You will show faithfulness to Jacob,
    and covenant loyalty to Abraham,
As you have sworn to our fathers
    from days of old.

The phrase עורי כימי קדם, 'awake as in the days of old', implies a contrast between Yahweh's apparent sleepy state and his past state of vigilance and activity. In the mourning lament there is always a longing for the glorious, beautiful past (e.g. 2 Sam. 1.19-27; Lam. 1.1).

---

12. M.K. Wakeman, *God's Battle with the Monster* (Leiden: E.J. Brill, 1973), p. 59 n. 3.
13. Wakeman, *God's Battle*.

Lament: Recollecting Yahweh's Mighty Deeds (Verses 9c-10). The longing for the past leads to the recollection of Yahweh's mighty deeds at the primeval creation and at the exodus from Egypt.

הלוא את־היא המחצבת רהב מחוללת תנין׃
הלוא את־היא המחרבת ים מי תהום רבה
השׂמה מעמקי־ים דרך לעבר גאולים׃

> Was it not you that hacked up Rahab,
>   that pierced the dragon?
> Was it not you that dried up the sea,
>   the waters of the great deep?
> That made the depths of the sea into a road
>   for the redeemed to cross over?

It is significant that the first two lines of this text are very similar in syntax and refer both to creation and exodus. The last line is slightly different in that it begins with the attributive participle השׂמה, 'that made', presupposes the interrogative clause הלוא את־היא, 'was it not you?' and points only to the exodus. The word ים, 'sea', present in both v. 10a and v. 10b, provides a link between the two lines.

Rahab is the name of a mythological sea serpent or dragon which has not been discovered in any extra-biblical text up to now. It means literally 'arrogant boasting'.[14] It appears as a sea monster defeated at the time of creation in Ps. 89.11:

אתה דכאת כחלל רהב בזרוע עזך פזרת אויביך׃

> You crushed Rahab like a carcass;
> with your mighty arm you scattered your enemies.

The name Rahab occurs also in Job 9.13 and 26.12; it is used as a metaphorical name for Egypt in Ps. 87.4 and Isa. 30.7. Here, in v. 9c, it could refer both to the chaos monster at the time of creation and to Egypt the oppressor at the time of the exodus.[15] As the synonymous parallelism suggests, Rahab and the dragon (תנין) are one and the same. Yahweh broke the heads of the dragons (ראשׁי תנינים) in the waters at creation (Ps. 74.13). Pharaoh, King of Egypt, is referred to as 'the great dragon' (התנין הגדול, Ezek. 29.3). He is further said to be 'like a dragon in the seas' (כתנין בימים, Ezek. 32.2). Thus in mythic language, both Rahab and the dragon represent Yahweh's adversaries at creation and exodus.

14. Motyer, *Prophecy*, p. 409 n. 3.
15. J. Day, 'Rahab', *ABD*, V, pp. 610-11.

'The sea', ים, is parallel to 'the deep', תהום, in v. 10a. The drying up of the sea also refers both to the creation account (Gen. 1.2, 6-10) and to the crossing of the Reed Sea (Exod. 14.21-22). There could be an additional allusion to the story of the Flood which mentions 'the great deep' (Gen. 7.11) and 'the deep' (8.2). Although the Canaanite myth of Baal's defeat of the sea god Yam makes no specific reference to creation,[16] the Babylonian creation epic *Enūma elish* describes Marduk's defeat of the sea monster Tiamat. The fusion of both Canaanite and Babylonian myths in v. 10a may be intended as a polemic against such myths, emphasizing Yahweh as supreme over both Baal and Marduk.

The גאולים, 'redeemed' (v. 10b), in the immediate context of the Reed Sea experience, are the people of Israel who were delivered from bondage in Egypt:

אני יהוה והוצאתי אתכם מתחת סבלת מצרים ... וגאלתי אתכם...

'...I am Yahweh. I will free you from the forced labor of the Egyptians...I will redeem you...' (Exod. 6.6).

נחית בחסדך עם־זו גאלת ונהלת בעזך אל־נוה קדשך:

In your covenant love you led the people you had redeemed,
you guided them by your strength to your holy dwelling (Exod. 15.13).

ויגער בים־סוף ויחרב ויוליכם בתהמות כמדבר:
ויושיעם מיד שונא ויגאלם מיד אויב:

He rebuked the Reed Sea, and it dried up,
   he led them through the deep as through a desert.
He saved them from the power of the foe,
   and rescued them from the power of the enemy (Ps. 106.9-10).

In Isaiah 40–55, the qal active participle גאל, 'redeemer', occurs as a title of Yahweh ten times (41.14; 43.14; 44.6, 24; 47.4; 48.17; 49.7; 49.26; 54.5, 8). It is a technical term for the nearest relative (Lev. 25.25, 48-49) who is bound to protect the honor and property of the family. This is not only a duty, but also a right. The prophet Jeremiah had the right of redemption, and so he bought the field of his uncle's son Hanamel (Jer. 32.6-9). In the case of Ruth, there was another גאל who had priority of rights over Boaz (Ruth 3.12; 4.4). This גאל was willing to redeem the property of Elimelech from Naomi but was unwilling to marry Ruth in order to maintain the name of Ruth's deceased husband on his inheritance (Ruth 4.6). So he gave his right of redemption to

16. J. Day, 'God's Conflict with Dragon and Sea', *ABD*, II, pp. 228-31.

Boaz who accepted both responsibilities (Ruth 4.6, 9-10). In this Isaian context, Yahweh identifies himself as his people's nearest relative. Yahweh has the right to redeem his people. Moreover, he is willing to do it, and he alone has the power to do it.

In Isaiah 40–55, Yahweh is the active subject of the root גאל five times. Yahweh redeems his people by restoring the broken covenant relationship (43.1), forgiving their sins (44.22) and setting them free from Babylonian oppression (48.20). Yahweh's act of redemption brings glory to him (44.23) and joy to his people (52.9).[17] In light of this, the word גאולים in 51.10b points to those who will take part in a new exodus from Babylonian oppression. Mention of deliverance at the Reed Sea here leads to the petition in the following verse.

Petition: Mourning Turned to Joy (Verse 11). This verse is an unintroduced quotation from Isa. 35.10. Other examples of unintroduced quotations are found in the narrative of the prophet's vision (Isa. 40.1-11).[18] Yahweh's opening speech (40.1-2) is reported without an introduction. The prophet introduces the speech of the first angel (40.3-5) by קול אמר, 'a voice cries out' (v. 3a), and the speech of the second angel by קול אמר, 'a voice says' (v. 6a). But the reply of the second angel (v. 8) to the prophet's speech (vv. 6ab-7) lacks any introduction. The prophet's own address to Jerusalem (vv. 9-11) is also unintroduced.[19]

J.J. Ferrie shows that Isa. 35.10 is an integral part of Isaiah 35 which pictures a rainstorm theophany in which Yahweh prepares a well-watered highway in the desert for the safe return of his people.[20] The גאולים, 'redeemed', in 35.9 are the פדויי יהוה, 'those ransomed by Yahweh', in 35.10 who will depart from Babylon (48.20) and travel on the דרך הקדש, 'the holy way' (35.8), to Zion. The quotation of 35.10 in 51.11 is appropriate. Jerusalem the mourner connects the גאולים from Egyptian bondage (51.10) with the גאולים from Babylonian exile in

---

17. H. Ringgren, 'גאל', *TDOT*, II, pp. 350-55.

18. I understand this passage to report a heavenly council scene similar to that found in 1 Kgs 22.19-23 or Isa. 6. Yahweh presides over his royal court and issues a decree reported in Isa. 40.1-2. Angels or Yahweh's messengers, members of the heavenly council, begin to implement Yahweh's decree with specific commands. One such angel may be speaking in v. 3, another in v. 6. See Clifford, *Fair Spoken*, pp. 72-73.

19. Ferrie, 'Meteorological Imagery', pp. 27-29, 184.

20. Ferrie, 'Meteorological Imagery', pp. 180-83.

Yahweh's oracle (35.9) and cites Yahweh's promise in 35.10 as an implied prayer in order to urge Yahweh to action:

ופדויי יהוה ישובון ובאו ציון ברנה
ושמחת עולם על־ראשם ששון ושמחה ישיגון נסו יגון ואנחה:

> Those ransomed by Yahweh will return,
> they will enter Zion with a joyful cry.
> Eternal joy will be upon their heads,
> gladness and joy will meet them,
> sorrow and sighing will have fled.

The root פדה, 'to ransom', stands in parallelism to גאל in Hos. 13.14; Jer. 31.11; and Ps. 69.19. It is used of the redemption of the firstborn (Exod. 13.13, 15) and for Yahweh's redemption of Israel from Egypt (e.g. Deut. 7.8; 9.26). 'Those ransomed by Yahweh' (Isa. 35.10 = 51.11) are those who will be delivered from Babylonian captivity. They will go home to Zion. Inexpressible joy will be the mark of the redeemed / ransomed who used to sigh from sorrow under the enemy's yoke. The word רנה means a loud ringing cry. The root רנן denotes a cry of distress in Lam. 2.19. In this context רנה is a cry of joy.

The image represented by שמחת עולם, 'eternal joy', on the heads of the returning exiles has been thought to refer to a special type of crown or headdress, based on Isa. 61.3 (NRSV).[21]

לשום לאבלי ציון לתת להם פאר תחת אפר
שמן ששון תחת אבל מעטה תהלה תחת רוח כהה

> To provide for those who mourn in Zion—
> to give them a garland instead of ashes,
> The oil of gladness instead of mourning,
> the mantle of praise instead of a faint spirit.

However, the wearing of a special headdress at the end of a mourning period is not attested elsewhere in the Bible, nor in the ancient Near Eastern literature.[22] The command to the prophet Ezekiel, פארך חבוש עליך ונעליך תשים ברגליך, 'bind on your turban, put your sandals on your feet' (Ezek. 24.17), at the death of his wife means that the prophet is not to mourn for his wife with any outward rituals. When his wife was alive, he had a turban on his head and wore sandals. Now that she is dead, he must go on as usual, with a turban on his head and sandals

21. Anderson, *A Time to Mourn*, p. 47, esp. n. 104.
22. Anderson, *A Time to Mourn*, pp. 45-47.

on his feet. That same command is repeated to the whole community of
the exiles; when they hear of the fall of Jerusalem and the destruction of
the temple, they are to do what Ezekiel did:

ופארכם על־ראשיכם ונעליכם ברגליכם לא תספדו ולא תבכו

> Your turbans shall remain on your heads, your sandals on your feet. You
> shall not mourn or weep (Ezek. 24.23).

Mourners in the ancient Near East and in biblical times did not anoint
themselves during the mourning period (e.g. 2 Sam. 14.2; Dan. 10.3).
Anointing one's head with oil is the ritual termination of mourning (cf.
2 Sam. 12.20). The interlinear parallelism in Isa. 61.3 between פאר,
'crown, headdress', and שמן ששון, 'oil of gladness', and between אפר,
'ashes', and אבל, 'mourning', points to the understanding of שמחת
עולם, 'eternal joy' (51.11b) as שמן ששון, 'oil of gladness', which is
poured on the heads of mourners to mark the ending of the mourning
sequence.

The accumulation of words expressing joy ששון ושמחה, 'gladness and
joy', conveys emotional intensity. When Yahweh comforts Zion, gladness and joy will be there (Isa. 51.3) to meet the returning exiles. Joy is
the reverse of mourning. Mourning will cease when Yahweh fulfills his
promise to bring back the exiles. Then there will be no more place for
'sorrow and sighing', יגון ואנחה:

והפכתי אבלם לששון ונחמתים ושמחתים מיגונם:

> I will turn their mourning into joy,
>   I will comfort them, and give them gladness for sorrow
>   (Jer. 31.13b; NRSV).

The prayer lament in 51.9-11 is different from the funeral lament in
that it does not dwell on the dead but takes hold of Yahweh's promise
and waits in expectancy for Yahweh's response. This prayer reflects
faith on the part of Zion; yet Zion's faith is still faltering[23] under the
weight of her present experiences of suffering, as shown by her fears
expressed in the following verses (ותיראי, 'that you fear', in 51.12, and
ותפחד, 'that you dread', in 51.13).

---

23. Contra Motyer (*Prophecy*, p. 410) who maintains that 'the impassioned
prayer of v 9 modulates, under the influence of historical certainties (10), into the
key of confident faith'.

Second Stanza: The Divine Comfort (Verses 12-16)
Assurance and Reproof (Verses 12-13). The double אנכי אנכי matches
the urgency of Zion's repeated appeal in v. 9. Yahweh, who does not
slumber or sleep (Ps. 121.4), is alert as ever and ready to help. Yahweh
hears the implied lament underlying Zion's recollection of his mighty
deeds in the past and the unspoken petition beneath her citation of his
promise. Yahweh hears the sighs and groans of sorrow of a people
oppressed and dejected. Yahweh sees the anguish and the fears of a
people living in exile, disspirited, uncertain about the future. So Yahweh comes to their rescue: he asserts that he himself is to be their מנחם,
'comforter'. The act of comforting belongs to the mourning context.
Yahweh knows Zion is mourning the fall of Jerusalem and the exile of
the surviving captives. In times of mourning a מנחם is greatly desired,
for he can alleviate the sufferings of the mourners by showing sympathy through identification with them in their pains, by speaking words
which lift up their spirits, by giving timely advice which may guide
them through the maze of their pain and loss.

In view of my foregoing discussion of the functions of the מנחם, what
does it mean for Yahweh to assert himself as the מנחם of Zion? It is
obvious that by reason of his nature, Yahweh does not assume the state
of mourning. Of the 38 occurrences of the root אבל, 'to mourn', in MT,
only one, and that in the hiphil conjugation, has Yahweh as subject
(Lam. 2.8, 'he caused to mourn'). Yahweh does not comfort as human
beings do, in the processual usage of the verb. Yahweh comforts by
bringing about the cessation of mourning (cf. Isa. 52.1-2; 61.2-3; Jer.
31.13). Yahweh can do so because only he can redress injustices (cf.
Isa. 28.17; 35.4), punish the oppressor (cf. 51.22-23), restore the waste
places (cf. 35.1-2; 51.3) and set the captives free (cf. 42.7; 51.14; 61.1).
By his very nature, Yahweh can comfort effectively, in the resultative
nuance of the root.

In this instance, Yahweh starts the comforting process by asking Zion
to reflect on her identity / status, מי־את, 'who are you?' (v. 12b). The
three rhetorical questions in Zion's frantic appeal:

(v. 9c) ‎הלוא את־היא המחצבת רהב...
(v. 10a) ‎הלוא את־היא המחרבת ים...
(v. 10b) ‎השׂמה מעמקי־ים דרך...

Was it not you that hacked up Rahab...
Was it not you that dried up the sea...
That made the depths of the sea into a road...

are answered by Yahweh's threefold rebuke:

(v. 12b) מי־את ותיראי מאנוש ימות...
(v. 13a) ותשכח יהוה עשך...
(v. 13b) ותפחד תמיד כל־היום...

> Who are you, that you fear human beings who die…
> [Who are you,] that you forget Yahweh your maker…
> That you dread continually, all day long…

Yahweh further reminds Zion of the true nature of the object of her fears: מאנוש ימות ומבן־אדם חציר ינתן , 'human beings who die, mortals who ought to be considered as grass' (v. 12b). The word אנוש comes from the root אנש which means 'to be weak'.[24] Indeed, a characteristic of אנוש is to be mortal, ימות (lit. 'who keeps dying'). The Old Testament emphasizes the frailty and transience of human life:

אנוש כחציר ימיו כציץ השדה כן יציץ:

> As for mortals, their days are like grass;
>   they flourish like a flower of the field (Ps. 103.15; NRSV).

The noun אנוש stands in parallelism with בן־אדם, 'son of man', who 'ought to be considered as grass', that is, who is by nature as fleeting and transitory as grass. The בני־אדם are created by God, as the psalmist makes clear in Ps. 89.48:[25]

זכר־אני מה־חלד על־מה־שוא בראת כל־בני־אדם:

> Remember how short my life is;
>   for what vanity you created all human beings!

By her constant fear of mere created human beings who die like the grass which withers (v. 12b; cf. 40.6-8), Zion seems to have forgotten her identity as the people of Yahweh, 'his own special possession, dearer to him than all other peoples' (cf. Exod. 19.5-6). Because of her insecurity and restlessness, Zion seems to have forgotten the fact that Yahweh, the creator of heaven and earth, is her 'maker' (v. 13a). It is Yahweh who 'formed her in the womb' (Isa. 44.2), who brought her into being. And if Yahweh gave her the right and privilege of existence, no human oppressor can ever annihilate her. The modifier 'your' in the phrase 'your maker' (עשך) means that Yahweh by his choice had

---

24. F. Maass, 'אנוש', *TDOT*, I, pp. 345-48.
25. I change MT אני מה־חלד to read מה־חדל אני (cf. Ps. 39.5).

committed himself to Zion, and not that Zion could claim Yahweh to be her own.[26]

Zion had thought that Yahweh had forgotten her (49.14). Instead, she had forgotten who Yahweh is, and her identity in relation to Yahweh. Yahweh as the 'maker' of Zion is qualified by two attributive participial phrases: נוטה שמים, 'who stretched out the heavens', and ויסד ארץ, 'and who laid the foundations of the earth'. The formula נטה שמים, 'to stretch out the heavens', is used in parallel with expressions about the creating of the earth: יסד ארץ, 'to lay the foundations of the earth', in 51.13, 16 (emended); רקע הארץ, 'to spread out the earth', in 42.5; 44.24; עשה ארץ, 'to make the earth,' in 45.12. Thus the idiom נטה שמים seems to be derived from an ancient creation tradition and is used by Second Isaiah to magnify Yahweh as the supreme creator. The imagery associated with this formula is that of pitching the heavens as a sacred cosmic tent where Yahweh appears in order to create, to reign, and to redeem:

הישב על־חוג הארץ וישביה כחגבים
הנוטה כדק שמים וימתחם כאהל לשבת:

He is the one enthroned above the horizon of the earth
and its inhabitants are like grasshoppers,
The one who stretches out the heavens like a curtain,
and spreads them out like a tent to reign there (Isa. 40.22).

הוד והדר לבשת: עטה־אור כשלמה
נוטה שמים כיריעה: המקרה במים עליותיו
השם־עבים רכובו המהלך על־כנפי־רוח:

You are clothed in glory and splendor,
wrapped in light as with a garment.
You stretch out the heavens like a tent,
you set the beams of your* chambers on the waters,
You make the clouds your*[27] chariot,
you ride on the wings of the wind (Ps. 104.1b-3).

In this text, Yahweh's creative activity in stretching out the heavens is set within the context of a theophany. The heavens are Yahweh's 'tent' where he manifests himself as creator and king. The theophanic dimension of the formula 'stretching out the heavens' is confirmed by two other passages which have no direct connection with creation:

26. Motyer, *Prophecy*, p. 411.
27. Here, MT has the third person possessive adjective, equivalent to 'his'.

יהוה הט־שמיך ותרד נע בהרים ויעשנו:
שלח ידיך ממרום פצני והצילני
ממים רבים מיד בני נכר:

> Yahweh, stretch out the heavens and come down!
>   Touch the mountains so that they smoke!
> Stretch forth your hand from on high!
>   Set me free and rescue me
> from the mighty waters, from the hand of aliens (Ps. 144.5, 7).

Here, the psalmist calls on Yahweh to come to his rescue. In Ps. 18.10-17, Yahweh does stretch out the heavens and comes down to deliver the psalmist from his enemy.

To sum up, the phrase נוטה שמים describes Yahweh as the supreme creator who stretched out the heavens in the primeval act of creation, and who continually appears in his heavenly 'tent' to rule the universe and to come to the help of his children in distress.[28]

The formula יסד ארץ, 'to lay the foundations of the earth', is used three times in Second Isaiah (48.13; 51.13, 16). It stems from a creation tradition that stresses Yahweh's primordial victory over the chaotic forces and his subsequent ordering of the cosmos which he continues to uphold. This is made clear from the other occurrences of the formula יסד ארץ in Job 38.4; Pss. 24.2; 78.69; 89.12; 102.26; 104.5; Prov. 3.19; and Zech. 12.1. When Yahweh laid the foundations of the earth, he shut in the sea (ים) with doors when it burst forth from the womb (Job 38.4, 8). Yahweh crushed Rahab when he founded the heavens and the earth, the world and all that is in it. Yahweh rules over the raging of the sea even now (Ps. 89.9-11). When Yahweh founded the earth, he covered it with the deep (תהום). Then Yahweh rebuked the chaotic waters, and they fled to the place appointed for them, whence they cannot pass the boundary set by Yahweh (Ps. 104.5-9). The phrase יסד ארץ in Isa. 51.13, 16 follows the description of Yahweh's battle with the chaotic forces in 51.9-10: Rahab, the dragon, the sea, and the great deep. Thus, the tradition history of יסד ארץ is connected with Yahweh's cosmic battle and subsequent victory over the chaotic forces.

The formula יסד ארץ is also associated with the praise of Yahweh as the all-powerful ruler of the cosmos (Ps. 89.6-13), the king over all the earth (Pss. 24.7-10; 102.13; Isa. 40.21-23), the ultimate creator, the first

---

28. N.C. Habel, 'He Who Stretches out the Heavens', *CBQ* 34 (1972), pp. 417-30.

and the last (Isa. 48.12). The founding of the earth is further associated with the founding of Zion in Ps. 78.68-69:

וַיִּבְחַר אֶת־שֵׁבֶט יְהוּדָה אֶת־הַר צִיּוֹן אֲשֶׁר אָהֵב:
וַיִּבֶן כְּמוֹ־רָמִים מִקְדָּשׁוֹ כְּאֶרֶץ יְסָדָהּ לְעוֹלָם:

But he chose the tribe of Judah,
   Mount Zion, which he loves.
He built his sanctuary like the high heavens,
   like the earth, which he has founded forever.

This close association is shown by the use of the same root יסד for the establishment of Zion / the temple:

כִּי יְהוָה יִסַּד צִיּוֹן וּבָהּ יֶחֱסוּ עֲנִיֵּי עַמּוֹ:

For Yahweh has founded Zion,
   and the needy among his people will find refuge in her (Isa. 14.32b).

הָאֹמֵר לְכוֹרֶשׁ רֹעִי וְכָל־חֶפְצִי יַשְׁלִם
וְלֵאמֹר לִירוּשָׁלִַם תִּבָּנֶה וְהֵיכָל תִּוָּסֵד:

Who says of Cyrus, 'He is my shepherd,
   and he shall carry out all my purpose';
And who says of Jerusalem, 'It shall be rebuilt,'
   and of the temple, 'Your foundations shall be laid' (Isa. 44.28; NRSV).

The verb יסד is used again in Isa. 54.11 in connection with the founding of new Zion.

In summary, the phrase יסד ארץ is an 'earth-creation' formula, with connotations of the primordial cosmic battle with chaotic forces, of Yahweh as the supreme victorious creator, and of the founding of Zion.[29]

In order to dispel Zion's fear, Yahweh reminds her of his greatness, his power over the cosmos, not only in days long ago (בימי קדם) but even now. He is still stretching out the heavens to come down and deliver his people. He still intervenes to save. He laid the foundations of the earth, he will cause the foundations to be laid for a new Zion.

The second rebuke 'that you forget Yahweh your maker' (v. 13a) is enclosed within two rebukes about fear, ותירא, 'that you fear', in v. 12a, and ותפחד, 'that you dread', in v. 13b. Zion dreads the fury of המציק, 'the oppressor'. The root צוק occurs in Judg. 14.17 where Samson is harassed by his wife's nagging to explain his riddle, and again in

---

29. T.M. Ludwig, 'The Traditions of the Establishing of the Earth in Deutero-Isaiah', *JBL* 92 (1973), pp. 345-57.

Judg. 16.16 where Delilah pesters Samson into revealing the secret of his unusual strength. Aside from one more occurrence in Job 32.18 where Elihu feels constrained by the spirit to speak to Job, the root צוק always refers to the distress brought about by a siege (Deut. 28.53, 55, 57; Isa. 29.2, 7; Jer. 19.9). The word מציק in Isa. 51.13c thus recalls the atrocities of the siege in 587 BCE. The מציק is described by the clause כונן להשחית, 'he has planned to destroy'. The polel perfect כונן is transitive, and used of the archer's aiming his bow and arrow:

אם־לא ישוב חרבו ילטוש קשתו דרך ויכוננה׃

> If one does not repent, he [God] will sharpen his sword,
> he has bent and aimed his bow (Ps. 7.13).

כי הנה הרשעים ידרכון קשת כוננו חצם על־יתר

> For, see, the wicked bend the bow,
> they fit their arrow to the string (Ps. 11.2a).

כי תשיתמו שכם במיתריך תכונן על־פניהם׃

> For you will put them to flight;
> you will aim at their faces with your bows (Ps. 21.13).

Even though the oppressor has set up or planned everything in order to destroy, he is but אנוש or בן־אדם. Elihu tells Job:

הן־זאת לא־צדקת אענך כי־ירבה אלוח מאנוש׃

> But in this you are not right. I will answer you:
> God is greater than any mortal (Job 33.12).

Yahweh contrasts his supreme power in creation to the transience of human oppressors who fade away like the grass or the flower of the field. The oppressors can do no more harm than what has been given them to do. Surely they are no match for Yahweh. They are of no account. They are only creatures under the power of the creator, as Isa. 54.16 (NRSV) says:

הן[30] אנכי בראתי חרש נפח באש פחם
ומוציא כלי למעשהו ואנכי בראתי משחית לחבל׃

> See it is I who have created the smith
> who blows the fire of coals,
> and produces a weapon fit for its purpose;
> I have also created the ravager to destroy.

---

30. *Kethib* is הן; *qere* is הנה.

The remedy for fear is to remember Yahweh, to trust in him who has surpassing power over the whole cosmos:

באלהים בטחתי לא אירא מה־יעשה אדם לי:

In God I trust; I am not afraid.
What can a mere mortal do to me? (Ps. 56.12)

Promise of Salvation (Verse 14). Yahweh reiterates his promise of salvation in three parts: (1) the oppressed who are stooping down under the burden of forced labor will soon be released; (2) they will not die and go down to the pit; (3) they will not lack bread.

The צעה, 'one stooping down', recalls Jer. 48.11-12 where Moab, which has not gone into exile, is compared to wine resting on its dregs, wine which has never been poured from vessel to vessel. So Yahweh will send צעים, 'decanters' (lit. tilters), to Moab who will stoop down and tilt the wine jars to pour the wine into other vessels, straining the dregs at the bottom of the jars. This is a figure for exile. Life in exile is a life of continuous fear: והיו חייך תלאים לך מנגד ופחדת לילה ויומם ולא תאמין בחייך:, 'your life shall hang in doubt before you; night and day you shall be in dread, with no assurance of your life' (Deut. 28.66; NRSV).

The second part of the promise is ולא־ימות לשחת (lit. 'he will not die to the pit'). The exiles who have had no assurance about their life now have Yahweh's promise that they will survive the exile. The צעים will be set free and return home to Zion. The word שחת, 'pit', is parallel to שאול in Ps. 16.10, where the dead go. Yahweh's promise of life takes away the fear of death and mourning.

The last part of the promise is ולא יחסר לחמו, 'and he will not lack bread'. Famine was a constant fear in the life of the people in biblical lands. Irregular rainfall easily led to drought, crop failure and loss of cattle and herds. The ravages of war increased the rate of starvation. Accordingly, the promise of divine deliverance is often accompanied by the promise of plenty, for example, Isa. 49.9-10 (NAB):

לאמר לאסורים צאו לאשר בחשך הגלו
על־דרכים ירעו ובכל־שפיים מרעיתם:
לא ירעבו ולא יצמאו ולא־יכם שרב ושמש
כי־מרחמם ינהגם ועל־מבועי מים ינהלם:

Saying to the prisoners: Come out!
To those in darkness: Show yourselves!

Along the ways they shall find pasture,
  on every bare height shall their pastures be.
They shall not hunger or thirst,
  nor shall the scorching wind or the sun strike them;
For he who pities them leads them,
  and guides them beside springs of water.

Just as fasting is a rite of mourning, so eating and drinking are rites of joy. The command to bring offerings to the house of Yahweh goes together with the command to eat and rejoice before Yahweh (Deut. 12.6-7, 11-12, 17-18).[31] One aspect of rejoicing as the antitype of mourning is expressed through eating and drinking, as in Isa. 22.12-13:

ויקרא אדני יהוה צבאות ביום ההוא
לבכי ולמספד ולקרחה ולחגר שק:
והנה ששון ושמחה הרג בקר ושחט צאן
אכל בשר ושתות יין אכול ושתו כי מחר נמות:

The Lord, Yahweh of hosts, called on you,
  on that day,
To weep and mourn,
  to shave your head and put on sackcloth.
But look! There was gladness and joy,
  killing oxen and slaughtering sheep,
Eating meat and drinking wine:
  'Let us eat and drink, for tomorrow we die!'

Yahweh's promise of bread anticipates the termination of mourning in Isa. 52.1-2. A related passage in Jer. 31.11-14 brings together the concrete terms by which Yahweh comforts Zion, that is, redemption from exile, homecoming, bountiful harvests and festive celebrations.

Assurance and Affirmation (Verses 15-16). The ואנכי, 'for I am / as for me, I am...', is emphatic. Since Zion seems to have forgotten Yahweh her maker (v. 13), Yahweh now reminds Zion again of who he is in relationship to her, and of his power over the cosmos, in order to confirm his promise in v. 14.

The promise of release is enclosed within two self assertions of supremacy by Yahweh (vv. 13, 15-16). Yahweh's promise is firmly grounded on who he is: ואנכי יהוה, 'For I am Yahweh'. Yahweh's self-revelation began with the exodus event. He is the one who answered Moses' question about his name by uttering the enigmatic אהיה אשר

31. Anderson, *A Time to Mourn*, pp. 19-26.

אהיה, 'I am who I am' (Exod. 3.14). Yahweh is the source of all created beings. Yahweh, the almighty God, has condescended to be the God of Israel (e.g. Exod. 6.7; Lev. 26.12), the God of Zion, to take the people of Israel into his own special care and protection. The expression רגע הים, 'who stirred up the sea', echoes the chaos battle of vv. 9-10, as confirmed by its occurrence in Job 26.12-13:

בכחו רגע הים ובתבונתו מחץ רהב:
ברוחו שמים שפרה חללה ידו נחש בריח:

By his power he stirred up the sea,
    by his cunning he crushed Rahab;
By his wind the heavens were made fair,
    his hand pierced the fleeting serpent.

The exact words רגע הים ויהמו גליו יהוה צבאות שמו are found in Jer. 31.35-36:

Thus says Yahweh,
    who gave[32] the sun to shine by day,
    and[33] the moon and the stars to shine by night,
Who stirred up the sea so that its waves roared,
    whose name is Yahweh of hosts:
If this fixed order were ever to be removed
    from my sight, says Yahweh,
Only then would the offspring of Israel cease
    to be a nation in my presence forever.

Both Isa. 51.15 and Jer. 31.35c may be quoting a well-known creation hymn, other parts of which are found in Amos 4.13; 5.8; 9.5-6.[34] The passage in Jer. 31.35-36 argues from the permanence of the cosmos to the permanence of the covenant Yahweh made with his people Israel. In the same way, Isa. 51.15 leads from Yahweh the creator of the

---

32. Scholars do not agree on the tense of the two attributive participles נתן, 'who gave' (v. 35a), and רגע, 'who stirred up' (v. 35c), and the following *wayyiqtol* ויהמו, 'so that they [its waves] roared' (v. 35c). NAB, NIV and NRSV render all three as timeless presents and so understand them as referring to a *creatio continuo*. REB translates all three with past tenses. Just as in the note to Isa. 51.15, the *wayyiqtol* of the action verb וַיֶּהֱמוּ is a past tense, and so the two preceding participles also have a past value, pointing to the initial act of creation. This may be what MT had in mind. It would also be possible to revocalize וְיֶהֱמוּ and render all three forms as timeless presents. See Ferrie, 'Meteorological Imagery', p. 198.

33. I omit חקת with LXX; it may be a dittography from v. 36a.

34. Motyer, *Prophecy*, p. 412 n. 1.

cosmos to the covenantal relationship between Yahweh and his people in 51.16. Yahweh cites his own words to Zion: עמי־אתה, 'you are my people'.

Yahweh reminds Zion that he is יהוה צבאות, 'Yahweh of hosts', a title which appears in context of battles (e.g. Israel's battle with the Philistines, 1 Sam. 4.4; war against the Amalekites, 1 Sam. 15.2) and kingship over the heavenly court (e.g. Isaiah's call vision, 6.3, 5). Yahweh of hosts is the divine warrior who won the cosmogonic battle and who is enthroned as king of the divine council. Thus, Yahweh, the God of Zion, is ready to fight for his people.[35]

Most commentators think that 51.16a is out of place.[36] They focus on its affinities with the Servant Songs (49.2; 50.4) and the prose passage 59.21. But once it is recognized that 51.11 is a quotation from 35.10 by Zion, the mourner who reminds Yahweh of his promise of deliverance, then 51.16a appears as Yahweh's admission that he did make that promise. This implies Yahweh's assurance that his words will be ful-filled. Yahweh goes on to remind Zion of his continuing protection. The word צל, 'shade / shadow', denotes a place of refuge and protection (cf. Ps. 17.8, 'Hide me in the shadow of your wings', בצל כנפיך תסתירני). The phrase בצל ידי, 'in the shadow of my hand', occurs only here and in 49.2. The hand and the arm of Yahweh (v. 9) represent Yahweh in action, actively working to create (e.g. 66.2a, ואת־כל־אלה ידי עשתה, 'all these things my hand has made'), to redeem (e.g. 50.2b, הקצרה קצרה ידי מפדות, 'Is my hand shortened that it cannot redeem?'), and to re-dress injustice (e.g. 59.15b-16; NRSV):

וירא יהוה וירע בעיניו כי־אין משפט׃
וירא כי־אין איש וישתומם כי אין מפגיע
ותושע לו זרעו וצדקתו היא סמכתהו׃

> The Lord saw it, and it displeased him
>   that there was no justice.
> He saw that there was no one,
>   and was appalled that there was no one to intervene;
> So his own arm brought him victory,
>   and his righteousness upheld him.

Zion's fears should have been assuaged by now. Yahweh's comfort-ing speech assures her of her privileged status as his own special

35. C.L. Seow, 'Lord of Hosts', *ABD*, III, pp. 304-307.
36. E.g. Westermann, *Isaiah*, p. 244; North, *Second Isaiah*, p. 214.

people, entitled to his care, protection and deliverance. Yahweh is able to accomplish his promises because he is the supreme warrior king over all creation who not only won the primordial battle against the chaotic forces, but also intervened in history to deliver the people of Israel from Egyptian bondage, leading them through the Reed Sea as on dry land. Yahweh continues to stretch out the heavens to come down and help his people. He laid the foundations of the earth and continues to uphold the cosmic order. The comforting thought for Zion is that Yahweh, the supreme creator of the whole world, has bound himself to protect his covenant people.

Third Stanza: The Prophet's Comfort (Verses 17-23)
The First Command to Get Up (Verse 17a). In the first stanza, Zion called upon Yahweh to awake, to act on her behalf. She thought Yahweh did not know or did not care about her plight. However, Yahweh comforted her and reassured her that he is her God and that her captives will soon be released. Basing himself on Yahweh's promise of deliverance (v. 14), the prophet now calls on Zion to rouse herself. The hithpolel reflexive התעוררי (v. 17a) has a stronger connotation than the qal עורי (v. 9). The duplication of the imperative denotes urgency. Actually, when Zion called upon Yahweh in the lament prayer, she had already been roused from her lethargic numbness caused by so much suffering and pain. However, she is still seated on the ground, in mourning posture, and so the prophet calls on her to prepare to get up and get done with her mourning. The imperative קומי, 'get up', in v. 17a anticipates the קומי in 52.2a.

Reasons for Zion's Mourning (Verses 17b-20).

1. *Yahweh's cup of wrath (v. 17b-c).* The prophet tries to comfort Zion by letting her know that he sympathizes with her in her great sufferings.
 The wrath of the oppressor in v. 13c turns out to be an instrument of Yahweh's own wrath (v. 17b). Jerusalem underwent all those fears and sorrows because she had drunk and drained the cup of Yahweh's wrath, from his hand. She had borne the full measure of his judgment. I already noted in my comment on Lam. 1.12 that 'wrath' is not an attribute of Yahweh. It only describes the way he reacts to sin and carries out his judgment against sinners. The 'cup of Yahweh's wrath' as a metaphor for his punishment occurs also in Pss. 11.6; 75.9; Jer. 25.15-29; Ezek. 23.31-34. According to Jer. 25.18, as a result of drinking the

cup of wrath, Jerusalem and the towns of Judah became 'a desolation and a waste, an object of hissing and of cursing'. Jeremiah 51.7 further specifies that this cup in Yahweh's hand is Babylon. Apparently this cup of Yahweh's wrath keeps on refilling, for after it had been drunk and drained by Jerusalem, it is to be passed on into the hands of her oppressors (v. 23), for them to drink and drain.

2. *Loss of children (vv. 18-20)*. The prophet goes on to describe the plight of Jerusalem. She had many children, but in her times of need, they are all gone. She has no מנהל, 'one who leads or guides'. The root נהל has connotations of leading to a place where there are springs of water to quench the thirst (cf. Isa. 49.10), to refresh the weary (cf. Ps. 23.2). In Exod. 15.13, Yahweh guided (נהלת) his people out of Egypt to his 'holy abode' in Canaan. The psalmist (31.4) implores Yahweh to guide him out of the hidden net of the enemy. The root נהל in Isa. 40.11 and 49.10 occurs in contexts of comfort (40.1-11; 49.8-13). It is part of the task of the מנחם to lead and guide. Note the similarity of sound between מנהל, 'one who guides, leads', and מנחם, 'one who comforts'. The weary mourner needs guidance out of her distress to a place and / or a state of rest.

Zion has no one to take her by the hand (מחזיק בידה) either. The phrase חזק ביד also belongs to the context of assurance, comfort and deliverance. Yahweh takes his servant Israel by the right hand and says:

כי אני יהוה אלהיך מחזיק ימינך
האמר לך אל־תירא אני עזרתיך:

> For I, Yahweh your God,
>   take you by your right hand;
> It is I who say to you: 'Do not fear,
>   I will help you' (Isa. 41.13).

In Jer. 31.32, Yahweh took Israel's ancestors by the hand (החזיקי בידם) to bring them out of the land of Egypt. Thus the role of the מנחם would also include 'taking by the hand'. Jerusalem the mourner has no one to guide her, no one to take her by the hand. She has no מנחם.

The imagery in v. 18 recalls a passage in *The Tale of Aqhat*. Danil, Aqhat's father, had no son before Aqhat was born. Danil spent seven days in the temple of the gods pleading for the gift of a son. Then Baal implores El on behalf of Danil and enumerates the duties of a son:

> Wilt thou not bless him, O Bull El, my father,
>   Beatify him, O Creator of Creatures?

So shall there be a son in his house,
A scion in the midst of his palace:
Who sets up the stelae of his ancestral spirits,
In the holy place the protectors of his clan…
Who takes him by the hand when he's drunk,
Carries him when he's sated with wine…[37]

Verse 20 explains why the children of Jerusalem cannot fulfill their role as מנחמים for her. They lie 'unconscious [עלפו] at the corner of every street'. The hithpael of the root עלף in Amos 8.13 refers to fainting from thirst, and in Jon. 4.8 to fainting from the heat of the sun. Here, Jerusalem's children have fainted from the heat of Yahweh's wrath; they have been 'filled' with it (המלאים חמת־יהוה), since they have drunk and drained the cup of 'his wrath' in v. 17bc. Consequently, they are helpless at the hands of their oppressors, like antelopes caught in a net, struggling to be freed, to the point of exhaustion, but to no avail. The תאו, 'antelope', appears only here and in a list of clean wild deer in Deut. 14.5.

The phrase גערת אלהיך, 'the blast of your God', is in synonymous parallelism with חמת־יהוה, 'the wrath of Yahweh'. The root גער means 'to scream, cry out'. The גערה of Yahweh is often manifested in the context of his victory over the waters (e.g. Pss. 18.16 = 2 Sam. 22.16; 104.7), against the enemies (e.g. Pss. 76.7; 80.17). Here, the blast is aimed against his own people. The expression בראש כל־חוצות, 'at the corner of every street', recalls the description of Jerusalem's children 'who faint from hunger at the corner of every street' in Lam. 2.19d.

Enclosed between the two laments for Jerusalem's children (vv. 18 and 20) is a solemn statement about the terrible calamities that befell her. Those calamities are spelled out in four words, but are grouped as two: שתים הנה קראתיך, 'two things have happened to you'. The first two words השד והשבר, 'devastation and destruction', describe the effects of the war upon the city in terms of buildings and structures, the last two והרעב והחרב, 'famine and the sword', refer to the ravages of war upon human beings. The two rhetorical questions מי ינוד לך, 'who can grieve with you?' and מי ינחמך (emended), 'who can comfort you?', imply a negative answer: no human being can possibly show enough sympathy to assuage Jerusalem's grief; no human being can possibly say or do anything to comfort her. Her damages are beyond repair. Her loss is too great. These questions echo those in Lam. 2.13:

---

37. ANET, pp. 149-55.

מה־אעידך מה אדמה־לך הבת ירושלם
מה אשוה־לך ואנחמך בתולת בת־ציון
כי־גדול כים שברך מי ירפא־לך:

> What can I say to you, to what can I compare you,
>> O daughter Jerusalem?
> To what can I liken you, that I may comfort you,
>> O virgin daughter Zion?
> For great as the sea's [ruin] is your ruin!
>> Who can heal you?

Similar questions are asked at the destruction of Nineveh:

והיה כל־ראיך ידוד ממך ואמר
שדדה נינוה מי ינוד לה
מאין אבקש מנחמים לך:

> Then all who see you
>> will shrink from you and say,
> 'Nineveh is devastated;
>> who will bemoan her?'
> Where shall I seek
>> comforters for you? (Nah. 3.7; NRSV)

These two categories of calamities also recall the two kinds of punishment that will be inflicted upon Babylon in Isa. 47.9:

ותבאנה לך שתי־אלה רגע ביום אחד
שכול ואלמן כתמם באו עליך

> Both these things shall come upon you
>> in a moment, in one day:
> Bereavement and widowhood, in full measure,
>> shall come upon you.

The number 'two' may be a way of expressing the totality of destruction, as is the duplication of synonymous parallel cola in vv. 18 and 19:

ואין מחזיק בידה	//		אין־מנהל לה	
מכל־בנים גדלה	//		מכל־בנים ילדה	
(emended) מי ינחמך	//		מי ינוד לך	

The verb נוד means to assuage the pain of the mourner by nodding the head sympathetically as a sign of grief. The parallel piel נחם should probably be taken as a processual usage of the term, that is, to alleviate the mourner's grief by adopting the mourning gestures. No human מנחם can bring any relief to Jerusalem since her destruction is so great. The resultative meaning of נחם, that is, to bring about the cessation of mourning, is solely Yahweh's prerogative. It should be noted that the sequence נוד and נחם occurs in similar contexts of mourning (e.g. Nah. 3.7; Job 2.11; 42.11; Ps. 69.21).

Punishment of Zion's Oppressors (Verses 21-23). With the word לכן, 'therefore', at the beginning of v. 21 the prophet introduces a new decision by Yahweh based on previous events. Because Jerusalem has drunk to the dregs the cup of Yahweh's wrath, because she has suffered those two kinds of losses, Yahweh her Lord, who is master over her and over all that ever happens to her, will take up her cause and exercise justice for her.

Jerusalem is called עניה, 'afflicted one', because of all the pains and hardships she has endured. She desperately needs to be comforted. The word עניה occurs in another passage (54.11) where her need to be comforted is explicitly spelled out, together with the comforting promise of restoration:

עניח סערה לא נחמה
הנה אנכי מרביץ בפוך אבניך ויסדתיך בספירים:

O afflicted one, storm-tossed, and not comforted!
I will lay your pavements with jewels [read בַּנֹפֶךְ],
   and your foundations [read וִיסֹדְתַיִךְ] with sapphires!

The phrase ושכרת ולא מיין, 'drunk but not with wine', carries on the imagery of כוס חמתו את־קבעת כוס התרעלה, 'the cup of his wrath, the chalice, the cup of staggering' (vv. 17b-c, and 22b-c in reverse order). The metaphor of drunkenness describes the lethargic stupor which envelops Jerusalem, the lonely mourner. The new decision from her God, who 'contends for his people' (יריב עמו, v. 22a), will arouse her out of that torpor. The phrase יריב עמו implies the exercise of justice, cf. Jer. 50.33-34:

כה אמר יהוה צבאות
עשוקים בני־ישראל ובני־יהודה יחדו
וכל־שביהם החזיקו בם מאנו שלחם:
גאלם חזק יהוה צבאות שמו
ריב יריב את־ריבם למען הרגיע את־הארץ והרגיז לישבי בבל:

Thus says Yahweh of hosts:
Oppressed are the people of Israel,
   and so too are the people of Judah;
All their captors hold them fast
   and refuse to let them go.

> Strong is their redeemer, whose name is Yahweh of hosts;
> He will surely plead their cause
>> that he may give rest to the earth,
>> but unrest to those who live in Babylon.

Yahweh will exercise justice by taking the cup of his wrath out of Jerusalem's hand and placing it in the hands of those who caused her to suffer (vv. 22b-23). Jerusalem has had her share of suffering. Although the poem in 51.9–52.2 does not mention sin, mention of the justice of Yahweh implies that Jerusalem suffered for the sins she committed against Yahweh. This is made clear in Mic. 7.9:

זעף יהוה אשׂא כי חטאתי לו
עד אשׁר יריב ריבי ועשׂה משׁפטי
יוציאני לאור אראה בצדקתו׃

> The wrath of Yahweh I will endure
>> because I have sinned against him,
> Until he takes up my cause,
>> and executes judgment for me.
> He will bring me forth to the light;
>> I will see his justice.

Now her tormentors, who treated her cruelly, will bear the chastisement of their sins. They will have to drink the cup of Yahweh's wrath. The grounds for the judgment and the verdict passed on Babylon are spelled out clearly in 47.6-11 and 51.23. Babylon did not have compassion on Yahweh's people. She laid a heavy yoke even on the aged. One of the ways by which Babylon humiliated Jerusalem was to make her lie down for her tormentors to walk over her (51.23). Such treatment of the defeated by conquerors is recorded in Josh. 10.24, Zech. 10.5 and Bar. 4.25. Whereas in ages past, at the first exodus, Yahweh made a road in the depths of the sea for his people to cross over, now his people make their backs like the ground for their oppressors to walk on. Yahweh will avenge his people by making their oppressors 'eat their own flesh' and 'drunk with their own blood' (49.26). This vindication is what Jerusalem has been asking for from Yahweh in Lam. 1.21-22. Her request is indirect and more subdued in Lam. 2.20-22 and Isa. 51.11.

The prophet's command קומי on behalf of Yahweh at the beginning of the stanza (v. 17a) reverses the command of her tormentors שׁחי, 'bow down', at the end (v. 23b). The command קומי marks the beginning of the end, the end of Jerusalem's mourning. BDB connects שׁחי

with the root שׁחה which is related to another root שׁחח, used in contexts of mourning:

כרע־כאח לי
התהלכתי כאבל־אם קדר שׁחותי:

As though I grieved for a friend or a brother,
I went about as one who laments for a mother,
   bowed down and in mourning (Ps. 35.14).

נעויתי שׁחתי עד־מאד כל־היום קדר הלכתי:

I am stooped and utterly bowed down;
   all day long I go around mourning (Ps. 38.7).

To bow down and to lie prostrate on the ground (v. 23c) are postures of mourning.

Fourth Stanza: End of Zion's Mourning (52.1-2)
Command to Change Garments (Verse 1). The call עורי עורי לבשׁי עזך, 'Awake, awake, put on your strength', addressed to Zion is almost the exact duplicate of the appeal made to the 'arm of Yahweh' in 51.9. The difference lies in the presence of the pronoun suffix ך- and in the tone as perceived through the context. Whereas the command to Zion is an excited cry of joy, bringing relief, the appeal to Yahweh is charged with fear and anxiety. Moreover, strength is an attribute of Yahweh while Zion has no strength of her own. She is constantly in fear (v. 13b). The phrase עזך, 'your strength', is parallel to בגדי תפארתך, 'your glorious garments', in v. 1b. Thus the strength that she is told to put on is her glorious garments, just as Queen Esther put on 'royalty', that is, her royal robes (ותלבשׁ אסתר מלכות, Est. 5.1). Zion no longer needs her mourning garb. Her days of mourning are over. She needs to take off the sackcloth that she has been wearing and put on her glorious garments to indicate her new status. The psalmist experiences a similar change when his prayer has been heard:

הפכת מספדי למחול לי פתחת שׂקי ותאזרני שׂמחה:

You have turned my mourning into dancing;
   you have taken off my sackcloth
   and clothed me with joy (Ps. 30.12; NRSV).

Jerusalem's glorious garments are also a sign of her being set apart for Yahweh, since she is 'the holy city' (עיר הקדשׁ, v. 1b; 48.2; Neh. 11.1). Moses was commanded to have sacred garments made for Aaron,

'for his glory and beauty' (Exod. 28.2, לכבוד ולתפארת). The holiness
of Jerusalem rests on the divine presence symbolized by the ark of the
covenant which David brought up from the house of Obededom (2 Sam.
6.12-19). While Zion was under Yahweh's wrath, gentile nations
invaded her sanctuary (cf. Lam. 1.10; 2.7, 20c). Now that Zion resumes
her real status as 'a kingdom of priests, a holy nation' (cf. Exod. 19.6),
no person uncircumcised or unclean can enter her gates. This is Yahweh's promise of protection from defilement. Circumcision is the sign
of the covenant God made with Abraham and his offspring after him
(Gen. 17.9-14). Any uncircumcised male is cut off from the community
of God (Gen. 17.14). He does not belong to the people of God and
therefore cannot partake of his holiness. Yahweh is holy and enjoins his
people to be holy (Lev. 11.44-45; 19.2; 20.7-8, 24-26; 22.32-33). Foreigners must submit to circumcision if they want to be part of God's
community. Any unclean person is forbidden to enter Zion, the holy
city (cf. Isa. 35.8), lest it become defiled. The clause לא יוסיף־יבא־בך
עוד, 'will no longer enter you' (v. 1c), echoes לא־תוסיפי לשתותה עוד,
'you will no longer drink it' (v. 22c).

Second Command to Get Up (Verse 2). Verse 2 adds some further
graphic details about terminating the mourning ceremony. Zion / Jerusalem is commanded to shake off the dirt she has been sitting in, to get
up, and to take her seat on the throne. Here, שבי (v. 2a) is short for ישב
על כסא המלוכה, 'to sit on the royal throne' (1 Kgs 1.46; 2.12). Compare
Isa. 10.13 where יושבים refers to kings. *BHS* and other commentators[38]
propose reading the adjective שביה, 'captive', for the sake of parallelism
with v. 2b. This suggestion misses 'a beautiful pun, identical sounds
with opposite meanings!'[39] The alliterative wordplay on שבי versus
שביה contrasts 'the present captivity of Jerusalem with her approaching
enthronement'.[40] The hithpael imperative התפתחי (lit. 'loose yourself';
v. 2b, emended), harks back to the niphal infinitive construct להפתח,
'be released, be let loose' (51.14). The promise in v. 14 becomes a
command in 52.2b. Yet daughter Zion is still captive (שביה בת־ציון,
'captive daughter Zion', v. 2b). She cannot perform all those antici-
patory commands by herself. She needs the strength of Yahweh which
she had asked for in vv. 9-11. She needs Yahweh to act first, to open the

38. E.g. Westermann, *Isaiah 40–66*, p. 247.
39. Motyer, *Prophecy*, p. 416.
40. K. Holter, 'A Note on שבי/שביה in Isa 52.2', *ZAW* 104 (1992), pp. 106-107.

way. After all, her own strength or her glorious garments come ultimately from Yahweh, her God, who 'contends for his people' (v. 22a).
The imagery of weakness and dependency implied in שׁביה at the end of
the stanza contrasts markedly with עֻזֵּךְ, 'your strength', in the opening
line (v. 1a).

Conclusion

In summary, the prayer of lament by Jerusalem, the chief mourner, in
51.9-11 has been answered positively. Yahweh the מנחם reassures his
people of his care and protection, of his supreme power over the forces
of nature and humanity, of his coming deliverance (vv. 12-16). Yahweh
knows and understands the sufferings his people are going through; he
will redress injustices (vv. 17-23). Yahweh provides a way for his
people to end the mourning period and to start on a new beginning
(52.1-2). Their oppressors will in turn drink and drain the cup of
Yahweh's wrath.

The spirit of fear and dejection at the start of the poem gives way to
joy and confidence. Yahweh has comforted the mourner Zion not only
by showing sympathy and understanding, but also by effecting deliverance and redressing injustices, thereby inducing the termination of
mourning. Captive daughter Zion is commanded to get up from the dirt
of her mourning, to remove the fetters of servitude, to put on new garments befitting her new status, and to take her seat on her throne. Yahweh's promise in 35.10 quoted by Zion in her prayer in 51.11 is about
to be realized:

> Those ransomed by Yahweh will return,
>   they will enter Zion with a joyful cry.
> Eternal joy will be upon their heads,
>   gladness and joy will meet them,
>   sorrow and sighing will have fled.

Chapter 5

CONCLUSION

The presence of the מנחם, 'comforter', is indispensable in times of
mourning (cf. Jacob's sons and daughters in Gen. 37.34-35; David's
envoys to King Hanun of the Ammonites in 2 Sam. 10.1-2; Job's
friends in Job 2.11-13). The plaintive lament about the lack of a מנחם in
Lamentations 1 suggests that the literary setting of the poem is a
mourning ceremony. Lamentations 2 grieves over the destruction of
Jerusalem and the whole land of Judah, and laments the humanly
impossible task of comforting in the face of such tragic circumstances.
The poem in Isa. 51.9–52.2 confirms the human incapacity to comfort
and presents Yahweh as the divine מנחם, who alone can terminate the
mourning process.

The mourning ceremony setting allows for the interchange of speakers in all three poems, and helps one to follow the continuous line of
thought from one speaker to the next, even if the speakers are not
expressly addressing each other, as in Lamentations 1. Commentators
often fail to follow the flow of ideas and attribute this apparent lack of
coherence, in the case of Lamentations 1 and 2, to their alphabetic
acrostic form,[1] and in Isa. 51.9–52.2, to 'occasional borrowing' and
'subsequent additions'.[2] The contributions to the field of biblical studies
which result from reading these poems against the literary setting of a
mourning ceremony will now be brought together under two headings:
first, on the macro-level, the flow of thought from one verse to the next;
and second, on the micro-level, the contextual meaning of words. The
three poems will be treated consecutively with respect to both headings.

1. E.g. Westermann, *Lamentations*, pp. 131-35.
2. E.g. North, *Second Isaiah*, pp. 213-14.

Lamentations 1

At this mourning ceremony, Lady Jerusalem, the chief mourner, voices her sufferings out loud, while a second speaker laments her fate sympathetically, and, at one point, helps her to articulate her prayer. The fresh insights gained from this study are gathered here under the two headings mentioned above.

Flow of Thought

Lamentations 1 is composed of two main sections of 11 stanzas each. The first section is mainly spoken by the second speaker. Jerusalem interrupts with two brief appeals to Yahweh at vv. 9c and 11c. The main speaker of the second section is Jerusalem. The second speaker interrupts with a brief comment on Jerusalem's need for a comforter. Besides these general observations, different commentators identify disruptions in the flow of thought at different points. These disruptions will be dealt with in the order of verses.

1. Hillers thinks that v. 6 is not closely linked to v. 5 in thought, and that v. 6 follows right after v. 5 probably because the idea of the children going into exile (v. 5c) suggests the departure of the glory from Zion (v. 6a), and also because לִפְנֵי רוֹדֵף, 'before their captors' (v. 6c), echoes לִפְנֵי־צָר, 'before the foe' (v. 5c).[3]

What has not been noted so far is that vv. 1-2 and vv. 7-9b describe Lady Jerusalem in mourning, and that vv. 3-6 explain the cause of her mourning. Verses 3 and 4 explain the cause of Jerusalem's mourning in terms of events happening in Judah, outside the capital city of Jerusalem: for example, the Judahites have been taken into exile (v. 3a), the roads leading to Zion are deserted (v. 4a). Verses 5 and 6 go together because they describe events which occur inside the city: for example, the children (inhabitants) of Jerusalem have also been led into exile (v. 5c), Zion has lost her splendor (v. 6a), her princes are taken captive and led away, starving (v. 6bc).

2. Hillers sees no close connection between the first colon of v. 9a (טֻמְאָתָה בְּשׁוּלֶיהָ, 'her filth is on her skirt') and its second colon (לֹא זָכְרָה אַחֲרִיתָהּ, 'she gave no thought to her future').[4] The connection between the two cola of the verse depends on the contextual meaning of

---

3. Hillers, *Lamentations*, pp. 67, 85.
4. Hillers, *Lamentations*, p. 86.

particular words in that verse. This point will be dealt with under my second heading on contextual meaning.

3. Westermann sees no intrinsic connection between v. 9c and v. 11c on the one hand, and vv. 10a-11b on the other. Furthermore, the five bicola in vv. 10a-11b do not show any clear flow of thought. Verse 10 is a complaint about the enemy while v. 11ab describes the misery of the population gripped by famine.[5] Indeed, most scholars explain v. 9c and v. 11c as 'brief ejaculatory prayers' by Jerusalem which interrupt the speech of the second speaker.[6] Hillers even suggests that the second part of the poem spoken by Jerusalem may begin at v. 11c.[7]

In the setting of the mourning ceremony, the whole unit from v. 9c to v. 11c is a prayer addressed to Yahweh. Jerusalem begins the prayer in v. 9c, but is too exhausted and too upset to say anything else. The second speaker continues her prayer in vv. 10-11b, expanding on what Jerusalem may have meant by כִּי הִגְדִּיל אוֹיֵב, 'for the enemy has gone too far!' The second speaker brings to Yahweh's notice that the enemy has shown contempt for Yahweh by invading his sanctuary and taking away the temple vessels. The enemy further offended Yahweh by reducing his people to starvation. Jerusalem then gathers up her strength and finishes the prayer by reminding Yahweh that the enemy has despised her (v. 11c).

This prayer ultimately concerns Yahweh's honor. It amounts to saying: 'O Yahweh, please look at what the enemy has done to your temple, to your people. Please Yahweh, act for your name's sake!'

4. Commentators are also disturbed by the apparent lack of connection between the description of what Yahweh did to Judah in vv. 12-15 and the description of the agony in vv. 16-17a. Furthermore, the proper sequence of v. 16c and v. 17bc seems to be disrupted. According to Westermann, v. 17bc belongs to the 'accusation against God' and should follow v. 15.[8]

However, within the setting of the mourning ceremony where many voices can find expression, vv. 12-16 form the address by Jerusalem to the passers-by. She describes for them her sufferings and her loneliness, hoping to receive sympathy and comfort from them. She has no com-

---

5.   Westermann, *Lamentations*, pp. 130-31.

6.   E.g. Hillers, *Lamentations*, pp. 79, 88; Provan, *Lamentations*, pp. 46-47; Reyburn, *Lamentations*, pp. 26-27.

7.   Hillers, *Lamentations*, pp. 79, 88.

8.   Westermann, *Lamentations*, pp. 135-36.

forter among her own children who have been terrified into silence by the enemy. Jerusalem must have broken into tears by now at the memory of her children (v. 16). The second speaker comes in at this point (v. 17) and notes that her appeal to the passers-by has been fruitless. She can find no מנחם among them since they have become her enemies, and that at Yahweh's command.

Contextual Meaning of Words
The mourning ceremony setting gives a fresh meaning to words and phrases, and often eliminates ambiguities in Lamentations 1.

1. In the context of mourning, the word בדד in v. 1a, with the following imagery of widowhood in v. 1b, depicts loneliness and desertion rather than solitary security as suggested by A. Ahuviah.[9]

2. The distinction should be made between אהביה, 'those who have loved her', or blood relatives (v. 2b), and רעיה, 'her friends' (v. 2c), and מאהבי, 'my lovers' (v. 19a), who are the political allies of Judah. Blood relatives and friends are usually present at mourning ceremonies to comfort the mourner. See exegesis of vv. 2 and 19. The Tanakh, NRSV and CEV do not distinguish between אהביה in v. 2b and מאהבי in v. 19a.

3. The mourning setting suggests the interpretation of היא ישבה בגוים, 'she sits as a mourner among the nations' (v. 3b), as referring to the present plight of exile, and not to the past, when Judah dwelt as an independent nation among others, as some commentators have argued.[10]

4. Since the מנחם is a special figure at a mourning ceremony, the lack of a comforter in v. 2b is explained in part by the betrayal of Zion's former allies in v. 2c. This public violation of an existing covenant treaty is behind the verb הזילוה, 'they despise her' (v. 8b).

5. The word ערותה, 'her nakedness' (v. 8b), has been commonly explained in terms of Jerusalem's being punished for her sins through the shameful exposure of her body.[11] Actually, this expression refers to Lady Jerusalem's being girded with sackcloth from the hips down, leaving the upper part of her body bare for beating as part of the mourning practice.

9. A. Ahuviah, 'איכה ישבה בדד העיר רבתי עם (Lam 1:1)', *Beth Mikra* 24 (1979), pp. 423-25, cited by Provan, *Lamentations*, p. 35.

10. Rudolph, *Klagelieder*, pp. 211-12; Hillers, *Lamentations*, pp. 66-67, 82.

11. E.g. Hillers, *Lamentations*, p. 86; Provan, *Lamentations*, pp. 44-45; Reyburn, *Lamentations*, p. 25.

6. Similarly, the word טמאתה, 'her filth' (v. 9a), has been usually interpreted as designating menstrual blood.[12] In fact, it is the dirt on which Jerusalem has been sitting as a mourner. It also refers metaphorically to her sins mentioned in vv. 5b and 8a. The sackcloth she wears is at the same time a mourning garb and a penitential garb. The connection between the first colon of v. 9a, טמאתה בשוליה, 'her filth is on her skirt', and the second colon, לא זכרה אחריתה, 'she gave no thought to [lit. 'did not remember'] her future', is that the first colon describes the physical and moral status of Jerusalem. She is seated in the dirt, girded in sackcloth. Her sackcloth has dirt on it. This dirt also represents her sins. She is in mourning as well as in penitence. When she committed those sins in the past, she did not think of their consequences. So she suffered punishment for her sins. She now finds herself on the ground, mourning her dead and repenting of her sins. This imagery is supported by the next colon in v. 9b, ותרד פלאים, 'thus she has fallen astoundingly', that is, she is defeated, conquered by the enemy, and she has descended from the throne, the seat of honor, to sit on the ground, to mourn the defeat of her people. She has fallen from her former status as 'princess over the city-states' to her present plight of a 'forced laborer' (v. 1c).

7. The adjectives שוממין (v. 4b), שממה (v. 13c) and שוממים (v. 16c) carry the nuance of being terrified into the silence of mourning.

8. The adjectives דוה (v. 13c) and דוי (v. 22c) refer to the state of being weakened to the point of fainting, even of death, due to much sorrow and weeping.

Lamentations 2

The voices of Lady Jerusalem and the second speaker in Lamentations 1 are also heard at this mourning ceremony. The difference with the first poem is that here, the second speaker voices his own sorrow and fulfills his role of comforter by advising Jerusalem to call on Yahweh for mercy.

As in the case of Lamentations 1, the mourning setting interpretation provides new insights first for the flow of thought and then for the contextual meaning of words in Lamentations 2.

---

12. Hillers, *Lamentations*, p. 86; Provan, *Lamentations*, p. 45; Reyburn, *Lamentations*, p. 25; Westermann, *Lamentations*, p. 129.

Flow of Thought

In a cursory reading of the poem, one notes a major division only between the first 9 verses which focus on the destructive acts of Yahweh, and the remaining 13 verses which present a mixture of themes: the dejection of Jerusalem's people (v. 10), the poet's own grief (v. 11), the starving and dying children (v. 12), Jerusalem's sufferings (v. 13), the blaming of the false prophets for Jerusalem's collapse (v. 14), the mockery of Jerusalem by her enemies (vv. 15-16), Yahweh's fulfillment of his word (v. 17), the call on Jerusalem to cry out to Yahweh for mercy (vv. 18-20), and the description of suffering with comments on Yahweh's role in that suffering (vv. 21-22).[13]

Westermann offers another structure: the accusation against God (vv. 1-9a), the complaint of the community (vv. 9b-13), the complaint about enemies framed by the confession of guilt (vv. 14-17), and finally the summons to Zion followed by the petition to Yahweh (vv. 18-22).[14]

These two ways of structuring the poem disregard the problem of address. No account is taken of who is speaking or who is being addressed. However, paying attention to the interaction of the two speakers in this poem discloses the setting of a mourning ceremony and the continuity in the flow of thought from one verse to the next.

Speech of the Second Speaker or מקונן *(Verses 1-19).* The מקונן begins with a description of the mourning ceremony (vv. 1-10): Jerusalem is cast to the ground (vv. 1b, 2c), her outer and main walls are mourning (v. 8c) with the gates sunk into the dirt and the bars shattered (v. 9a), her few surviving people are seated on the ground, girded in sackcloth, with dirt strewn on their heads (v. 10). The cause of the mourning is given in vv. 2-9. The poet laments the destruction of Judah (vv. 2-5), then that of Jerusalem (vv. 6-9).

At this point, the מקונן can no longer control his emotions and bursts into tears as he recalls the poignant scene of the starving and dying children in the streets of Jerusalem (vv. 11-12).

Then he addresses Jerusalem and tries to comfort her. He admits that her ruin is unprecedented in history and can only be compared to the primordial ruin of the sea (v. 13). Human beings cannot comfort her. Her prophets have not heard from Yahweh, therefore what they say is empty and misleading (v. 14). Neighbors behave like enemies. They

13. Reyburn, *Lamentations*, p. 41.
14. Westermann, *Lamentations*, pp. 148-49.

mock her (vv. 15-16). Yahweh sent destruction because he was true to his word while Jerusalem sinned against him (v. 17). Only Yahweh has the power to heal. The מנחם finally advises Jerusalem to pray to Yahweh (vv. 18-19).

Speech of Jerusalem (Verses 20-22). Jerusalem listens to the מנחם's advice and prays to Yahweh. She admits her guilt—Yahweh's wrath (a reaction to her sins) is mentioned in vv. 21c and 22b—but she is still full of bitterness because of her severe sufferings, so she does not offer any petition for healing or restoration; she only cries out from her agony to Yahweh against Yahweh himself. Her cry lays out before Yahweh the incomprehensibility of what has happened to her.

This mourning ceremony is heavy with anguish, bitterness and sorrow. The human מנחם seems unable to alleviate the sufferings of Lady Jerusalem. Yet his advice to appeal to Yahweh's compassion is the only and best advice Jerusalem can be given at this time.

Contextual Meaning of Words
The mourning ceremony setting helps to choose between various meanings of the same word and to grasp with more poignancy the personification of inanimate objects like walls and gates.

1. The *hapax legomenon* יעיב has been explained as a denominative verb from עב, 'dark cloud'.[15] The cloud is the symbol of Yahweh's presence (cf. 1 Kgs 8.10-11) and not of his wrath. The context of wrath and the mourning ceremony setting favor, however, the alternative meaning of 'to detest, abhor', from *ועב, the root from which תועבה, 'abomination', is derived. Jerusalem is cast down to earth because the Lord abhorred her, that is, she has become an abomination to the Lord. The following eight verses explain this 'being cast down to earth' as a military defeat (השיב אחור ימינו מפני אויב, 'he [the Lord] turned back his [Israel's] right hand before the enemy', v. 3b) and destruction by the enemy. Public mourning usually followed a military debacle (e.g. Josh. 7.6; 1 Sam. 4.12-13; 2 Sam. 1.2, 11-12). The pattern of the people's sins leading to Yahweh's wrath, then Yahweh's wrath causing the people to be defeated in battle, is typical of the book of Judges (cf. Judg. 2.7-8).

2. Verse 1b, השליך משמים ארץ תפארת ישראל, 'He cast down from heaven to earth the glory of Israel', contrasts the past greatness of Jeru-

15. See p. 102 above.

salem with her present ruin. It also evokes the posture of mourning:
Lady Jerusalem is now seated on the ground.

3. Verse 2c, הגיע לארץ חלל ממלכה ושריה, 'He brought down to the
ground in dishonor the kingdom and its princes', also conveys the picture of mourning. The whole land and its leaders have been defeated
and are now seated on the ground, in mourning.

4. Commentators are puzzled by the comparison כגן, 'like the garden', in ויחמס כגן שכו, 'he demolished his tent like the garden' (v. 6a).[16]
Enclosed within v. 1 and v. 10 is a two-part description of the devastation: the devastation of Judah in vv. 2-5, and the devastation of Jerusalem in vv. 6-9. This distinction helps to make sense of the comparison
כגן. Yahweh destroyed Jerusalem, that is, his booth / tent (שכו) as he
destroyed 'the garden', which is the whole land of Judah.

5. Verse 8c, ויאבל־חל וחומה יחדו אמללו, 'He caused to mourn the
outer and main walls, together they grieve', and the first colon in v. 9a,
טבעו בארץ שעריה, 'her gates have sunk into the ground', depict a
mourning scene with the heaps of ruins from the outer and main walls
and the city gates personified as mourners seated on the ground.

6. Verse 10 portrays the mourning ceremony with all the surviving
inhabitants of Jerusalem represented by the two opposite poles of the
population: the elders and the virgins. They are seated on the ground in
terrified silence, girded with sackcloth, with dirt strewn on their bowed
heads.

7. Scholars question the use and the meaning of the hiphil of עוד in
מה־אעידך (v. 13a). I have established above (p. 105) that the fundamental sense of the hiphil of עוד is 'to repeat [words]'. This meaning is
appropriate here, for the poet desires to comfort Jerusalem (ואנחמך,
'that I may comfort you', v. 13b). Human compassion requires relatives
and friends to comfort mourners and those who are distressed. To
deride instead of to comfort is the attitude of the enemy. To comfort
involves participation in the mourning rites and speaking kind words,
giving advice to the mourners. Thus it seems fitting to translate
מה־אעידך by 'what can I say to you'. This understanding of אעידך
reveals an a:b::b´:a´ chiastic pattern in the four verbs of v. 13ab:
מה־אעידך::מה אדמה־לך::מה אשוה־לך::ואנחמך, 'what can I say to you: to
what can I compare you::to what can I liken you: that I may comfort
you'.

---

16. E.g. Provan, *Lamentations*, pp. 64-66; Reyburn, *Lamentations*, p. 52; Westermann, *Lamentations*, p. 150.

Isaiah 51.9–52.2

In Lamentations 1 and 2, Jerusalem, the chief mourner, speaks only after the lament of the other voice. Here, Lady Jerusalem speaks first, as Job is the first one to break the mourning silence in Job 3. The interaction between Yahweh, the prophet, and Jerusalem at this mourning ceremony will be treated under the heading 'flow of thought'; some fresh insights into the meaning of particular words will be dealt with under the second heading on 'contextual meaning of words'.

Flow of Thought
The limits of the poem in Isa. 51.9–52.2 have been clearly defined in the section on Poetic Structure (pp. 157-61). This poem begins with a lament by a mourner (51.9-11) and closes with the divine older to the mourner to cease mourning (52.1-2).

1. The speaker of the lament in 51.9-11 can be identified as Lady Jerusalem, the chief mourner, for Yahweh responds to her need for a מנחם in v. 12a, and the prophet, speaking for Yahweh, commands her to get up (51.17a; 52.2a), shake off the dirt she has been sitting in (52.2a), put on her glorious garments (52.1b) and take her seat on the throne (52.2a). In other words, Jerusalem is urged to terminate her mourning.

2. Isaiah 51.11 is almost identical with 35.10. Commentators are divided as to which is original and which is secondary.[17] The connection between 51.9-10 and 51.11 is thought to be loose.[18] However, once it is realized that Isaiah 35 describes a desert transformed by the rain and a highway through it, by which Yahweh's people released from exile will come back to Zion, it becomes apparent that 35.10 is integral to the chapter.[19] Thus its quotation in 51.11 is a prayer by Jerusalem, the weary mourner, urging Yahweh to fulfill his promise of deliverance.

3. North finds a loose connection between vv. 12-14 on the one hand, and vv. 15-16 on the other hand. Moreover, v. 16a does not flow smoothly into v. 16b.[20] Westermann is also puzzled by the intrusion of

---

17. Westermann, *Isaiah*, p. 243.
18. North, *Second Isaiah*, pp. 212-13.
19. See the exegesis of this verse and the relevant notes above.
20. North, *Second Isaiah*, p. 214.

v. 16a within the unity of vv. 15-16 which proclaim Yahweh the creator who elects Zion to be his people.[21]

The setting of the mourning ceremony helps to put these verses into the proper perspective. In the unit of vv. 12-16, Yahweh answers the prayer lament of Jerusalem the mourner by assuring her that he is her מנחם. Yahweh can perform his role far better than any human מנחם since he is the creator of the cosmos. In v. 13, Yahweh reminds Jerusalem that he created the heavens and the earth. In v. 15, which quotes from the same hymn as Jer. 31.35, Yahweh stresses the fact that he also created the roaring sea. The same order of creation—heavens, earth and sea—is recorded in Gen. 1.6-10. In v. 16a, Yahweh confirms his promise of deliverance and affirms that it was he who made Jerusalem utter that promise in her prayer (v. 11). Yahweh assures her of his continuing protection. The permanence of the cosmos, heavens, earth and sea should assure Jerusalem of the permanence of the covenant Yahweh made with her, by which covenant she became his own people.

Contextual Meaning of Words
In this mourning ceremony, Jerusalem the chief mourner breaks the mourning silence first, and appeals to Yahweh to fulfill his promise concerning the return of the exiles (vv. 9-11).

1. Yahweh introduces himself as the מנחם of Jerusalem (v. 12a). The logical implication is that Jerusalem is in mourning and needs a comforter. Yahweh exhorts her not to fear human beings who are transient like grass, and reassures her that her captives will be set free, and that food will not be lacking (v. 14). There is no need to change לחמו, 'his bread', to לחו or לחמו, 'his vigor', for the promise of bread is the answer to the dread of famine in v. 19b.

2. The command to Jerusalem to arise (קומי in v. 17a and 52.2a) suggests that Jerusalem has been sitting on the ground in mourning.

3. The two rhetorical questions in v. 19, מי ינוד לך, 'who can grieve with you?', and מי ינחמך (emended), 'who can comfort you?', occur in a context of mourning.

4. The command in 52.1b, לבשי בגדי תפארתך, 'put on your glorious garments', shows that up to now Jerusalem has been wearing mourning sackcloth.

5. The command in 52.2a, התנערי מעפר קומי שבי ירושלם, 'Shake the dirt off yourself, get up, sit enthroned, O Jerusalem', is a clear definitive

21. Westermann, p. 244.

order to Jerusalem to terminate the mourning sequence, to get up from the dirt on which she has been sitting in mourning, and to take her seat on the throne.[22]

Hopefully, the highpoints selected above will serve to remind the reader in summary fashion of the detailed argumentation presented in this study. The three texts treated here are all made up of combined words, words that often signify something a good deal more precise in their specific cultural contexts than the generic definitions of dictionaries. The intended audience for these texts shared the cultural context of their authors, immediately understood implicit references and inferred the total picture being presented. Modern interpreters who come to the texts from other, very different cultures are incapable of grasping the texts in this way, without an extraordinary effort to become familiar with their ancient cultural contexts—an effort that at times borders on the impossible due to the paucity of sources.

The three texts I have studied are some of the easiest to establish in the historical setting in which they were composed. Lamentations 1–2 date from the beginning of the exile. The all but total despair that pervades the texts points to the immediate effect of the trauma of Jerusalem's fall. By contrast, in the context of Second Isaiah, Isa. 51.9–52.2 dates from a period toward the end of the exile, during the rise of Cyrus. But the relevant history that can be pieced together from both Old Testament and Mesopotamian sources is extremely limited, and for the most part only a few hard dates are known, as well as the names of the kings who were players in the drama and battles lost and won.

We have no detailed account of the siege and fall of Jerusalem in 587 BCE, central for this study, but we can be certain that it was bloody. The besiegers attempting to enter a walled city had to go over, through or under the wall purposely designed by military architects to keep the besiegers in the direct, short line of fire of the defenders. The losses among the besiegers were inevitably bloody and numerous. Once the

---

22. North (*Second Isaiah*, p. 218) comments that '"sit down" reads oddly after "stand up"' and suggests reading שְׁבִיָּה, 'captive', instead of שְׁבִי, 'sit enthroned'. Westermann (*Isaiah*, pp. 246-47) realizes that the call to Zion in 51.17 summons her to rouse herself from mourning, yet he also suggests reading שְׁבִיָּה. J.D.W. Watts (*Isaiah 34–66* [WBC, 25; Waco, TX: Word Books, 1987], p. 210) retains MT שְׁבִי but explains the contrast with קוּמִי by referring to 1 Sam 28.23; 2 Sam 19.9 (BDB, p. 442).

wall was breached, the defenders could hardly expect humane treatment. In addition, a besieging army of necessity had to secure the countryside to prevent attacks from the rear during the siege and to gather provisions and forced labor to support the siege. After the fall of the city, there may be added the exile of the pillars of the Judean political and economic scene and the necessity to pay tribute to Babylon. There are traces of information available in these areas, but detailed information about the wretched state of Judean society during the exile as well as about the Judean exiles in Babylon is difficult to read out of the cryptic language of the texts studied. These details of history, which were clear to the authors of the texts and to their intended audience, remain obscure to us. It would be well worth the effort to gather them. That has not been attempted here.

Ultimately, of course, it must be admitted that the authors of these texts were more interested in the theological interpretation of the history they lived through than the details of that history. That involves the doctrine of divine retribution with faint glimmers of forgiveness in Lamentations 1–2, and clear forgiveness in Isa. 51.9–52.2, and the doctrine of divine control of history. This too raises serious theological questions which I have not attempted to treat.

Other materials in the texts deserve extensive analysis: the picture of the LORD as warrior, of Lady Jerusalem, both extensively present in all three texts, and the picture of the cup in Isa. 51.17, 22. What connotations did the ancient audience hear in this mysterious language? What feelings did it convey?

A serious, total interpretation of the three texts in this study would involve a detailed, contextual treatment of all the elements gathered and the vocabulary in which they are presented. It is clear that I have not attempted such an ambitious reading. I have been endeavoring simply to present a coherent reading of each of the texts in their common literary setting, namely, the Israelite mourning ceremony. Such a reading involves a literary adaptation of the mourning rites occasioned principally by the death of a loved one. The city Jerusalem, even personified, is not a lady. Some of her children, the Judeans, are dead; many are not. The connection between these texts and the Israelite mourning rites has been generally recognized. I have pushed this insight further than has been done previously and have been able to explain a significant number of details on the basis of these mourning rites more satisfactorily than previously. There are places where I have perhaps exaggerated;

but in every case my explanations based on mourning practices seem to me at least plausible.

I have not included Lamentations 3–5 in this study because they are not 'Jerusalem mourning ceremony' texts in the sense that they do not present Lady Jerusalem in mourning and in need of a מנחם. The obvious complement for Lamentations 1–2 is Isa. 51.9–52.2 which marks the end of the mourning rites presented in the former texts.

BIBLIOGRAPHY

Ackroyd, P.R., 'יד', *TDOT*, V, pp. 393-426.

Albrektson, B., *Studies in the Text and Theology of the Book of Lamentations* (STL, 21; Lund: C.W.K. Gleerup, 1963).

Alt, A., *'Hic murus aheneus esto'*, *ZDMG* 86 (1932), pp. 33-48.

Anderson, G.A., *A Time to Mourn, a Time to Dance: The Expression of Grief and Joy in Israelite Religion* (University Park, PA: Pennsylvania State University Press, 1991).

Artzi, P., 'Mourning in International Relations', in B. Alster (ed.), *Death in Mesopotamia* (Copenhagen Studies in Assyriology, 8; Copenhagen: Akademisk, 1980), pp. 161-70.

Barthélemy, D., *et al.*, *Critique textuelle de l'Ancien Testament. II. Esaïe, Jérémie, Lamentations* (OBO, 50.2; Fribourg: Editions Universitaires, 1986).

Baumann, A., 'אבל', *TDOT*, I, pp. 44-48.

Bechtel, L.M., 'Shame as a Sanction of Social Control in Biblical Israel: Judicial, Political, and Social Shaming', *JSOT* 49 (1991), pp. 47-76.

Bergman, J., and E. Johnson, 'אנף', *TDOT*, I, pp. 348-60.

Boadt, L., 'Intentional Alliteration in Second Isaiah', *CBQ* 45 (1983), pp. 353-63.

Boyce, R.N., *The Cry to God in the Old Testament* (SBLDS, 103; Atlanta: Scholars Press, 1988).

Bracke, J.M., '*šûb šebût*: A Reappraisal', *ZAW* 97 (1985), pp. 233-44.

Bright, J., *A History of Israel* (Philadelphia: Westminster Press, 3rd edn, 1981).

Brockelmann, C., *Hebräische Syntax* (Glückstadt: J.J. Augustin; Neukirchen Kreis Moers: Buchhandlung des Erziehungsvereins, 1956).

Clements, R.E., and G.J. Botterweck, 'גוי', *TDOT*, II, pp. 426-33.

Clifford, R.J., *Fair Spoken and Persuading: An Interpretation of Second Isaiah* (New York: Paulist Press, 1984).

—'Second Isaiah', *ABD*, III, pp. 490-501.

Collins, T., 'The Physiology of Tears in the Old Testament: Part 1', *CBQ* 33 (1971), pp. 18-38.

—'The Physiology of Tears in the Old Testament: Part 2', *CBQ* 33 (1971), pp. 185-97.

Conrad, J., 'זקן', *TDOT*, IV, pp. 122-31.

Cooper, J.S., *The Curse of Agade* (Baltimore: The Johns Hopkins University Press, 1983).

Couroyer, B., 'L'arc d'airain', *RB* 72 (1965), pp. 508-14.

—'Corne et arc', *RB* 73 (1966), pp. 510-21.

—'*nḥt*: "Encorder un arc" (?)', *RB* 88 (1981), pp. 13-18.

Cross, F.M., 'Studies in the Structure of Hebrew Verse: The Prosody of Lamentations 1.1-22', in C.L. Meyers and M. O'Connor (eds.), *The Word of the Lord Shall Go Forth: Essays in Honor of David Noel Freedman in Celebration of his Sixtieth Birthday* (ASORSVS, 1; Winona Lake, IN: Eisenbrauns, 1983), pp. 129-55.

Dahood, M., 'Textual Problems in Isaiah', *CBQ* 22 (1960), pp. 400-409.

Day, J., 'God's Conflict with Dragon and Sea', *ABD*, II, pp. 228-31.
—'Rahab', *ABD*, V, pp. 610-11.
Dempsey, D., 'The Verb Syntax of Second Isaiah and Deuteronomy Compared' (PhD dissertation, Washington, The Catholic University of America, 1988).
Dhorme, E., *A Commentary on the Book of Job* (New York: Thomas Nelson, 1967).
Dietrich, E.L., 'שוב שבות: Die endzeitliche Wiederherstellung bei den Propheten', BZAW 40 (1925), pp. 32-37.
Dobbs-Allsopp, F.W., *Weep, O Daughter of Zion: A Study of the City-Lament Genre in the Hebrew Bible* (BibOr, 44; Rome: Pontifical Biblical Institute, 1993).
Driver, S.R., *A Treatise on the Use of the Tenses in Hebrew and Some Other Syntactical Questions* (Oxford: Clarendon Press, 1881).
Droin, J.-M., *Le livre des Lamentations: 'Comment?' Une traduction et un commentaire* (Geneva: Labor et Fides, 1995).
Eising, H., 'זכר', *TDOT*, IV, pp. 64-82.
Erlandsson, S., 'בגד', *TDOT*, I, pp. 470-73.
Everson, A.J., 'The Days of Yahweh', *JBL* 93 (1974), pp. 329-37.
Fabry, H.-J., 'הדם', *TDOT*, III, pp. 325-34.
Feldman, E., *Biblical and Post-Biblical Defilement and Mourning: Law as Theology* (New York: Ktav, 1977).
Ferrie, J.J., Jr, 'Meteorological Imagery in Isaiah 40–55' (PhD dissertation, Washington, The Catholic University of America, 1992).
Ferris, P.W. Jr, *The Genre of Communal Lament in the Bible and the Ancient Near East* (SBLDS, 127; Atlanta: Scholars Press, 1992).
Fitzgerald, A., 'BTWLT and BT as Titles for Capital Cities', *CBQ* 37 (1975), pp. 167-83.
—'Hebrew Poetry', *NJBC* (1990), pp. 201-208.
Fox, N.S., 'Clapping Hands as a Gesture of Anguish and Anger in Mesopotamia and in Israel', *JANESCU* 23 (1995), pp. 49-60.
Freedman, D.N., 'Acrostics and Metrics in Hebrew Poetry', *HTR* 65 (1972), pp. 367-92.
—*Pottery, Poetry, and Prophecy* (Winona Lake, IN: Eisenbrauns, 1980).
Gaster, T.H., *Thespis* (New York: Gordian, 1975).
Gordis, R., *The Song of Songs and Lamentations* (New York: Ktav, 3rd edn, 1974).
Gottwald, N.K., *Studies in the Book of Lamentations* (SBT, 14; London: SCM Press, 2nd edn, 1962).
—'Review of Iain W. Provan, *Lamentations*', *CBQ* 55 (1993), pp. 550-52.
Guinan, M.D., 'Lamentations', *NJBC*, pp. 558-62.
Haag, H., 'בת', *TDOT*, II, pp. 332-38.
Habel, N.C., 'He Who Stretches out the Heavens', *CBQ* 34 (1972), pp. 417-30.
Hamp, V., 'בכה', *TDOT*, II, pp. 116-20.
—'טבח', *TDOT*, V, pp. 283-87.
Hasel, G., 'זעק', *TDOT*, IV, pp. 112-22.
Hillers, D.R., 'History and Poetry in Lamentations', *CurTM* 10 (1983), pp. 155-61.
—*Lamentations* (AB, 7A; Garden City, NY: Doubleday, 2nd edn, 1992).
Hoffner, H.A., 'אלמנה', *TDOT*, I, pp. 287-91.
Holladay, W.L., *Jeremiah 1* (Hermeneia; Philadelphia: Fortress Press, 1986).
—*Jeremiah 2* (Hermeneia; Minneapolis: Fortress Press, 1989).
Holter, K., 'A Note on שביה/שבי in Isa 52.2', *ZAW* 104 (1992), pp. 106-107.
Hunter, J., *Faces of a Lamenting City: The Development and Coherence of the Book of Lamentations* (BEATAJ, 39; New York: Peter Lang, 1996).

Jacob, E., 'Mourning', *IDB*, III, pp. 452-54.

Jahnow, H., *Das hebräische Leichenlied im Rahmen der Völkerdichtung* (BZAW, 36; Giessen: Alfred Töpelmann, 1923).

Jenni, E., *Das hebräische Piel* (Zürich: EVZ-Verlag, 1968).

Jepsen, A., 'חזה', *TDOT*, IV, pp. 280-90.

Johnson, E., 'אנף', *TDOT*, IV, pp. 280-90.

Kaiser, B.B., 'Poet as "Female Impersonator": The Image of Daughter Zion as Speaker in Biblical Poems of Suffering', *JR* 67 (1987), pp. 164-82.

Kaiser, O., *Klagelieder* (ATD, 16; Göttingen: Vandenhoeck & Ruprecht, 3rd edn, 1981).

Kellermann, D., 'בצע', *TDOT*, II, pp. 205-208.

Kraus, H.-J., *Klagelieder* (BKAT, 20; Neukirchen–Vluyn: Neukirchener Verlag, 3rd edn, 1968).

—*Psalms 1–59* (Minneapolis: Augsburg, 1988).

Kuntz, J.K., 'The Contribution of Rhetorical Criticism to Understanding Isaiah 51.1-16', in D.J.A. Clines, D.M. Gunn and A.J. Hauser (eds.), *Art and Meaning: Rhetoric in Biblical Literature* (JSOTSup, 19; Sheffield: JSOT Press, 1982), pp. 140-71.

Kutscher, E.Y., *The Language and Linguistic Background of the Isaiah Scroll (1QIsa^a)* (STDJ, 6; Leiden: E.J. Brill, 1974).

Lemaire, A., 'Abécédaires et exercices d'écolier en épigraphie nord-ouest sémitique', *JA* 266 (1978), pp. 221-35.

Levenson, J.D., 'Zion Traditions', *ABD*, VI, pp. 1098-1102.

Lipiński, E., *La liturgie pénitentielle dans la Bible* (LD, 52; Paris: Cerf, 1969).

Lohfink, N., 'Enthielten die im Alten Testament bezeugten Klageriten eine Phase des Schweigens?', *VT* 12 (1962), pp. 260-77.

Ludwig, T.M., 'The Traditions of the Establishing of the Earth in Deutero-Isaiah', *JBL* 92 (1973), pp. 345-57.

Maass, F., 'אנוש', *TDOT*, I, pp. 345-48.

McCurley, F.R., *Ancient Myths and Biblical Faith* (Philadelphia: Fortress Press, 1983).

McDaniel, T.F., 'Philological Studies in Lamentations: I', *Bib* 49 (1968), pp. 27-53.

—'Philological Studies in Lamentations: II', *Bib* 49 (1968), pp. 199-220.

Malina, B.J., *The New Testament World: Insights from Cultural Anthropology* (Louisville, KY: Westminster/John Knox Press, 1981).

Mayoral, J.A., *Sufrimiento y esperanza: La crisis exílica en Lamentaciones* (ISJ, 29; Navarra: EVD, 1994).

Meek, T.J., and W.P. Merrill, *The Book of Lamentations* (IB, 6; Nashville: Abingdon Press, 1956), pp. 1-38.

Miller, J.M., and J.H. Hayes, *A History of Ancient Israel and Judah* (Philadelphia: Westminster Press, 1986).

Miller, P.D., Jr, *Genesis 1–11: Studies in Structure and Theme* (JSOTSup, 8; Sheffield: University of Sheffield, 1978).

Mintz, A., 'The Rhetoric of Lamentations and the Representation of Catastrophe', *Prooftexts* 2 (1982), pp. 1-17.

Moran, W.L., 'The Ancient Near Eastern Background of the Love of God in Deuteronomy', *CBQ* 25 (1963), pp. 77-87.

Motyer, J.A., *The Prophecy of Isaiah* (Downers Grove, IL: InterVarsity Press, 1993).

Muilenburg, J., 'The Book of Isaiah: Chapters 40–66', *IB*, V, pp. 381-773.

Napier, B.D., 'Prophet, Prophetism', *IDB*, III, pp. 905-906.

North, C.R., *The Second Isaiah* (Oxford: Oxford University Press, 1964).

Olyan, S.M., 'Honor, Shame, and Covenant Relations in Ancient Israel and its Environ-
    ment', *JBL* 115 (1996), pp. 201-18.
Plöger, O., 'Die Klagelieder', in E. Würthwein *et al.*, *Die fünf Megilloth* (HAT, 1.18;
    Tübingen: Mohr Siebeck, 2nd edn, 1969), pp. 127-64.
Praetorius, F., 'Threni I, 12. 14. II, 6. 13', *ZAW* 15 (1895), pp. 143-46.
Preuschen, E., 'Die Bedeutung von שבות שוב im Alten Testamente', *ZAW* 47 (1929),
    pp. 17-44.
Preuss, H.D., 'דמה', *TDOT*, III, pp. 250-60.
Provan, I.W., *Lamentations* (NCBC; London: Marshall Pickering; Grand Rapids: Eerd-
    mans, 1991).
Re'emi, S.P., 'The Theology of Hope: A Commentary on Lamentations', in R. Martin-
    Achard and S.P. Re'emi (eds.), *God's People in Crisis: A Commentary on the Book
    of Amos; A Commentary on the Book of Lamentations* (ITC; Grand Rapids: Eerd-
    mans, 1984), pp. 73-134.
Reviv, H., *The Elders in Ancient Israel* (Jerusalem: The Hebrew University, 1989).
Reyburn, W.D., *A Handbook on Lamentations* (United Bible Societies Handbook Series;
    New York: United Bible Societies, 1992).
Ringgren, H., 'גאל', *TDOT*, II, pp. 350-55.
—'חמר', *TDOT*, V, pp. 1-4.
Rudolph, W., *Das Buch Ruth, das Hohe Lied, die Klagelieder* (KAT, 17; Gütersloh: Gerd
    Mohn, 2nd edn, 1962).
Sakenfeld, K.D., *The Meaning of Hesed in the Hebrew Bible: A New Inquiry* (HSM, 17;
    Missoula, MT: Scholars Press, 1978).
Salters, R.B., 'Lamentations 1.3: Light from the History of Exegesis', in J.D. Martin and
    P.R. Davies (eds.), *A Word in Season* (JSOTSup, 42; Sheffield: JSOT Press, 1986),
    pp. 73-89.
Seitz, C.R., 'The Divine Council: Temporal Transition and New Prophecy in the Book of
    Isaiah', *JBL* 109 (1990), pp. 229-47.
Seow, C.L., 'A Textual Note on Lam 1.20', *CBQ* 47 (1985), pp. 416-19.
—'Lord of Hosts', *ABD*, III, pp. 304-307.
Seybold, K., 'הפך', *TDOT*, III, pp. 423-27.
—'חשב', *TDOT*, V, pp. 228-45.
Shea, W.H., 'The *qinah* Structure of the Book of Lamentations', *Bib* 60 (1979), pp. 103-
    107.
Skehan, P.W., and A.A. Di Lella, *The Wisdom of Ben Sira* (AB, 39; New York: Doubleday,
    1987).
Smart, J.D., *History and Theology in Second Isaiah: A Commentary on Isaiah 35, 40–66*
    (Philadelphia: Westminster Press, 1965).
Smith, W.F., 'Prayer', *IDB*, III, pp. 857-67.
Stählin, G., 'σάκκος', *TDNT*, VII, pp. 56-64.
Talmon, S., 'Wilderness', *IDBSup*, pp. 946-49.
Toombs, L.E., 'Hunting', *IDB*, II, pp. 662-63.
Torrey, C.C., *The Second Isaiah: A New Interpretation* (New York: Charles Scribner's
    Sons, 1928).
Wagner, S., 'אמר', *TDOT*, I, pp. 328-45.
Wakeman, M.K., *God's Battle with the Monster* (Leiden: E.J. Brill, 1973).
Wallis, G., 'חמד', *TDOT*, IV, pp. 452-61.
Warmuth, G., 'הדר', *TDOT*, III (1978), pp. 335-41.

Watts, J.D.W., *Isaiah 34–66* (WBC, 25; Waco, TX: Word Books, 1987).

Westermann, C., *Isaiah 40–66* (OTL; Philadelphia: Westminster Press, 1969).

—*Praise and Lament in the Psalms* (Atlanta: John Knox Press, 1981).

—*Lamentations: Issues and Interpretation* (Minneapolis: Fortress Press, 1994).

Wiklander, B., 'זעם', *TDOT*, IV, pp. 106-11.

Williamson, H.G.M., *Ezra, Nehemiah* (WBC, 16; Waco, TX: Word Books, 1985).

Yadin, Y., *The Art of Warfare in Biblical Lands* (2 vols.; Jerusalem: International Publishing, 1963).

Zobel, H.-J., 'בדד', *TDOT*, I, pp. 473-79.

—'גלה', *TDOT*, II, pp. 476-88.

INDEXES

INDEX OF REFERENCES

OLD TESTAMENT

INDEX OF AUTHORS

JOURNAL FOR THE STUDY OF THE OLD TESTAMENT
SUPPLEMENT SERIES